SUCCESSFUL CREATIVITY IN DIRECT MARKETING

by John Watson

The *only* comprehensive guide
to the creative techniques that
produce better results in mailings,
press, TV and radio.
Features over 70 examples.

Foreword by Drayton Bird

**THE INSTITUTE OF
DIRECT MARKETING.**

"When Aeschines spoke,

they said, 'How well he speaks'.

But when Demosthenes spoke,

they said, 'Let us march

against Philip'.

I'm for Demosthenes."

David Ogilvy

'Confessions of an Advertising Man'

FOREWORD

I owe a lot to John Watson.

We first worked together in 1975. Then, in 1976, with remarkable prescience he told me he thought anyone starting a direct marketing agency was bound to do well. In 1977, I made one of my few good decisions: I went into partnership with him.

He is one of the best copywriters I have ever met; and in some respects the best.

He is able to look at problems from a slightly different angle, and come up with distinctly better solutions uncannily fast. And he has a remarkable ability to charm money out of customers' pockets.

In this book he reveals some of his secrets. If you read it, you too will owe John Watson a lot.

Drayton Bird

SUCCESSFUL CREATIVITY IN DIRECT MARKETING

by John Watson

First published as Hardback 1993.
This Paperback edition 1995.

Published by
The Institute of Direct Marketing,
No. 1 Park Road, Teddington,
Middlesex TW11 0AR.

ISBN: 0 9518692 1 3

Typeset by Direct Art, London.
Type Design by Gino Conte.
Printed and bound in Great Britain by
RPM Offset, London.

THE INSTITUTE OF
DIRECT MARKETING

CONTENTS

INTRODUCTION

T HIS book is all about getting better responses through the use of creative techniques. And surprisingly, of all the factors that affect response rates in direct marketing, creativity is one of the most important yet one of the least understood and least recognised.

Indeed, in almost any discussion of what factors most affect the performance of direct marketing promotions, lists, offer and media will often be given pride of place, with creative usually coming last.

I do not disagree with this simply because of my own creative background, but because in over 20 years of involvement in all aspects of direct marketing – including those important ones of lists, offer and media – it has been my experience that creative plays a much greater role. Indeed, in many cases, it plays the *greatest* role of all.

In fact, the right kind of creativity can often be the difference between the success and failure of a direct marketing promotion.

I have seen promotions that have failed no matter how good the list work, how clever the selections, how cheap the production and how powerful the offer; yet once the right creative is used, that promotion works.

Naturally, I have to assume that your listwork, selections, production and offer *are* right; the one time that creativity makes no difference at all is when other elements are so poor as to negate the creative message. But these days, when so much on the 'technical' side is good, it would be useful to see the same effort put into creativity.

Simple changes to headlines, to body copy or to art direction can dramatically change the numbers. I have seen cases where the difference between one headline and another is the difference between success and failure. I have seen cases where simply changing the art direction style can triple and even quadruple response.

Why, then, is creative not generally regarded as being top of the list?

The problem is, I suspect, that most direct marketing is run by people who are comfortable with numbers; and when such almost magical effects as doubling response through the change of a few words happens, the process defies logic and therefore can be ignored. Perhaps more creative people running direct marketing businesses would redress the balance.

In addition, the increasing use of sophisticated technology together with the wider application of powerful statistical methods has meant that the role of creative, if ever acknowledged sufficiently, has become downplayed. People forget simple facts, if they ever knew them, such as the plain fact that long mailing letters work a great deal better than short mailing letters. But how many packs these days do you see where good, strong, long mailing letters are being used? It's not that they don't work anymore – it's just that people have sadly forgotten that they do work.

It also has to be said that getting the 'right kind of creative' is more difficult than it should be. Good direct marketing creative people are surprisingly thin on the ground;

and it has to be confessed that there are many bad ones who do not help the overall reputation of the creative process.

So it seems to me that the time is right to put creative back where it belongs – not at the top of the pile, but sharing the stage with the many other techniques that are available.

This book, then, is an attempt to give creative the role it should have, by explaining the underlying reasons why certain techniques work, and then by going on to explain in some detail exactly how those techniques should be applied.

The fundamental standpoint of the book is looking at creativity wholly from the point of view of getting better responses; I am sure I have as a result ignored many techniques that could properly be regarded as creative, but which do not, in my view at least, make a significant contribution to getting those results.

In the main, this book is concerned with consumer direct marketing; this is the area where most activity comes from and where most of the testing is done. The business-to-business direct marketer may not feel there is much to interest him or her – but the fact remains that most of the techniques described here are directly applicable to *every* field of direct marketing.

The book is aimed primarily at two groups of people. First, of course, it is aimed at creative people themselves, creative people who intend to make, or who are making, a serious professional commitment to direct marketing. It is written for those people in the hope that it will mostly guide (and now and then inspire) them towards improving their craft, by giving them a detailed understanding of the basic techniques that will produce better results.

The second group of people it is aimed at are those who are responsible for briefing and approving direct marketing creative work, be they on the client side or the agency side. Their work is no less 'creative' because they are not directly involved with the process of creation itself, and a deeper understanding of the processes involved will help explain what is good, what is bad, and how to recognise it when they see it.

From the beginning, let me say that this book is unashamedly about technique and formula. It is based on solid, traditional direct marketing values. To some, who are more concerned with image, this book will mean nothing. There has been a trend in recent years to denigrate these supposedly traditional values as being 'formula driven' and lacking in 'true' creative values.

I am not going to take on that argument here, except to point out that those who have been loudest in those arguments have been some of the fastest to go out of business, while those of us who have stuck to the 'formula' have prospered, through good times and bad.

The success of WWAV, an agency dedicated above all else to practical, hard-nosed, response-oriented creativity, must surely be the most eloquent argument in favour of this approach.

Most of the statements in this book are based on demonstrated fact, and not on opinion, belief or preference (unless otherwise stated). Nothing is said that I have not had personal experience of either seeing happen or having heard about it happening from sufficiently reliable sources. In saying this I am not claiming infallibility: one of the things you learn quickly in direct marketing is that what works for one type of organisation may not work for another. But I have tried as far as possible to keep clear of those more contentious techniques and concentrate on those that broadly work for *most* people.

This is not to say that all you need to do is read this and you can go off to become a successful writer or art director in direct marketing. The formula is really about the basics - it provides the ingredients of creativity, without which the dish cannot be created. But individual skills play a great part. Using the same ingredients, a good cook makes a much better dish than a bad cook, and your own judgement, intuition and creativity play a vital role, one that cannot be learned from a book. But equally, no cook, however brilliant, can make a good dish from poor ingredients.

I hope, at least for creative people, that I am not offering recipes, simply a list of ingredients. It's up to you to put them together in the way that will best succeed on the day.

So, this is *not* meant to be a 'rule book'. Do not attempt to use it as such. When, for example, I say that long letters work better than short letters, don't get too upset if you find this is not the case, or you have already found that it is not the case. Nothing is absolute; there are *always* exceptions. But equally, just because you may discover the odd exception, don't claim that it overturns the rules, either. If I can offer another metaphor, this book is like a volume describing how to make a car – it would suggest that four wheels, one in each corner is a good idea; and that normally the engine goes in the front. *Most* cars accord to this 'rule'; yet within this rule you have variations as wide as a Panda to a Ferrari – and there are even some oddities with three or six wheels. So don't get upset with the 'rules' – use them intelligently.

A word or two about how to get the best from this book.

It is written in sections that are designed as nearly as possible to be free-standing. Thus if you are mainly interested in Headlines, then by reading that Chapter alone you will be able to make good use of this book, without necessarily having to read other Chapters to make sense of it. This means there is inevitably some repetition, particularly of some of the basic rules which apply to almost all direct marketing activities, and where you find them I hope they do not become too tedious.

The first section is about general principles, and the second section relates those principles to specific direct marketing creative tasks.

Even if you only need to read about specific applications, you should still find Chapters 1 and 2 – 'Why Things Work' and 'Propositions: Key to Success' useful in setting the scene. In particular, 'Why Things Work' is an attempt to explain the underlying rationale behind the somewhat illogical world of direct marketing.

All of the illustrations used are of work created by WWAV in London or WWAV North. This is not because I think that only WWAV produces the best work, but because I know that work better and can comment on it more accurately. There are many other cases I would like to have shown, particularly some of those from Reader's Digest, but unless I know them to be successful it would be better not to feature them. I am grateful to those clients who have agreed to allow me to use their work.

Lastly, while this book bears my name, it would be wrong to claim that I could have written it without substantial contributions from the many people I have had the good fortune to work with over the years. All of them have had some bearing on what I have written here, and it would be impossible to acknowledge the full extent of the debt; however, all of those people who have made WWAV what it is today – the people who work (and who have worked) at WWAV, the suppliers who help us, and the clients who use us deserve especial thanks.

In particular, I would like to thank a number of people who read the manuscript and were kind enough to make comments: Rinalda Ward, Chris Albert, Lynne Pearson, Gordon Brown, Maria Phillips, Bob Nash, Drayton Bird and Glenmore Trenear-Harvey. I cannot guarantee to have followed all of their advice, but their help was enormous. And special thanks to Jeanine Berigliano, my PA, who turned a very scrappy text into something readable and who gave invaluable help in sorting out the illustrations.

John Watson

<u>About this Paperback edition</u>
The success of the first hardback edition of this book has now led to this paperback edition – at a price that will hopefully render it more affordable for greater numbers of people. For this edition, nothing has been cut or reduced in any way, apart from, of course, the price.

<u>September 1995.</u>

PART ONE
Principles

WHY THINGS WORK

*Certain creative techniques produce significant differences
in response. Exactly why this is so remains unexplained.
In this section, an attempt is made to provide a logical
rationale of why, for example, long copy outperforms short,
and some of the other oddities in successful direct
marketing creativity.*

SOME of the strangest things work in direct marketing. A letter that is considerably longer...pages longer...than the sort you would normally receive will produce more response – sometimes much more response – than a shorter, briefer, easier-to-read letter will.

A mailing, stuffed to overflowing with individual sheets of paper, so many that you hardly know where to start, will produce five and ten-fold increases in response over a mailing that is short, sharp and to the point.

A press advertisement, set in small type, with copy so long that it seems as though it would take you half an hour to read, looking as grey as the editorial matter around it, will overwhelm in response terms a witty, punchy ad that gleams out of the page to grab your eye.

And a TV commercial that is so long that you could comfortably get up, put the kettle on, make a cuppa and return to the armchair while it's still running, will set more phones ringing within seconds than the most spectacular, wittiest and superbly directed product the finest advertising minds in London agencies can create.

With due deference to Drayton Bird's excellent 'Commonsense Direct Marketing', very little of this *is* commonsense. Why should things that seem duller and more boring actually work *better* than things that seem brighter and more interesting? And by 'work', I do not mean by a few points. Some of the stranger creative techniques I shall describe in this book produce *differences in response of hundreds of per cent*. The application of some of these curiosities makes the difference between a successful campaign and an abject failure.

They are techniques that have been developed over very many years and in split-test after split-test, statistically reliable improvements of a very significant order have almost always been noted.

So, to return to the question, why do these things work?

TOWARDS AN EXPLANATION

Rather than simply a blunt assertion that such things work, what is needed is a rational explanation for such phenomena which will be most helpful for those who have to approach the task of creating such strange mailings, ads and TV commercials every day.

Over countless numbers of mailings, ads, and even a commercial or two, I have attempted to develop a theory that holds some water. It is not perfect. But it goes some way to explaining why the 'rules' of direct marketing actually make a lot more sense than they seem to at first glance.

Like any good theory in science, it is merely a hypothesis that can only be tested by observation: can the hypothesis predict the results in advance? On a surprisingly large number of occasions, I have to confess that yes, it really can – not to percentage levels (yet!), but certainly given one piece that conforms to the theory and one piece that doesn't, *you can reasonably expect to choose the winning item in about 75% of the cases.*

A PROPOSED THEORY OF WHY THINGS WORK

The theory, then, goes something along these lines:

> **"A conventional advertisement, designed to influence the greatest number of people, has to be aimed at as many people as possible. A direct marketing advertisement, designed to achieve sales as cost-efficiently as possible, has to appeal more strongly to only those people most likely to purchase."**

Please note, by the way, that I am using the word 'advertisement' to cover ads, mailings, inserts, commercials, and all the rest of the direct marketing promotional opportunities available.

So, what does this theory mean in practice? And how can I justify it anyway?

The basis for this theory can be most easily seen in the briefing notes for an advertisement or a mailing: typically this is a definition or assumption of a target audience. A brief for a fundraising mailing may say something along the lines of:

> **"Out of the total file of 350,000 we have selected 100,000 that are the most recent donors and whose average value over the last 12 months exceeds £25."**

The assumption in this case is, of course, that I am writing to those 100,000 donors. Another example will be with creating a newspaper advertisement or a TV commercial. I am going in the Daily Mail with a product aimed at ABC1 readers. Of the 4.3 million readers of the Daily Mail, only 53% fall into this category, and therefore I am writing my ad to some 2.4 million people.

With the TV commercial, if I am making a commercial to run on Channel 1 network during the afternoons, some 2.3 million will in theory see my commercial. Naturally enough, my commercial needs to appeal to all of them.

Naturally enough? Alas, no.

The single most common mistake made by people creating direct marketing advertisements or mailings is this: it is wrong to assume that you will ever get any more than a small percentage of those people who theoretically fall into your target taking the slightest notice of your work.

OF THE TARGET MARKET THAT ARE *SUPPOSED* TO BE INTERESTED IN YOUR PRODUCT OR SERVICE, ONLY A VERY SMALL NUMBER ACTUALLY *ARE* AT THE TIME YOU COMMUNICATE WITH THEM

Let's go back to those 100,000 people in the earlier example. We are mailing those 100,000 people because the statistics predict that those 100,000 are most likely to respond to – in this case – a further solicitation for funds. However, this is simply a statistical prediction. In effect, what the stats people are saying is "of all of the people on the file, these 100,000 people will show the greatest probability of responding". Note that they are not saying "these 100,000 people *will* respond".

In fact, it is the failure of the statistics, or the failure of the much vaunted 'targeting capabilities' of direct marketing, that causes much of the problem. We are writing to these 100,000 people because we know that somewhere within the group lie those people who *will* respond, and those people who *might* respond. But typically, the majority of them will *not* respond.

WHAT ABOUT THE 95% WHO DON'T RESPOND?

But what about the non-responders? Surely they are important? They are – but I think they should not simply be looked upon as a group of people who, because they don't respond, should be allowed to dominate the approach you make to that far more critical group who do.

It has been commented on many times about 'the 95% who don't respond'; and, indeed, I have known whole mailings altered in an attempt to appeal to them – for example, what looks like an 'aggressive' mailing is toned down for fear of upsetting those 95%.

The fact that they fail to respond is not because they are upset by an aggressive mailing, but simply because they do not happen to be in the market at the time you communicate with them. Our 'targeting' talents are not yet so refined as to be able to exclude them.

In other words, by worrying about those who don't respond and assuming (incorrectly, if you follow my logic) that they are not responding because they don't like the mailing, you are actually *reducing* your chances of success (and increasing the 95% who don't respond to 96%) if you soften or modify your approach.

Clear your mind of the problem by seeing the non-responders as a group of people you are having to talk to by 'accident', in order to talk to the people who are *most* interested. You are talking to a dozen people in a crowd, but you've got to talk to the entire crowd to get to the dozen people.

Think about a shop. Just because not everyone goes into it on the same day is no reason why that shop will change its tactics. Those that don't come in on a given day are not repelled. It's simply because they're not in the market for what that shop is selling on that day. Tomorrow, they could be.

Kwik-Save discount stores only get a minority of the population shopping in them. Imagine if they started worrying about the fact that a majority of the country didn't go into a Kwik-Save. They could as fairly conclude as some people do about mailings or ads that the reason is because the 'formula' is too strong. Thus Kwik-Save would throw away its 'niche' appeal, attempt to gain a wider audience, and probably perish in the process.

But I have been sidetracked; back to the people we are really interested in – those who *will* respond.

THERE ARE TWO MAIN REASONS WHY – NO MATTER WHAT YOU DO – YOUR AUDIENCE WILL NOT RESPOND

Out of my 100,000, then, I know for certain that not everyone I am 'forced' to write to will respond, whatever I say to them. I am in this case seeking an additional donation. Clearly not all of them have the money to give; not all of them will want to give; and for a variety of reasons there is little that a printed sheet of paper can do to them that will change their minds.

As I said earlier, there are two main reasons why they are not going to respond:

■ FIRST, they are not going to respond because they are simply not in the market at the time you communicate with them (I shall have a little more to say on this point later on – there are techniques that can bring them into the market a little earlier than they would otherwise be)

■ SECOND, they are not going to respond because our targeting techniques are not sufficiently accurate and we are communicating with people who would never be interested anyway.

I hesitate to suggest which of the two reasons are strongest. I suspect it varies greatly with the medium you are using. For example, a 'warm' list – or list of existing customers – ought to suffer mainly from the first problem, less from the second. A 'cold' list – people who haven't dealt with you before – is probably about half and half, given that we know relatively little about them. And press response probably suffers mostly from the second problem, given that statistics about press audiences are based on woefully small samples and in reality probably indicate little more about a Daily Mail reader than that they read the Daily Mail.

SHEER ENTHUSIASM FOR YOUR PRODUCT OR SERVICE ALWAYS PROVIDES A BEDROCK OF PEOPLE WHO WILL RESPOND, NO MATTER HOW YOU COMMUNICATE WITH THEM

So much for the non-responders. However, thankfully, I also know that some of them (sadly, always a minority) will donate no matter what I send them. There is always a small body of people who have such a feeling for your product or service, and who enjoy transacting business through direct marketing methods, that almost any message is enough to trigger off a response.

These are the great enthusiasts without whom none of our organisations would exist. In fact, this is why some very small files in specialist areas show dramatic response rates - 50% and 60% is not uncommon – in spite of creative material that you would otherwise think had all the hallmarks of failure. Gardening catalogues are some of the best examples. All over the country there exist small specialist growers who cater for the enthusiastic gardeners, rather than the Sunday morning garden centre shopper.

Fig. 1:
The difference creative makes (1).
These two advertisements are different only so far as creative treatment is concerned. Offer, price and product are identical; and, as an AB split, they were tested on the same day in the same publication, eliminating other variables. The Burglar ad produced 342 enquiries; the Simple ad 2,714 enquiries, a difference of 790%. The Burglar ad is conventional and tries to appeal to everyone; the Simple ad follows direct response rules and is targeted only to people interested in home insurance. Note the difference in copy length.

The difference creative makes (2).
The pack on the right was the original control pack to invite prospective buyers to visit Craigendarroch, an up-market time ownership development. It worked well. But the pack on the left (which was actually more expensive) created more glamour about the product. The result was, on a head-to-head test, the expensive pack produced a 107% increase in response, and reduced the sales cost of weeks sold by two-thirds. The offers were the same in both packs; but the successful pack used better creativity to dramatically improve the cost performance.

1

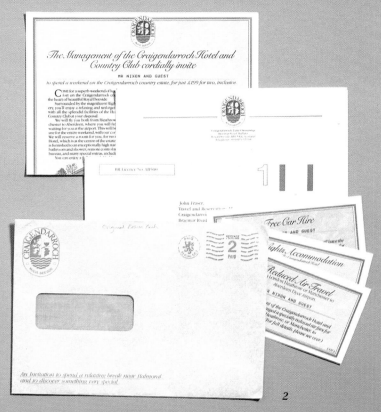

2

Typically their catalogues consist of little more than Xeroxed listings of plants, often by Latin names. Their customers, I imagine, eagerly peruse these listings for some sought-after treasure and spend at a rate that would make the average order values of most catalogue companies turn 'Day-Glo chartreuse' with envy.

With little in the way of the creative techniques discussed in this book, the sheer enthusiasm of the file means that almost any type of communication will work, and the gains in response that would undoubtedly come from using a more professional approach would simply be too small to justify either the effort or the cost.

DEFINING THE NUMBERS

Let us return to our 100,000 supposed audience. We have already seen that there will be those who – for reasons of not being in the market or for reasons of complete disinterest through inadequate targeting – will not respond. We have equally seen that there are also those who respond whatever we do to them.

Can we put some numbers on these groups? I think by looking back over typical response levels we can achieve a reliable feel for the normal sizes of these groups within the file. On a warm mailing, for instance, we would not be surprised to see a 5%-10% response level on many products. On a cold mailing, 1%-2% is probably more common. On a press ad, .05% to .1% is the general range.

(These are, let me stress, simply general levels. I have seen many, many cases of response levels much higher and much lower – but if I try and take account of those at this stage my already weak grasp of maths will be unable to cope with the modest demands that will be needed, so for now I shall take those as general numbers.)

So by taking a warm mailing such as our 100,000 donors, we would expect around a 10% response level on a fair day. From this, we can probably derive some idea of the size of the groups we're attempting to identify.

To do this, we have to know what kind of effect a professional, hard-hitting mailing would have to that file. Again, you will have to accept some general numbers, but I have often seen mailings that have produced a 25% uplift on response; sometimes it can be much more, although only in exceptional cases will it exceed 100%. But a good, competent piece of creative work should beat a mediocre piece by 25%.

A SPECTACULAR UPLIFT AGAINST A CONTROL STILL ONLY BRINGS ANOTHER 10% OF THE TOTAL AUDIENCE INTO THE RESPONSE ARENA

Back to our 100,000. If we assume that perhaps 5% of the file will respond to anything, and 10% is the average for a reasonable piece, a 25% uplift on the 10% will look like this:

> *'Core' response*..*5,000*
> *Control response*..*10,000*
> *25% uplift on control*....................................*12,500*

Thus we have gained an additional 2,500 replies from 100,000 people – a 25% uplift on the control response, bear in mind, is 'only' another 2.5% replies on the total file. Yet 25% is generally considered a very good effort.

Even if we took the blue sky route and said that our marvellous new pack would produce a 100% uplift, this is what we get:

'Core' response...*5,000*

Control response...*10,000*

100% uplift on control...................................*20,000*

Again, although we have achieved a spectacular 100% improvement, we have gained another 10,000 replies which is still only an extra 10% of the total file that we have persuaded to reply to us.

And if you accept the idea that 5% would have responded anyway, the improvement is somewhat less than it seems.

Thus for a remarkable effort, we still have 80% of the file who have not responded. Using a more realistic uplift figure than the one I just have, we are in fact left with 87.5% who have remained unmoved.

I think from this (and these numbers are generally realistic) we can surmise that something like 80-90% of even a warm file must fall into the non-responding group. If this seems like a frighteningly high number, and suggests a very poor degree of targeting indeed, I doubt that it compares at all badly with other forms of promotional activity. Because we know the numbers, we can see exactly how many people are moved by our message, and how many aren't. If you compare these numbers with the cost-effectiveness of an above-the-line campaign, I suspect you would have to conclude that although our targeting is not perfect, it is quite a long way better.

THE MAGIC MARGIN

And so now we come to what I think is the *key* to successful creativity.

We have seen that in order to achieve a much higher response to a communication, we only need a fairly small number of additional replies – small, that is, compared to the size of the whole file.

We know that we are highly unlikely to get them from our non-responding category.

We know that we needn't worry about those who will respond in any event. *Thus we need to work hard on converting a small additional number of those who fall into the 'might if pushed' category.*

This is 'The Magic Margin' – the small percentage of people who if they can be persuaded to reply, can provide you with 25% uplifts on your control, or even (and yes, it really does happen) very much more.

(The biggest increase I have personally seen, and this technique was exactly the one employed, was in the order of 800%.)

Can we know more about this group? Fortunately, if you accept the logic of this theory so far, these people fall into a clearly definable group.

They are not highly enthusiastic – otherwise they would be our natural responders. But they are in the market or inclined to reply – otherwise they would be in our non-responders group.

£1000+ TO INVEST?

ARE YOU LOOKING FOR:

The opportunity for real growth .... ✓

An investment with security.................................... ✓

Regular withdrawal option...................................... ✓

Immediate access to your money .... ✓

A bonus of up to 2.5%... ✓

If your money is sitting in a bank, building society, or national savings account, it could be working harder. With Dual Growth Bond, half of your investment goes into gilts or high interest building society accounts. The other half is invested by a leading City stockbroker mainly in the UK stockmarkets, giving you a perfect balance of security and the prospect of high growth. Your money isn't tied up either. You can make withdrawals at any time without delay or take a regular monthly cheque from your investment.

Taking more than the growth rate would reduce your capital over time.

Homeowners, a leading U.K. Friendly Society, currently manages over £500 million on behalf of 250,000 investors. Our objective is to beat the best building society rates.

SELL YOUR SHARES

A special service from Homeowners.

CALL 0800 591137 or tick box on coupon.

The value of investments can fall as well as rise, and you may not recover the amount invested.

Minimum investment is £1000. Return the coupon now for full details of this hardworking, flexible investment including a bonus of up to 2.5%.

You'll be under no obligation whatsoever.

Cut the coupon now or phone or write to us quoting the reference below.

PHONE FREE 0800 591137 PHONE NOW

Please quote ref: [ ]   MEMBER OF LAUTRO.

Send to: Homeowners Friendly Society, FREEPOST, Springfield Avenue, Harrogate, North Yorkshire HG1 5BR.

Mr/Miss/Mrs/Ms _____
BLOCK CAPITALS
Address _____
_____

Postcode _____ Tel. No. _____ Date of Birth _____
TICK FOR DETAILS OF SHARE SELLING SERVICE ☐

HOMEOWNERS FRIENDLY SOCIETY

Fig. 2:
Targeting your audience.
This ad for Homeowners Friendly Society boasts what most people would regard as a very dull headline. Yet this ad has remained the control for several years; clever creative styles have come nowhere near its cost-effectiveness. It works because it simply targets the people it wants to talk to, and ignores everyone else. Anybody without £1,000 to invest will miss this ad. Fine, we don't want them. Anyone thinking of investing £1,000 or more now, finds this headline irresistible.

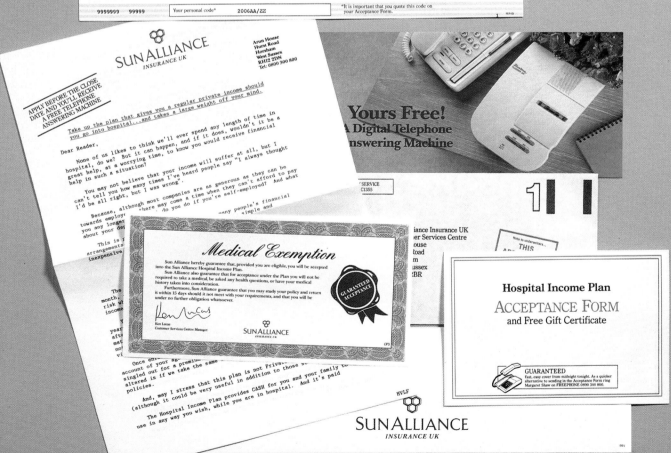

Fig. 3:
The more you tell.

This pack for Sun Alliance, virtually unchanged for 10 years, exemplifies the fundamental creative rule of direct mail – use long copy and as many items of paper as you can within the package. Apart from the drama of the large cheque, the letter runs to four pages, there is a medical exemption certificate, a gift flyer, an all-copy brochure plus the reply device and return envelope... 7 items in all. This package is mailed successfully to both house files and to cold lists, and despite repeated attempts it has not yet been possible to find another pack that works better.

THE PEOPLE YOU MOST WANT TO TALK TO ARE THE PEOPLE
WHO MOST WANT TO HEAR FROM YOU

That statement sounds tediously obvious. Yet it lies at the heart of why certain creative techniques really do work.

The people you need to aim your message at – to the exclusion of others if necessary in order not to dilute it – are the people who are in your market place NOW and want to buy…but for one important problem. They are 'waverers' – the people who are interested in your product, but for whatever reason are not yet convinced. They have not 'gone over the top' and they are the people who need to be worked on. They have a number of characteristics:

   INTEREST Because they are in the market and looking around for something very like what you're offering, they have a high degree of interest in the subject.

   WILL Typically, they probably want to buy – but because they're not that enthusiastic, they need someone to push them over the edge. They are like the people who walk into a car showroom and ask questions about a new car. The salesman knows full well that they've virtually decided to buy, but also knows that they are seeking justification: they need someone to tell them, emotionally, that they've made the correct decision.

   But they also have PROMISCUITY, again as a function of their interest. In other words, they'll be looking around, comparing prices and value, teetering on the edge of replying but not quite there.

It must be said quickly that the above characteristics are very strong ones as described here, and in the real world while the prospect will display tendencies in those directions it is rare to get them so clearly and easily defined. Usually it is because we are selling low capital goods items. You would certainly encounter the above characteristics if you were selling a car or a house; you encounter them rather more gently when selling accident insurance or a book.

But I think it aids the understanding of this issue if we assume those characteristics are present, even if subtly.

Our task is to shift them from wavering to replying, and because we now
have a clear idea of the sort of person they are, the creative techniques we
can use to achieve this shift become a great deal clearer.

First, we know they are interested. Therefore we can afford to talk to them as an interested person – we have no need to develop their interest in the first place. This, as you will see, makes the job a great deal easier.

How do we get their attention in the first place? Largely the process of 'self-selection' works for us. If the prospect is interested in a car, then I need to say I want to talk to him about a car, or a specific type of car.

If I fail to do this – to attract his or her attention by talking about something of immediate interest to that person - I have lost my argument already. This is why 'tricky' headlines so rarely work in direct marketing: they are designed to attract the attention of the greatest number of people. But if we have already discovered that we only want the attention of the people most likely to reply, tricky headlines become useless and we soon understand the need for headlines that aim directly at the MOST INTERESTED PERSON.

I will discuss headlines in a lot more detail later. But for now, simply following the logic, the best headline will be the one that flags the interested person, then presents an argument that convinces the person that here is something they are interested in.

So headlines need to be TARGETED, and inevitably they have to be long – here is the first great oddity in the argument about creativity, where conventionally speaking a short snappy headline is supposed to be the ideal. In fact, a long headline usually works best.

It needs to be long in order to achieve the degree of targeting I am talking about – and in order to convey sufficient information to that small group of interested people that we have been looking at. Short headlines mean little information – long headlines mean maximum information, and as I hope has by now become obvious, *if people are interested, they want to know more.*

(Of course, long headlines do pose problems of readability. In Chapter 3, I discuss various techniques to get over that problem.)

BRINGING PEOPLE INTO THE MARKET

At this stage, I now need to divert from my theory simply to show that while it may aid understanding, there is always more to direct marketing creativity than meets the eye.

I have been attempting to prove that aiming your communication to the 'most likely to buy' sector is the route to success, and so, in most cases, it is. But I said earlier that it is possible to use techniques that rather than simply flag people's interest, actually work harder to create interest where it may not otherwise strongly be – bringing people into the market much earlier than would otherwise be the case.

I will deal with this subject in more depth, but essentially you can create headlines that go much further 'down' the level of waverers and provoke a response from people who didn't have the slightest inkling they were in the market at all. This is 'demand creation'; and in Chapter 10 I show how incentives and other promotional devices can be employed very effectively to persuade people to respond who have a lower level of interest than I am talking about here. But bringing more people into the market can be done by creativity alone. It's not always necessary to employ promotional devices, though these certainly have a powerful role to play.

Let's take a look at how you can write your headlines to appeal to the most interested group, or how you can extend the argument even further to bring more people into the market. Take a headline such as:

'LEARN TO PLAY THE PIANO IN 30 DAYS'

As I have been saying earlier, it quite clearly appeals to those in the marketplace already. If you have no interest in playing the piano whatsoever you will probably not even see that headline. But if you have an interest, it certainly gains your attention – and by adding a strong time close makes it sound very desirable.

But can we go further and pull in people who are not really interested at all? We can, by wringing the emotions in the way John Caples did with:

"THEY LAUGHED WHEN I SAT DOWN AT THE PIANO, BUT WHEN I STARTED TO PLAY..."

You may never have wanted to play the piano in your life before, but this ad will still catch your imagination. It works by appealing to a much more deep-rooted sense – a desire for respect, for prestige, to have some notice taken of us. In that way, of course, most people are 'in the market', and Caples brilliantly uses this deep-rooted emotion to sell piano courses. Clearly, to extend the marketplace like this requires copywriting skills of a very rare order indeed.

But back to the more basic levels of creativity. However we choose to gain our reader's attention, by simply flagging their inherent interests, or like Caples by going for much deeper motives, attention alone is not sufficient. We have to move from attention to interest.

WHY LONG COPY WORKS

Your chosen headline technique will have flagged down your most interested person. They are ready to listen to you. And now we see why LONG COPY really does work: given that the only person we are interested in talking to is the person most interested in us, long copy – or more precisely defined as sufficient information required to make up the reader's mind for them – becomes perfectly reasonable.

THE MORE YOU TELL THE MORE YOU SELL

'The More You Tell, The More You Sell' in this context becomes, I hope, less of a slogan and more of a shorthand way of expressing a fundamental principle of the craft of direct marketing creativity.

The more information you can get into your communication, the better it will do, simply because the person who is reading it is interested – and because they are 'waverers' – like the person who goes into the car showroom – they are looking for justification, a rational reason why they should go ahead and do what it is you're asking for.

It should go without saying that the *quality of the copy is fundamental*. An empty piece of prose written to fill a page is hardly likely to do anything other than bore the reader. A dry list of product features is better, but still can be highly tedious. A lively, highly factual presentation of features, showing how they bring benefits to the reader, is going to work best of all.

Beware, then, the long copy for the sake of long copy approach. I have in my time been taken very seriously by a budding copywriter, who has then filled four pages of a letter with copy, as instructed. Sadly, the whole story that writer presented could have been easily condensed into about five paragraphs.

It is quality of information that counts, not quantity. But if you have a lot of

Fig. 4:
Asking for action.
One of the most important elements in successful direct marketing creativity is going hard for action; getting somebody to do something is, after all, the purpose of most direct promotions. This pack for the NSPCC shows the vigour with which action should be pursued. The headline on the letters starts with 'Will you give...' and the whole tone of the mailing is centred not just around the problems of abuse, but in telling you what you can do about it. Many otherwise good mailings fall at this last fence – they forget to demand action. Ensure that the 'close' is strongly in evidence in your mailings.

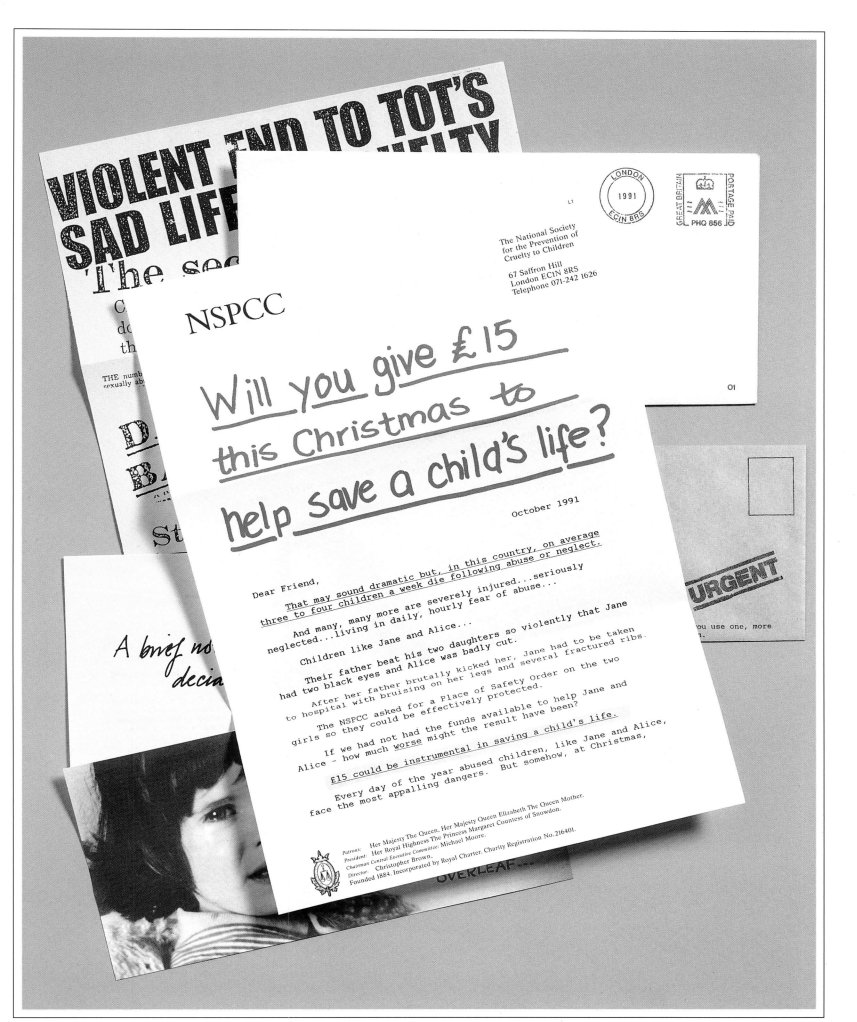

quality information to impart, then your reader who you know is interested really wants to hear the lot, down to the last nut and bolt of the details.

The most common criticism voiced against long copy is that 'nobody will read it'. If you follow my argument, then partially that statement is true – not everybody *will* read it. But the people who will read it, and read it in detail, are those people who are seeking as much information as they can find.

If you reduce the amount of detail because you're worried about boring people, you may well get more people reading you – but for those people who as waverers need convincing, you have simply not given them enough: almost certainly your piece will not do as well as it may have done.

WILL YOU HAVE A PROBLEM WITH YOUR IMAGE?

Shifting that Magic Margin of waverers to responders requires a great deal of concentration upon them – and them alone. It certainly requires a great deal of courage to produce advertising that deliberately sets out to ignore the majority of the people that could see the mailing or ad. But if you want your work to succeed, then this is exactly what you need to do – however many people might tell you that 'no one will read all of that'. Results will prove *you* right, and them wrong.

But arguments over 'image' will rage anyway. To create the kind of work I am talking about will not endear you to people who have not understood the point about focusing on the most interested and who see advertising in terms of image.

One of the most common areas where this problem arises is in press ads or TV commercials. Direct mail, because it is less public and therefore fewer people are concerned about image, seems more able to develop this necessary concentration of firepower.

The more public forms of advertising such as press or TV are likely to suffer from this 'image' problem to a much greater extent. And direct mail is rarely approved at high levels in the organisation , whereas even a modest sum spent on a TV commercial usually ends up on the Chairman's desk.

It requires therefore a much more determined attitude to make press and TV conform to the principles I have outlined above: and bluntly I think the fact that there are relatively few excellent examples of the kind of press ad I will be talking about, and even fewer examples of good TV commercials (good, of course, very much in a direct response sense), has something to do with this problem. What you can do about it is very little, other than stick to what you can see is going to work. Arguments over image are by their nature subjective; arguments over results become much more objective.

Some years ago, one of my partners went to a charity committee meeting, a charity that we had been sending out some strong direct mail for. "It's horrible" said Lady so-and-so. "It can't do us any good at all." My partner patiently explained how much money such horrible mailings had raised.

The following year, there was Lady so-and-so, chairing the meeting, when one of the audience stood up and began to complain loudly about the 'horrible' direct mail they were sending out. Lady so-and-so sternly told the objector about how much money was being raised. I gather the subject has not come up since.

THE CLOSE: THE MISSING INGREDIENT

Now we need to assume that we have gained our reader's attention and we have closely argued our case, presenting in benefit-oriented detail all of the facts we can muster. This is still not enough to achieve our ends.

Remember we are still dealing with the 'waverer'. We should by now have brought that individual a great deal closer to replying. We have in fact, if we have done our job properly, achieved a very high state of interest. What happens next is critical – *we need to close the sale.*

It is this 'close' that is so often missing in otherwise very workmanlike creativity. The reader is convinced, but left in many ways up in the air, with no clear idea of what to do next. I shall be dealing with closing in much more detail in other Chapters of this book. Closing a sale is a science almost in itself: but you need a clear idea of the type of person you are talking to before you appreciate why closing works.

Going back over this theory, if you have gained the interest of a 'waverer' they are still looking for an additional push for 'where to sign'. They want to respond. They are ready to respond. *But they still need a final confirmation that they are about to do the right thing.* An understanding of this frame of mind is vital for the creative person to be able to write convincing closes, not just hackneyed phrases such as the immortal 'so send off the coupon today'.

This hopefully also explains another oddity of direct marketing creative work – the almost childlike concentration that a good piece will have on telling the prospective customer what to do. It is not, of course, that the customer is thick. It is simply because they are on the edge – and you need to *push* them over.

DOES IT WORK?

At the beginning of this Chapter I suggested that any hypothesis had to be able to predict in advance a result for it to be taken seriously. I also suggested that this theory was not quite so scientific as to be able to do this, which is unfortunately true.

However, the general principle holds water extremely well. The next time you are asked to make a judgement about a piece of creative work – or you are judging your own – simply ask yourself the following questions:

> *"Have I aimed this at the small number of people who are going to be most interested in this idea?"*
>
> *"Have I flagged them with my headline and given them something sufficiently interesting to want to read more?"*
>
> *"Have I told them absolutely everything I can think of to convince them?"*
>
> *"Have I finally given them sufficient encouragement and sufficient rational reasons to reply now?"*

If you have chosen the route I suggest, and you can answer yes to the questions above, I would rate your chances of success as pretty high. If, on the other hand, you have not achieved all of these things, your chances of success will be low ∎

CHAPTER 1: SUMMARY

In Direct Marketing, the creative task is not to produce a mailing or ad that will appeal to the largest number of people, but to the much smaller minority who are most likely to buy. In writing to that small group, relatively inefficient targeting means that we are 'forced' to talk to a wider audience as well – but we don't really want them.

■

If we concentrate the message on those 'most interested' people, then the reason why long headlines, long copy, lots of pieces of paper in the pack and other oddities work so well is that we are talking to an interested audience. We can happily afford to ignore those people who are not interested.

■

There is no need to worry about 'the 95% who don't respond'. The reason they are not responding is not because you have upset them, but because we didn't really want to talk to them in the first place – but in order to find our 'most interested' audience, it is usually necessary, statistically, to have a large number of non-interested people at the same time.

■

In concentrating on the most interested, we can then achieve some spectacular improvements in response. A small number of people converted to replying can represent a large percentage improvement in response.

■

There will be those who will reply in any event, their interest is so high. There will be those who will never reply, because they are not in the market. The target to aim for is the 'waverer', the person who is interested but not yet convinced. Through the application of the right creative techniques, this person is duly convinced and replies.

■

The greatest mistake is to create a piece aimed at the widest possible audience. This inevitably gives you short headlines, short copy and convinces no-one. This is the first hurdle that creative people who want to be successful in direct marketing have to jump.

PROPOSITIONS:
KEY TO SUCCESS

*A proposition is the starting point for all creative work,
either in the form of a brief from marketing people, or in the
form of a propositional statement worked out by creative people.
Here, I will deal with how to create propositions that almost
automatically produce better and more responsive creative work.
The problem is, a lot of confusion seems to exist as to what
exactly a proposition is. Perhaps this will help.*

B EFORE you even start on the creative work, a great deal of preliminary thinking and planning has to be done. Trying to create a mailing or advertisement in a vacuum…trying to deal with a sheet of blank paper…is neither easy nor terribly productive. I have seen more time wasted through false starts – and I wasted more of my own time – by not having done the preparatory work than in almost any other way.

You can very rarely come up with a good piece from scratch. If you do, I assure you it's more by luck than judgement.

So, the most organised and productive way of doing the preliminary thinking is through the concept of developing a proposition before you even start the creative work proper.

Who should do this work? It can come from marketing people, but it can just as easily come from creative people too. It comes, best of all, from everyone sitting down together and addressing the fundamental issue: *what is it about this product or service that will make somebody buy it?*

A GOOD PROPOSITION IS HALF OF THE CREATIVE WORK DONE

The creation of the right proposition is so important that I would personally regard it as at least 50% of the creative effort required. Once a good proposition is in place, the writing and art direction of the rest of the work is, frankly, pretty straightforward. It is therefore your blueprint, your wiring diagram, your architect's plan. Everything else you will do, creatively, flows from that proposition. It makes sense then to devote as much time as practically possible to evolving and defining that proposition before you start work. But what exactly *is* a proposition?

DEFINING THE PROPOSITION

It is curiously difficult to define what a proposition is, because in terms of direct marketing, it can be very many different things. But I ought to try to define it to start with.

I think it's something like this:

A proposition is a short statement that gives a clear reason, backed up by some brief arguments, why the target audience will respond.

It is therefore a 'why' statement. 'Why' should someone respond?

Turn the idea around and look at it from the point of view of the prospect. Why should I be interested in this? What's in it for me? A good proposition statement will be essentially an answer to the question "Why should I respond? Because…"

There are any numbers of ways of answering the question. You should respond…

because it's the cheapest on the market

because it will last longer than any other

because it will make you rich

because you don't need a medical

because it will save lives

because it's green

…or whatever feature you happen to settle on. You can just as easily use 'exterior' factors such as incentives…

because it's a limited edition

because you could win £100,000

because you get a free clock radio

because it's a special price

PORTMANTEAU PROPOSITIONS

Now, you need to be very careful here. It is not much use in answering the "why should I buy?" question with an answer that contains EVERY reason why you would buy. This is no help at all – attaching a long list of product features is not going to give much guidance as to which one of them will make the *strongest* headline. Such all-encompassing propositions are quite wrong. You need to isolate a SINGLE selling point, not throw all of them in.

DOES IT MAKE A HEADLINE?

The most obvious place that a proposition gets translated into creative work is through the headline, although it should also have a powerful influence over the stance of the rest of the copy. This is why 'portmanteau' propositions are no good. *One* selling point is needed, around which the whole argument can then be built.

Does it need to be unique? The USP ('Unique Selling Proposition') concept is a good one; clearly if it is unique then you have a strong competitive advantage. But it is not vital. And in direct marketing terms, if the product itself does not have anything exciting in it, or at least not sufficiently exciting to generate the required level of response, then incentives can be introduced which can make perfectly reasonable propositions.

Unique or not, it needs to be single-minded. This point cannot be emphasised too strongly. The more you can focus on a proposition, the stronger the creative work will become.

But the $64,000,000 question is, how do you find the right proposition?

CREATING THE RIGHT PROPOSITION

Clearly, devising the right proposition is not simply a matter of scribbling down a couple of paragraphs. It should be…in fact, it must be…the culmination of a great deal of work.

How do you start?

There are three things that you need before you can write down a proposition:

1 *Past response data.*
2 *What other people in the market are doing.*
3 *What your own marketing requirements demand.*

Past response data is by far the most important of these. By going back over past data, you can see specifically what things *have* worked, and just as importantly what things have *not* worked. When looking through this data, it's always a good idea to make sure you have the creative material associated with it. A pack description on a computer spreadsheet is usually rather too terse to give you much idea of what the proposition was. Look through the creative material and even if a proposition was never written down at the time, you can usually see it clearly enough from the creative work.

ONE OF THE BEST GUIDES TO WHAT IS WORKING IS TO LOOK CAREFULLY AT WHAT YOUR COMPETITION IS DOING. ORIGINALITY MAY WIN PRIZES BUT IT RARELY WINS SALES

Looking through what other people are doing, by means of a 'swipe' file or press cutting service, also gives you a very good steer. Half an hour spent leafing through a competitor's press cuttings for the last 6 months is one of the most instructive things you can do.

Of course, the more often an ad or mailing is repeated, the chances are higher that it is doing well. This can tell you which ideas to use, and which ones not to. Is this plagiarism? Of course! *Originality may win prizes, but it rarely wins sales.* I am not suggesting for one minute that you copy word for word – simply that propositions being used frequently are clearly working and you should think about trying them. After all, every shop in the world, even Harrods, copies the same promotional technique from each other – the summer and winter sales.

A study of both these sources of data needs to be allied to your own needs on the marketing front. Propositions that generate large volumes of response are fine if that's what you need, but if your problem is conversion levels, average order value, bad debt, poor quality leads, or any one of the hundreds of problems beyond raw response that afflict us, you'll need to look at how you can employ propositions that will work to achieve those ends.

It may seem topsy turvy that I leave your own marketing requirements to last. This is because of the 'want' problem with propositions, rather than the 'why' virtue. The danger is if you concentrate on your own marketing problems too much, you simply end up creating a proposition that tells the prospect what you *want* them to do, rather than giving them a good reason *why* they should do it. Go through the disciplines of looking at what actually worked first. You will then rarely come up with a proposition that is doomed to failure.

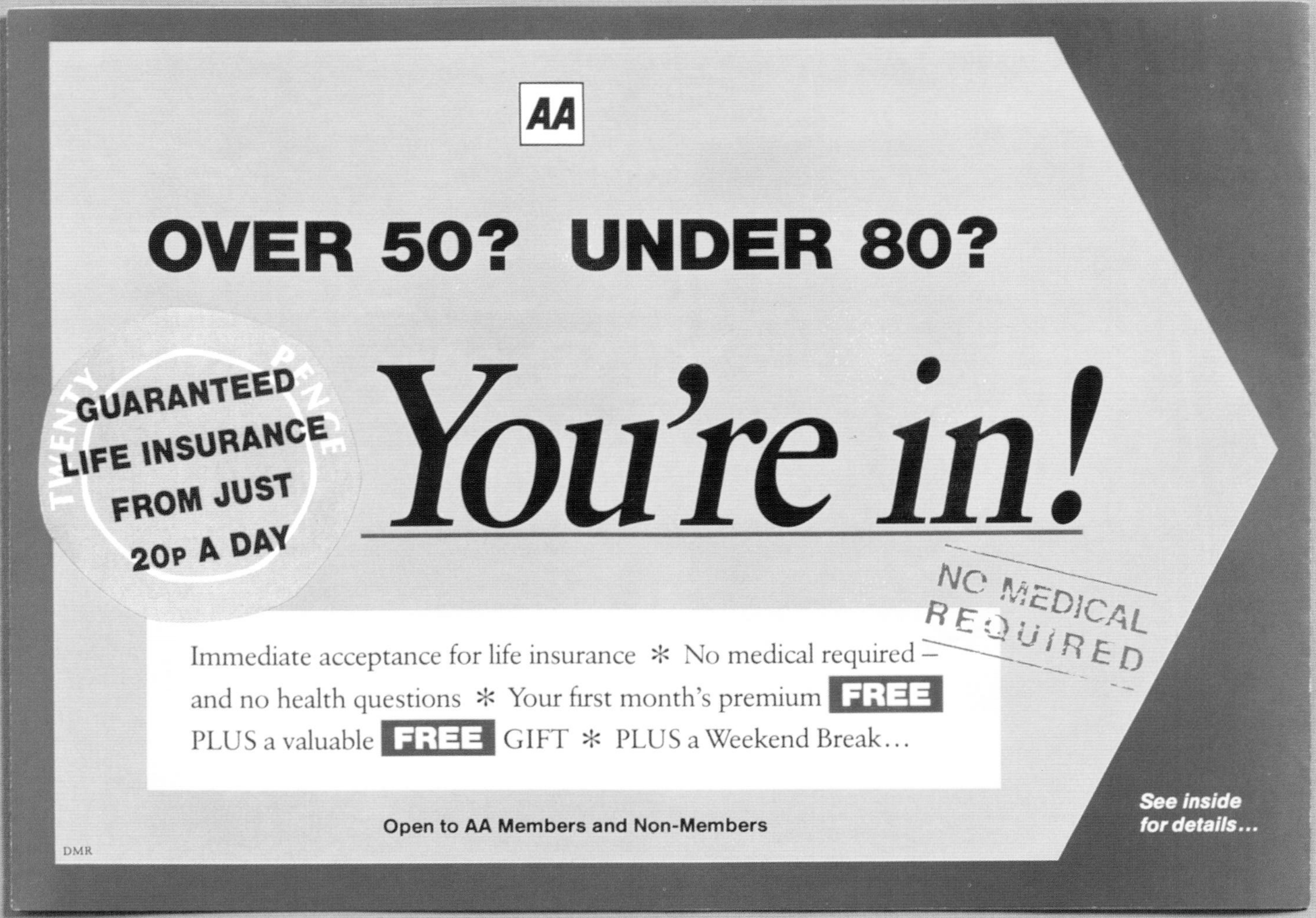

AA

OVER 50? UNDER 80?

You're in!

TWENTY PENCE
GUARANTEED LIFE INSURANCE FROM JUST 20p A DAY

NO MEDICAL REQUIRED

Immediate acceptance for life insurance ✳ No medical required – and no health questions ✳ Your first month's premium **FREE** PLUS a valuable **FREE** GIFT ✳ PLUS a Weekend Break…

Open to AA Members and Non-Members

See inside for details…

DMR

Fig. 5:
Concentrating on the proposition.
This insert for an AA Over 50s Plan has the main headline 'You're in', which comes directly from earlier, tested propositions revolving around guaranteed acceptance. Previous tests, as well as examination of competitive activity, showed this to be the winning proposition.

However, instead of saying simply 'Guaranteed Acceptance' we went to the 'emotional' heart of the proposition. Notice how additional overlines, panels and underlines amplify the main proposition, but still leave the feeling of 'acceptance' as the clear main message. This insert front cover was developed from a whole page press ad, shown in detail in fig. 56.

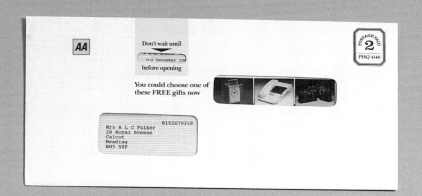

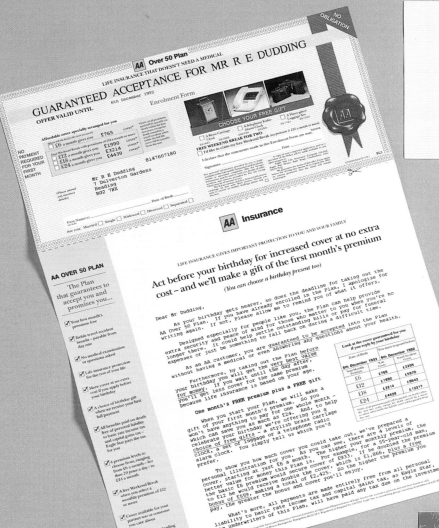

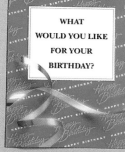

Fig. 6:
Propositions in mailings.
Like press ads mailings do better when you concentrate on the proposition. Here's the AA Over 50s product again, this time in a mailing format: here, the free gift offer is strongest. Notice how the proposition starts with the envelope showing the gifts (together with a time close) and then when the main letter is opened the top section continues to make the free gift strong. There's a strong subsidiary proposition working here – act now before your birthday. But see how the gifts still retain prominence.

'INTERROGATING THE PRODUCT'

A useful technique to help you develop the proposition is to 'interrogate' the product. What's it made of? Who made it? What's in it? You can gain answers to these questions by simply looking at the product; by carefully reading the literature; by visiting the factory; by talking to the designer. Never skimp on this information-gathering stage – you could discover a feature of the product that could transform your proposition.

HOW IT'S DONE: A LIVE EXAMPLE

I think we now need an example to try and clarify this concept. Unless you're used to thinking in propositions, it can be a very puzzling concept. I have seen many otherwise intelligent account people looking at me oddly when I expound this idea to them. But if you're brought up as a copywriter, you spend most of your time looking for headlines, and you tend to translate marketing needs into propositions that might (or might not) make good headlines.

Let's use a real case. It's a press ad, for an Over 50s Insurance Plan from AA Insurance Services. It's a bit of a cheat using a press ad because in many ways it's simpler than a mailing. But it may help explain the proposition concept more simply as well, so bear with me.

The product had been running in the press for some time. Like most successful ads, the old ad had done very well and as a result had had a fair number of runs in the press. This meant it started to tire and so we had to produce a new ad to beat it.

THE THREE STEP PROPOSITION FORMULA IN ACTION

The key here was in not simply creating a new ad, but to go through the process that I have outlined above.

First, we reviewed all the previous advertising. Then, we looked at competitive activity. We already had our marketing need: beat the existing control.

The key lay in what had gone on before. It was clear that the most powerful concept used in competitor activity was 'guaranteed acceptance'. How did we know? Simply by going through our press cuttings file and looking at all the competitors' ads. Because you have a thick sheaf of these, you have to look through them pretty quickly – you are in fact replicating very closely what happens when a prospect flicks through a newspaper. You don't have time to analyse every word – just pick up an impression of what they're saying. It was clear that variations on 'guaranteed acceptance' kept coming up most strongly.

THE VALUE OF PAST DATA

Our own past experience suggested the same thing. This was based not only on a review of previous results from the press activity, but just as importantly, from the activity of past mailings and even past clients marketing a similar product. Any source of data is useful.

The previous ad, although it had 'guaranteed acceptance' in it, didn't use it as the MAJOR PROPOSITION. It actually used a free gift approach, which is frighteningly difficult to beat. But given that it was tiring, something else needed to be used.

It seemed at this stage that 'guaranteed acceptance' had been isolated as a key ingredient – a reason 'why' the individual should reply. Naturally, you need to think quite deeply about why it should work: given a market of people over 50 who may have deep reservations about being rejected for a life insurance plan, it is a promising area.

All through the process, creative people needed to be involved. This is for a very simple reason: not every good proposition can be translated into a good headline or a good ad. A creative person has (or should have, if they're any good at their job) a strong sense of what propositions are likely to create strong ads or mailings. Can it be turned into a strong headline; does it allow the use of visual imagery to reinforce the point?

So, let us now attempt to write a proposition, using the earlier definition:

'A proposition is a short statement that gives a clear reason, backed up by some brief arguments, why the target audience will respond.'

Taking account of what we have discovered from past data, I think we could write a proposition along the lines of:

'The existing Over 50s control is tiring. A new ad should promote the benefits of guaranteed acceptance – if you're over 50 and you can say yes to a few simple health questions, we will guarantee to accept you into the plan.

The other benefits remain. In particular, a free gift will be sent on receipt of the first month's premium payment.'

That's it. From that proposition we were then able to develop a new ad style. You can see it here. The main headline is really very simple:

'YOU'RE IN!'

which is as dramatic and eye-catching a way of employing the proposition as we managed to come up with.

You can, I hope, see here that not only does the headline and whole approach of the ad hinge around the proposition, but it equally carefully follows the theory I outlined in the previous Chapter – it appeals *only to those people most likely to be interested*, and uses a carefully worked out proposition to do it with.

Inevitably it's not quite as simple as that: you will see that the headline is surrounded by a great deal of other material, and that material plays a vital part too – but we shall save that discussion for the Chapter on 'Headlines'.

We could of course have chosen any other proposition. Given the ability we have in direct marketing to test ads and mailings, we could select a variety of different propositions and give them a run. Or, equally, once we think we've found a proposition that works, we can create different material around it. Much as a good proposition will help you succeed, harder-working creative material can always give you better results.

PROPOSITIONS NEED TO BE HARD

We've seen how the creation of a proposition can help us towards good creative work. We've also seen how we arrive at the proposition. I hope you noticed along the way one very critical feature of the process: the 'promise' we use in the proposition is a very hard and specific one.

Fig. 7:
Same product, different propositions.
The 8 ads on the following pages are all for the same new product. Only the propositions are different. The problem was that the product was entirely new so we had little past experience to go on. Which approach would prove strongest? These approaches were selected from a number of possible propositions, then put into research prior to live tests in the media. The propositions were a) 'Care for your family' b) 'Don't rely on State benefits' c) 'The AA looks after your health' d) 'Two in one' e) 'Price/value' f) 'Choice' g) 'Free advice on healthcare' h) 'local/convenience'. In research, e) f) and g) came out tops, with e) and g) winning in live tests. There were many more possible propositions that could have been – this example shows how flexible propositions can be.

See overleaf ▶

A

Who suffers most when you don't have private medical insurance?

Protect your family now with AA Healthsure, up to £100,000 private health cover from around 66p a day

Choose the options that suit you best

Private Medical Cover up to £20,000 a year

Serious Illness Cash Sum £15,000

Monthly Income Protection Plan up to £400

Weekly Hospital Benefit up to £350

Easy to apply – no medical needed

Call in now for instant cover

ALL PAID TAX-FREE

Substantial cash sums you can rely on – tax-free

Free one-to-one advice for the cover that's best for you

For free expert advice visit your local AA Shop

AA Healthsure

LOOK IN YELLOW PAGES FOR THE ADDRESS OF YOUR LOCAL AA SHOP

SHOP OPENING HOURS Monday to Friday 9am to 5pm, Saturday 9am to 1pm

---

B

At last, a real alternative to depending on State Benefits if an accident or illness stops you working.

Protect your family now with AA Healthsure

£15,000 cash sum if you suffer a heart attack, cancer, stroke or other serious illness

Up to £20,000 a year to pay for private medical treatment

Up to £400 a month guaranteed if your income stops

Up to £50 for every day you spend in hospital

Up to £30 for every day you attend hospital as an out-patient

Up to £30 for every day you attend physiotherapy

Up to £30 for each day you spend convalescing

Up to £30 for every day you need 'day care'

Cover begins at just £6 a month

Easy to apply – no medical needed

Call in now for instant cover

Substantial cash sums you can rely on – tax-free

ALL PAID TAX-FREE

Free one-to-one advice for the cover that's best for you

For free expert advice visit your local AA Shop

AA Healthsure

LOOK IN YELLOW PAGES FOR THE ADDRESS OF YOUR LOCAL AA SHOP

SHOP OPENING HOURS Monday to Friday 9am to 5pm, Saturday 9am to 1pm

---

C

In these uncertain times, be sure you have enough healthcare cover.

Smiths Industries units cut sick pay
By Lisa Wood, Labour Staff

Cash shortfall forces Guy's to cut services

Health Cover? Call AA to the rescue.

Introducing AA Healthsure up to £100,000 private health cover from around 66p a day.

Choose the options that suit you best

Private Medical Cover up to £20,000 a year

Serious Illness Cash Sum £15,000

Monthly Income Protection Plan up to £400

Weekly Hospital Benefit up to £350

Easy to apply – no medical needed

Call in now for instant cover

£100,000 health cover from around 66p a day

ALL PAID TAX-FREE

Free confidential advice tailored to your needs

For free expert advice visit your local AA Shop

AA Healthsure

LOOK IN YELLOW PAGES FOR THE ADDRESS OF YOUR LOCAL AA SHOP

D

ANNOUNCING A MEDICAL BREAKTHROUGH

Now you can look after your physical *and* financial health with just one simple plan.

INTRODUCING AA HEALTHSURE – TOTALLY COMPREHENSIVE HEALTH COVER.

Choose the options that suit you best

Private Medical Cover up to £20,000 a year

Serious Illness Cash Sum £15,000

Monthly Income Protection Plan up to £400

Weekly Hospital Benefit up to £350

No medical needed

Call in now for instant cover

FREE confidential advice on the best cover for you

ALL PAID TAX-FREE

Cover starts at just £6 month

For free expert advice visit your local AA Shop

AA Healthsure

LOOK IN YELLOW PAGES FOR THE ADDRESS OF YOUR LOCAL AA SHOP

SHOP OPENING HOURS Monday to Friday 9am to 5pm, Saturday 9am to 1pm

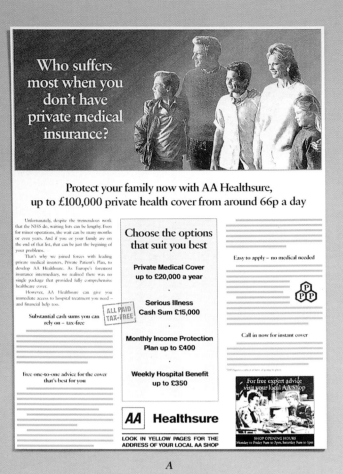

E

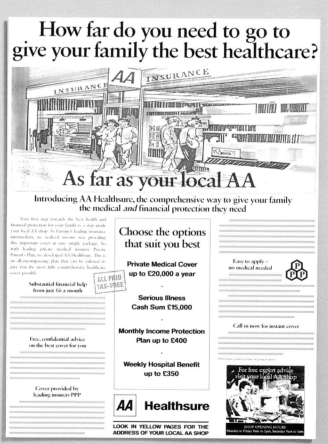

H

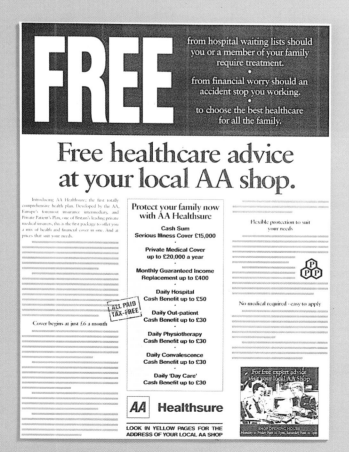

G

AA and Private Patients Plan introduce the first healthcare plan that's as individual as you are.

Now you can choose the type of cover you want from just £6 a month.

F

I have seen propositions created that are bound to fail because the promise is such a loose one. For example, a *bad* proposition for our Over 50s ad could be:

> *'The existing Over 50s ad is tiring. A new ad should be developed that*
> *presents all of the benefits in a much stronger way...'*

which is clearly a pretty woolly statement – but how many times have you seen such statements?

The art is in identifying the specific promise, or attribute, or benefit, or feature, or almost anything, that you think will form the basic trigger. IT DOESN'T MATTER IF YOU'RE WRONG – because you always need several such triggers to play around with first.

Incidentally, I am not aware of any rule that says you should only have a single proposition at a time when briefing. Try developing at least five, refining it down to three, and then looking at the creative results of the proposition. As I said earlier, sometimes the proposition may be technically good, but almost impossible to put over creatively. See how the creative work treats the proposition before you finally decide which one to start your testing process with.

TYPE OF SPECIFIC PROMISE THAT MAKES PROPOSITIONS WORK

What kind of promise can you use in propositions? There are a number of distinctly different types:

▪ PRODUCT FEATURES The example I used above, the AA Over 50s ad, used a product feature as the promise: in other words, a characteristic of the plan that could be used to over-ride the other characteristics. It would be seen by the audience to be the most important feature. This is the most usual place to find your promise: it has the great benefit of being highly specific, as well. An easy way to approach this is simply to list every single product feature, then pick the strongest ones.

▪ PRODUCT BENEFITS This is taking features a stage further. A benefit is what a product feature confers upon the user. Feature: guaranteed acceptance. Benefit to user: no need for embarrassing medicals. Every single product feature always has a corresponding benefit – or, more usually, benefits. Quite often a proposition will focus on the feature, and the copywriter will turn it into the benefit (this is dealt with later under 'Copy'). There is nothing to stop you using a benefit straight off, however.

▪ PROMOTIONAL PROMISES Frequently, using either features or benefits is not as strong as using promotional promises. If I refer back to the previous chapter you will see that sometimes you need additional promises to pull more of your audience into the market than would otherwise be the case. Therefore, should you have such an offer, this will then form your main proposition. It could be a prize draw, a time close, a competition, or a free gift. But as with the other cases above, you need to be very specific, and settle on one such element as your marketing plank.

THE OFFER?

Where does 'the offer' fit into all of this? Is it the same as the proposition?

Indeed it is, but I have deliberately refrained from calling it the 'offer' thus far for the very simple reason that most people think an 'offer' is literally that – a promotional device such as a free alarm clock radio – and that the product benefit is something else. This is not so. The 'offer' is the promise: it can be a promotional offer, but it can equally easily be the product feature or benefit that I have referred to. In the Over 50s example above, the 'offer' in this case was 'Guaranteed Acceptance'. In previous ads on the same product, the offer was in fact the famous Alarm Clock Radio. The offer – the promise – is an integral part of the proposition – in fact, it is no less than the proposition itself.

THE NEED TO DECIDE

I cannot stress too strongly that what you need to do to make the propositional route work for you is to take some hard decisions. It is a fact of life – albeit a sorry one – that marketing is full of compromise, usually because so many people with so many opinions are involved – that taking a clear decision is actually very difficult. It requires great courage or great foolhardiness!

Preparing a complete direct mail package on the back of a single specific proposition is, after all, risky. What if the client doesn't like it? What if it bombs?

I have no easy answers to those problems, except to say that the outcome of compromise in this area is usually failure. Weak propositions lead to weak creative work, which leads to poor results. Taking your courage in both hands, however, pick a proposition that is *strong and clear*, ensure that your creative work meets it, and you will more often than not get a good result.

And it should be said that getting a bad result in direct marketing is as useful as getting a good one, so long as you have used a specific proposition: you know, in future, which one *not* to use, which can literally give you a valuable competitive edge. *"If you're not getting any failures, you're not testing enough."*

The propositions you can come up with will actually give you an idea of what to test. Rather than just trying 'different' approaches, if you can generate a list of, say, five completely different propositions, then this will give you material to test five different ads – where the difference rather than being superficial is quite marked. Too often testing becomes a process where essentially the same propositions are tested against each other, but the creative work is slightly different. Not surprisingly the results are usually very close, and hardly worth the effort of the test.

JUDGING THE CREATIVE WORK

One of the most difficult things for anyone to do is judge creative work. The producer of the piece is usually too close to it; account people and clients, when the work is wrong, are generally unable to put their fingers on the reason why and start driving everyone potty by fiddling with small details.

The benefit of a propositional statement worked out in advance and agreed by all parties is that it gives you a base to judge the final work from, thus avoiding a purely

*Remember when AA men still saluted, when open roads stretched out
for miles across empty countryside…? Now a unique collection of Corgi models
pays homage to this Golden Age of British motoring.*

THE LEGENDARY JAGUAR XK120
YOURS FOR ONLY £1.
(+p&p)

1:43 scale replica. Actual size: 9.2 cms

The 1952 Jaguar XK120 – one of the all-time classic sports cars,
now reproduced in a 1:43 scale model from Corgi.

THE REVOLUTIONARY styling and technical innovation of the Jaguar XK120 took the motoring world by storm and influenced a whole generation of sports cars in Britain.

Now the sleek lines of this masterpiece in steel and chrome have been faithfully captured by Corgi in a detailed 1:43 scale die-cast model. It's the first car in a unique collection paying homage to the finest sports cars ever built…the days when the British motoring industry led the world.

You can own this beautiful model for the special price of £1 as your introduction to the Classic British Sports Car Collection. And in the months ahead you'll be sent seven further models representing some of the most famous names in British motoring…names like the Austin Healey, the MGA, the Triumph TR3A.

FREE Once you have received your first model, you can choose to take all the remaining cars at once and if you do, we'll send you the solid ash presentation stand featured below <u>completely free</u> (normal price £9.99).

All are available at the collector's price of £9.99 each. Every car is finished to the same high standards which have made Corgi one of the most famous model makers in the world.

To receive your Jaguar XK120 and start your collection, simply complete and return the coupon below – or telephone on 081-809 7814. <u>There's no need to send any money now.</u>

In the unlikely event that you are not satisfied for any reason, simply return the model within 28 days and you will have nothing to pay.

THE CLASSIC BRITISH SPORTS CAR COLLECTION

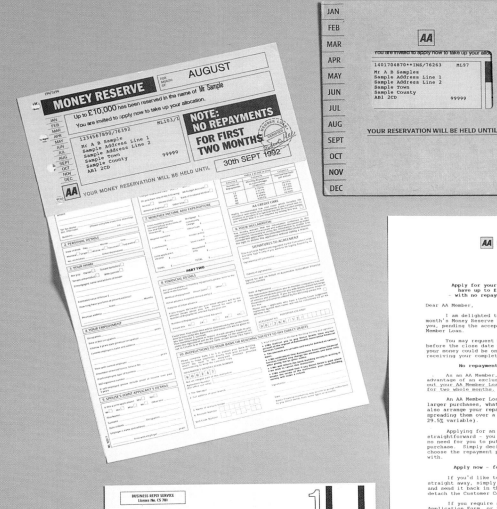

YOUR RESERVATION WILL BE HELD UNTIL

◀ Fig. 8:
Making the offer the proposition.

Propositions can be based on a feature of the product. But equally, where greater strength is required, an offer can become the proposition. Here, in an ad that launched Corgi into direct marketing, we used a traditional 'first one for £1' offer to get collectors started on the series. The headline was single-minded in its use of the offer as the main proposition; the copy goes on to amplify on the offer in detail. With such an emotional subject (to some, anyway!) it would have been easy to let the ad simply become overwhelmed by the car – it needs good discipline to ensure that the proposition dominates.

Fig. 9: ▲
Artificial propositions.

Sometimes propositions can be created purely as part of the process of designing a pack. With this loan product, there was nothing inherent in the product that differentiated it, nor were we able to make a 'hard' offer of gifts. We therefore created a proposition that

was loosely based around a time close, using months of the year, suggesting that only a certain amount was available for that month. This gave a 'shortage' feeling which seemed to inspire additional applications. When tested against a previous control, this approach significantly outperformed the old mailing.

subjective view and saving much time and heartache in the process.

Instead of looking at work and asking "Do I like it" (and if you didn't do it, the answer is normally that you don't like it as much as the person who did), with a proposition in front you, written down, you can compare the work with the proposition. You can then ask a more objective question: "Does it communicate the proposition we have agreed upon in a strong and compelling way?" If the answer is yes, you have a result. If the answer is no, you must reject the work.

Rejecting creative work is never easy. This is because too often a proposition is not in place and you tend to reject on what appears to be a subjective basis. Saying to someone who may have spent a week slaving over a package "I don't like it" is not the best route to love and affection within a creative department. When a mailing or an ad doesn't look or feel right to someone, it usually means it's weak – it's not 'selling' hard enough, it's not saying enough to convince someone to buy. *The underlying problem is almost always the lack of a proposition*, or a failure on the creative person's part to exploit the selling opportunities given by that proposition.

But once you have agreed upon the proposition, you can reject work that doesn't meet it on a rational and sensible basis. Rather than being subjectively critical of a week's work, you can simply say that it doesn't meet the proposition. Or, more likely, it doesn't make as much of the proposition as it could. Or, if the proposition has been correctly used, but it still seems weak, you can then begin a discussion that revolves around a much more productive area – is the proposition the right one anyway, or could something stronger be used?

By putting a great deal of work into defining the proposition in the first place, you not only make the chances of achieving the right creative work a lot higher, but you can then afford to focus on the bigger issues in direct marketing. And by doing this, you will be making a significant contribution to improving your results ■

CHAPTER 2: SUMMARY

*Before you commence any creative work, a proposition should be created
and agreed between creative people and marketing people.*

*A proposition is a brief statement that focuses on the main promise
you are going to use.*

*Good clues to which promise to choose come from three main sources: past
response data, competitive activity, and your own marketing requirements.
By looking through all of these you can derive a promise that will work.*

*The promise itself must be specific, not general. You need a lot of courage
to isolate a single promise from so many, and 'hang your hat' on it, so that the
whole piece revolves completely around it.*

*The promise – or offer – comes from one of three different areas. One, product
features – these are characteristics of the product. Two, product benefits – these
are generally the benefits that the product feature confers upon the purchaser.
Three, promotional promises such as free gifts or prize draws.*

*Don't worry about having a separate offer from the proposition.
The term is virtually interchangeable – the offer is the core of the proposition,
and can include not just promotional offers but can equally easily be
product features or benefits.*

*Once the creative work is produced, having an agreed, written proposition
allows you a more objective benchmark for judging that work. No matter how
good the creative work, it it fails to communicate the proposition, it is not doing
the job you want it to, and therefore you must reject it.*

HEADLINE TECHNIQUES

The headline, be it in an ad or a mailing, is the critical element. If you can't get your prospect interested with your headline, very little else is going to work. Writing headlines is seen as an inspirational process, yet in reality it involves a great deal more perspiration than inspiration. There are specific analytic stages that you need to go through which will help you create better and more powerful headlines.

HEADLINES are probably one of the most difficult jobs facing a copywriter. Sitting down and starting to try to write one is very similar to the feeling you get before you go on stage. If the headline is not good, if you fail to come up with the goods, almost nothing else is going to go right for you in the mailing or ad that you're trying to create.

You sit and sweat over drafts. Does it sell? Is it snappy? Does it communicate the proposition? Is it interesting? Does it select the right target audience? All of these things, and more, have to be achieved in just a few words.

It must be said that many copywriters add greatly to their difficulties by coming to rely on inspiration to a great extent to achieve all of these things. Frequently, pad after pad gets filled with endless variations on different headlines, each one crossed out until finally, hopefully, one emerges that seems to do the job. The problem is, by this time, the copywriter's brain is so full of the problem that it's difficult to know if the solution is correct or not.

I'd like to introduce you to what I think is a much easier way. Not only is it easier as far as the copywriter is concerned, it also has a much greater advantage: it can produce headlines that often work very well.

BACK TO BASICS

In order to do this, we need to go back to Chapters 1 and 2, because it is within the theory of what works, and then in the creation of a proposition, that the secret of writing a good headline really lies.

In Chapter 1, we learned about the need to isolate the 'Magic Margin' – the small minority of people who were 'waverers', upon whom we could exert the most influence for the best results. We discovered that they were defined as people who were already interested in the product or service that we were offering – or at least they were predisposed to be interested. We found that we needn't worry about people who weren't yet in the market, because there was little we could do to bring them to the market cost-effectively. They would get there in their own good time.

In Chapter 2 we learned about the preparatory work, employing the proposition concept – a simple statement of the main promise – or offer – that we would use; a

Fig. 10:
Good headlines aren't clever.
Most good headlines are the simplest possible expression of what the proposition is. On this ad for Scotts of Stow, the proposition was 'a cafetiere that keeps coffee hot for only £19.95'. With a few added adjectives to spice it up a little, the proposition becomes the headline. There's nothing clever in this line – it communicates the essential information quickly and clearly. Cleverness would only obscure the proposition. Note too how the headline is split into 3 – an overline talking about the virtues of 'plunger' cafetieres, the first headline giving the main proposition, then the second headline containing the price.

It's easy making real coffee in a 'plunger' cafetiere:
now this new insulated version keeps your coffee hot for hours.

The unique cafetiere that keeps fresh coffee piping hot for 2 hours or more.

MAKING fresh coffee is easy with a plunger-type cafetiere. Just add boiling water to the medium-ground coffee of your choice, wait 3-5 minutes then push down the plunger, and you've got really fresh coffee without fuss.

Trouble is, ordinary cafetieres let the coffee go cold in minutes. And with the price of fresh coffee, a jugful not drunk immediately is an expensive waste.

That's why this new insulated cafetiere from West Germany has already proved so popular. Made of heat-resistant borosilicate glass, the inner jug is surrounded by a layer of insulating material, protected in an elegant white, black or red outer jug. Naturally, with such a high quality cafetiere, the plunger incorporates a stainless steel filter.

Even the lid is insulated. The result? A **litre** of delicious fresh coffee that stays piping hot for 2 hours or even longer. Make a jug at breakfast, you'll still have some left for elevenses. Serve a jug after dinner, and your guests will still be enjoying it over the third brandy, without you having to keep popping out to put the kettle on.

And apart from the fact that it keeps your coffee hot, at just £19.95 it also costs quite a few pounds less than some conventional, non-insulated varieties.

To order your insulated cafetiere from Scotts of Stow, simply fill in the coupon and post today. Or telephone your order on 0793 706111, 9am to 9pm, 7 days a week. Either way, we gladly accept Access, Visa or MasterCard.

Your cafetiere will be sent to you within 14-28 days. If you're not completely delighted for any reason, simply return it within 3 months for a full, no-quibble refund.
☎ **Telephone Orders** – Call 0793 706111 to order on your Visa, Access or MasterCard.

SCOTTS of STOW

3 MONTHS' TOTAL CONFIDENCE GUARANTEE
If you're not delighted with your purchase for any reason whatsoever, simply return it within 3 months for a full, no-quibble refund. Post to: Scotts of Stow, Admail 222, The Square, Stow-on-the-Wold, Gloucs. GL54 1AF.

PLEASE SEND ME	CODE	PRICE	QUANTITY	TOTAL
Cafetiere Black	1058BK	£19.95		£
Cafetiere White	1058W	£19.95		£
Cafetiere Red	1058R	£19.95		£
I enclose my cheque/postal order (payable to Scotts of Stow Ltd) for:	PLUS P&P for one cafetiere add			£2.95
	PLUS P&P for two or more add			£3.95
£		ORDER TOTAL		£

or please debit my Visa/Access/MasterCard for the above amount.

Card No:

Expiry Date: _____ / _____

NAME (Mr/Mrs/Miss/Ms) _____
BLOCK CAPITALS PLEASE

ADDRESS _____

POSTCODE _____
Your postcode helps us to fulfil your order promptly.

SIGNATURE _____

Delivery U.K. excluding C.I. Subject to availability.

Occasionally we permit other carefully-screened organisations to write to you about products we feel may interest you. If you would prefer not to hear from them, please tick this box. ☐
Scotts of Stow Ltd. Registered Office: The Square, Stow-on-the-Wold, Gloucs., GL54 1AF. Registered No: 2548299 England.

ICEVS

Scotts of Stow's new Insulated Cafetiere, ONLY £19.95 +p&p.

ANOTHER SCOTTS of STOW SPECIAL OFFER

Scotts of Stow Ltd. Registered Office: The Square, Stow-on-the-Wold, Gloucs., GL54 1AF. Registered No: 2548299 England.

promise based on past results, competitive activity and marketing need that would form the creative platform we judged was going to work best – or was at least worth a try.

Armed with these two necessary tools – a theory and a proposition – you are now, and only now, ready to start the process of creating a headline that will work.

DON'T START UNTIL YOU'RE READY TO START

Of course, you could launch yourself at writing a headline before any of this is in place. You might be very lucky, or extraordinarily clever, and hit the mark straight off. I was never that lucky, and certainly never that clever, to be able to manage it.

What I have always found was that unless I went through the above two preparatory stages, I would flounder around for days and still not come up with anything satisfactory. But the moment I got my preparation right, the headline seemed almost to write itself.

Following the theory outlined earlier, I would form in my own mind as clear an idea of my 'waverer' as I could, even if possible thinking about somebody I knew who was of a similar character.

Then, with what I knew about the product, I would simply scribble down, with no thoughts of trying to write a 'headline', the basic promise – in other words, the proposition – that would appeal to most of them.

So long as I did this every time, headlines tended to come out in a way that seemed to me to be right. More importantly, when they actually ran, *they also worked*.

AN EXAMPLE

One of WWAV's most successful headlines was:

'CASH IF YOU DIE, CASH IF YOU DON'T'

which ran unbeaten for some five years and made the client, Lloyds Life (later Royal Heritage) a great deal of money. How did it come about?

The process followed very much the lines I described earlier.

The first step was reading through the product literature. Remember I referred in the previous chapter to sources of information for propositions, and I mentioned making a list of product features? This was this process – going through policy documents and sales literature and making a long list of the features that this particular plan actually offered. It's called 'interrogating the product'.

I admit that reading through a life insurance policy document does not sound like the most exciting thing you can think of doing; but to be a good copywriter you need a mind like a sponge, capable of soaking up masses of information of every description and churning it back out again. For an enquiring mind, even a life insurance policy document has its interests, if only temporary ones.

Having gone through that process, the next task was to look at what the competition was doing. At the time, there was a wide variety of approaches being used to sell insurance and investment products of all types: what was interesting was that you had to make a choice between plans that were investments, or plans that offered you 'straight' life insurance. There didn't seem to be much that *combined* the two ideas.

So, after some time spent going through this process – examining the product details and competitive activity – we developed a list of attributes, plus a clear idea of what propositions the competition was using. What now?

The first task in creating the headline was to conjure up in one's mind a picture of the 'waverer'. Obviously, somebody wholly disinterested in life insurance would find the whole thing very dull. Thus we were not going to worry about that group. Equally, there would certainly be many people who were highly expert on the subject, who – if this plan was any good – would buy it almost whatever our headline said.

So we were left with a group of people who we *guessed* were reasonably aware that they should have life insurance but they hadn't really done anything about it yet. The key was finding something in the proposition that would make them *act*.

From all the data we had, plus our product listing, one thing stood out: if you didn't die, the plan would actually give you money back – *before you died*. This certainly came as a revelation to us, as we assumed that life insurance was actually death insurance – you needed to be dead before it was any use to you. We reasoned that maybe the rest of the 'waverers' felt like that too. Why not tell them they don't have to die?

This then seemed like a reasonable proposition. The headline, as you can see, was the simplest, most concise presentation of this proposition. The earlier versions said much the same, but were much longer. The job was not 'creating' a headline – far from it. The headline was virtually written – but in longhand:

> *'A life insurance plan that pays out money if you die, but unusually also*
> *pays out money if you survive'*

was one of many early versions. It is a simple statement of the proposition. As such, it would probably do a reasonably good job, but certainly lacks bite and *precision*.

THE MR SHEEN APPROACH; POLISHING THE PROPOSITION

All that was now left was polishing up that proposition, to turn it from something rather long-winded to something rather more compelling.

Had this been a mailing, the polishing process would not have been quite so necessary, but would still be important. People reading mailings have more time, are more prepared to read long headlines. But we were working on a press ad. The medium we were planning to use was The Sun, and we needed the sort of *punch* that would help us compete with:

> *'FREDDIE STARR ATE MY HAMSTER'*
>
> or
>
> *'GOTCHA!'*

The polishing process is a simple one: you leave out as many words as you can without altering the central meaning. It is essentially editing. You don't just leave words out, of course. Sometimes you need to re-write small sections to make them shorter, punchier – faster to communicate, in other words, in a medium where time is simply not on your side.

If you wish to study this process, the newspapers are one of the best places to

Fig. 11:
Cash if you die...

This was one of the most successful press ad headlines run for an insurance product in the past decade. The headline is a classic of using the fewest possible words to express the broadest possible claim. The heart of the headline is a direct promise – of cash, whatever happens. Unusually for a direct response headline, this one appears to be relatively short, just 8 words. But don't be fooled...the smaller headline underneath the main headline is a critical part of the ad. The main heading acts as an attention-getter, while the sub-head converts attention quickly into interest. Thus the 'real' headline is actually 49 words long. (For the whole of this ad, see fig. 55.)

Fig. 12:
Multiple headlining gets more across.

In direct response there's little point in trying to think up short, snappy headlines – they simply don't work as well as long ones. But to make long ones work, you need to break them up into multiple headlines. This Compton and Woodhouse ad shows a classic way of doing this. There's a main headline, but down the left hand column runs a sequence of smaller headlines. These headlines are virtually a precis of the whole ad. The reader interested by the photo and main headline can discover a substantial part of the story by quickly scanning the smaller headlines.

look. Their sub-editors have to distil whole stories to just a few basic words. And remember, they don't have the luxury of time – they have just minutes to distil a complex story to its most significant feature, and then write a few words to represent that feature. Some newspapers do it in a very straightforward way – the Financial Times uses very simple headlines, but no less effective for that:

"Amalgamated issues profit warning as sales slump in last quarter."

The Sun would do it rather differently:

"City shock as '5 times a night' boss loses millions"

but the underlying story is the same.

Following a few hours polishing, we finally got the final headline:

"CASH IF YOU DIE, CASH IF YOU DON'T"

Yes, there is a certain amount of writing skill involved. It would be foolish to suggest that someone who cannot string words together is going to succeed simply by following these guidelines. Inspiration counts for something; so does a facility to use a few words of English to convey a thought that contains great interest. But a skilled writer using these guidelines is going to find it much easier to hit the mark.

This headline ran unchanged for, I think, about five years. The only thing that stopped it was when the client who backed it in the first place, John O'Rourke at Lloyds Life, packed it in and went to run a video shop, though I am happy to report that he has lately returned to the direct marketing fold. During those five years, we ran every headline we could think of in split tests to try and beat it, with little success – except when we simply added even more by way of information to the basic headline by making it a little longer and adding two boxed sub-headlines!

THE READER IS MUCH MORE INTERESTED IN WHAT YOU ARE SAYING, THAN HOW YOU ARE SAYING IT

It's worth looking now at another fundamental feature of a good headline: *it's the story that counts, not the way you tell it*, with all due deference to Frank Carson.

Too often writers get carried away with a need to create a 'clever' headline. Somehow, you feel you are not 'doing your job' unless something neat and witty is written. *This is one of the most dangerous blind alleys for a writer to get led up.* Given all that I have said before, I hope by now that it is clear that a good headline is *born from the product*, not from the writer's imagination. Sometimes it may be very dull to you, but is immensely interesting to the 'waverer'. I once wrote a headline for a new type of wheelbarrow. The headline was pithy to the point of apparent boredom:

"THE NEW BALLBARROW. ONLY £29.95"

You probably couldn't get a simpler expression of the proposition. It said it was new. It said what it was. It said how much it cost. If you weren't interested in barrows, it was probably the dullest headline you ever read. But if you were interested in barrows, it was riveting news. What on earth was a BALL-barrow? And whatever it was, as it was only £29.95, it was also something of a bargain. The result was that this was a hugely successful advertisement.

Again, I hope you can see how the headline comes from the proposition, and how the proposition is rooted in the product. It is hardly a *clever* headline. But it is a *good* headline.

Look, for example, at what must be the all-time most successful headline for the last forty or fifty years. It has built businesses worth millions around the world. The headline?

"3 BOOKS FOR £1"

Hardly great writing. But a very powerful offer. And expressed in the simplest, most economical way possible. Interestingly, Book Club Associates and its imitators have every now and then tried different approaches. I have personally written some of them. The essential headline remains unbeatable, and will do so until somebody comes up with a better offer, rather than a better headline.

When I have discussed the concept of rooting the headline in the product with other copywriters, I have often been met with stares of disbelief. It seems, somehow, much too *simple*. There remains a strong urge to be 'creative'. Again, in the same way that isolating a single proposition requires real courage, it requires equal courage on the part of a writer to allow themselves to be 'merely' a conduit of product information to a vaguely interested audience, in the 'hope' that it will ring a bell.

It's like swimming. You need faith that you will float. All the theories say you will. All the data says you will. It nevertheless requires a huge act of courage to fling yourself into the water for the first time.

GOING FURTHER THAN THE FEATURE

There is another class of headline that develops this thought much further. It is the benefit headline, as opposed to the feature headlines I have been talking about.

A feature headline would be:

"LEARN TO PLAY THE PIANO IN 30 DAYS"

which discusses the feature of the product. What, though, is the benefit conferred upon the prospect by this feature? We come back to the legendary:

"THEY LAUGHED WHEN I SAT DOWN AT THE PIANO, BUT
WHEN I STARTED TO PLAY..."

I hope you can see the powerful difference.

It must be said at this stage that benefit headlines are curiously out of fashion. While there is a great deal of evidence that they work in the United States, they are much less popular over here.

Given what I shall be saying about features and benefits later on, there is no real reason why benefit-oriented headlines should not have their place.

The fact that they do not, I can only put down to a number of factors. First, they are extraordinarily difficult to write well. I know very few writers who can do them – I certainly count myself among the number who can't. In Britain we have a much more reticent style, and it may be that Americans, who do not have the same fear of selling that we do, find it comes to them more naturally. Or it may be that the public simply finds them less acceptable, as by their very nature they are 'hype'.

Nevertheless, a serious practitioner of direct marketing should be prepared to try such headlines. How are they created?

The simple conversion of features to benefits is something I shall be covering in much more detail later, in Chapter 5.

But the technique is essentially simple. Here is a list of product features, and then an idea of the benefits that can be derived.

FEATURES	BENEFITS
Fast	Saves you time
Cheap	Makes your money go further
Easily available	No need to shop around
In 30 days	No need to wait for months

ad infinitum…the principle is that whatever feature a product offers, there is *always* a benefit that it gives to the prospect. People are actually a great deal more interested in benefits than features, but as I said it takes a clever writer to make them believable and sincere benefits, rather than just parodies of American direct response ads.

THE LENGTH OF A HEADLINE

The length of a headline is always a problem. A headline by definition is a short summary of the story that follows. But sometimes the story is complex – how can it be possible to shorten it down to the required 'snappiness' without losing some critical features or benefits?

In conventional advertising this is less of a problem, where you tend to be dealing with brands that offer one simple benefit. One of my favourite headlines from my days before direct response was for a new low-calorie ice cream. It said:

"SPOIL YOURSELF, NOT YOUR FIGURE"

I liked it because it had a benefit (rather than just saying *"NEW LOW CALORIE ICE CREAM"*), but mainly because it was short and simple. Actually, there wasn't anything else to say about it.

Life is rarely so simple for the direct marketer, where we have to wrestle with complex products that are being sold through the post.

This usually means that our headlines have to work harder, convey more information – and therefore, inevitably, have to be *longer*. Like the long copy argument, a long headline is not in itself a problem. It is usually, in fact, a virtue. Given the self-selected interested audience we are talking to with any headline, it needs to have a reasonable amount of information in it before it can hope to communicate with that specific audience.

But a very long headline runs into problems. Over a certain length it becomes very difficult to read – it ceases to stand out, and it contains so much information that no one feature stands out anymore, undoing the whole point of the headline. David Ogilvy, that doyen of direct marketing copywriting, maintains that headlines that go beyond 30 words become unreadable.

THE LABOUR PARTY SPONSORSHIP APPEAL

"What you can do right now to help Labour win" *Neil Kinnock*

Labour believes in freedom. Freedom from poverty, homelessness and oppression — both here and abroad. Just as important is the freedom to achieve, to question and to learn. The last six years have shown us how fragile those freedoms are. Now they must be rebuilt. Millions of people are looking to Labour to generate jobs, services and a better future.

But that isn't going to happen unless Labour wins victory at the polls — and has the money to mount the most powerful campaign possible when the election comes.

That's why, if you become a Labour Party Sponsor now, you will be giving us the resources we need to get into fighting condition. We have been doing a lot to lick Labour into shape. We want to do a lot more.

There is one great barrier to victory. And mundane as it may seem, that barrier is hard cash, or rather the lack of it. Labour simply cannot afford to be out priced by the Tories.

That's why I hope you'll Sponsor the Labour Party today. Please complete the form below and return it as soon as possible. And, if you complete the Banker's Order section, you'll be giving us an income we can rely on. Freedom doesn't come free.

SPONSORSHIP FORM

YES I want to help The Labour Party achieve victory, and continue the fight for a fairer society. *I wish to Sponsor as indicated below:

| INDIVIDUAL SPONSORSHIP | £12 ☐ £15 ☐ £25 ☐ £50 ☐ £_____ |
| UNWAGED SPONSORSHIP | £6 ☐ £10 ☐ £15 ☐ £20 ☐ £_____ |

*I do not wish to Sponsor, but I enclose a cheque/postal order for £_____

Name Mr Ms _____

Address _____

_____ Post Code _____

Enclose your Sponsorship remittance, or complete the Banker's Order section. In either case, ensure you complete the Name and Address panel.

BANKER'S ORDER

To (name of your Bank) _____

Address of your Bank _____

_____ Post Code _____

Your Bank Sort Code [__ — __ — __]
(the six figures at the top of your cheque)

Your Bank Account Number [☐☐☐☐☐☐☐☐]

Please pay the Co-Operative Bank, London Branch (08-03-08) for the account of The Labour Party (A/c No 580 10055)

the sum of [£ ____] amount in words _____

on __/__/1986 and thereafter the same amount on the same day

each ☐ month ☐ quarter ☐ year (please tick) until further notice.

Signature _____ Date _____ O/7/9

Return to The Labour Party, Room 313, FREEPOST, London SE17 1BR.

Fig. 13:
What you say is more important than how you say it.

This small space ad is part of a fundraising campaign that generated more than £2m for Labour before the 1992 General Election, one of the most successful political fundraising exercises ever. The headline concentrates on action – the proposition being that, as a Labour supporter, you want to do something. This ad simply says – 'here's what you can do'. It avoids political argument. It doesn't attempt to convert anyone. It assumes you are a Labour supporter and then simply provides a route for action. Note the 'right now' being underlined…for greater urgency; and note too the quote marks, which make headlines on small space ads stand out by giving them more 'life'.

Much as I respect Ogilvy's views on headline length, I suspect it is not as simple as 'going beyond 30 words' that causes difficulty for the reader. A headline longer than 30 words, if set in type consistent with the rest of the magazine or paper, remains readable. Headlines of many fewer words than 30, set in massive type taking up most of a whole page, are almost completely unreadable unless you happen to be on the other side of the room.

Nevertheless, a long headline does begin to lose impact: it may not matter so much in The Economist, but it starts to matter a great deal in the popular press and popular magazines. If you are to compete with the press, then it helps to do so on at least *equal* terms.

So, how do we overcome the problem – marrying a sensible amount of information in a headline, enough to gain the interest of the 'most likely to buy' reader, to impact and clarity?

MULTIPLE HEADLINING

The technique is simple. Rather than falling into the trap of just using short but not very effective headlines, or using long but rather unreadable headlines, we simply break up the headline into pieces, and *use several different headlines*.

To explain the technique, we need to return briefly to the proposition concept. From the proposition, we will have arrived at a simple headline. Let's go back to

"CASH IF YOU DIE, CASH IF YOU DON'T"

which while it encompassed the proposition in a way that caught the reader's eye, certainly left an uncomfortable feeling that there was more to tell – details that were sufficiently important to the argument that shouldn't have to wait for the body copy.

Rather than waste the brevity and impact of the original headline, we then simply used an underline.

> *"Should you put your money into a savings plan, or should you put your money into life insurance? Now you don't have to decide, because with Lloyds Life Linkplan there's now a policy that gives you both..."*

This meant that we caught our reader's attention with a simple statement, but then took that interest a little further. This is the 'precis' technique that newspapers are so fond of – and little wonder, in that it allows the use of bold and sharp headlines, but still gives the reader enough information to make the story interesting, rather than just attention-grabbing.

By the time the reader has got through the underline, the task of the body copy in explaining the full story then becomes much easier.

There are many useful variations on this multiple headline theme, all of them successful. Equally easily we could have used an overline:

> *"The AA arranges the insurance of more motorists than anyone else – offers competitive prices and instant cover – and gives you the service and claims assistance you'd expect from the AA"*

over the main headline:

"FIND OUT NOW WHY 150,000 MOTORISTS GET THE BEST CAR
INSURANCE DEAL BY GETTING THE AA ON THEIR SIDE"

Or just as easily, you can use a point-by-point approach:

"SAFE AT LAST

A new limited edition figure in fine bone china from Royal Worcester

Strictly limited to 12,500 figures only

Each figure individually numbered with a signed Certificate of
Authenticity in your name, bearing your personal figure number

The same figure number reserved for you personally throughout
the collection

Designed by Elisabeth Woodhouse; sculpted by Sheila Mitchell

Available only by direct subscription to Compton & Woodhouse;
the figure is not available from any shop

Send no money with your application"

And when the occasion demands it, we can use combinations of *all* these techniques.

Remember, it is the *total amount of information* you give which will determine the interest of your reader. Finding techniques like these allows you to increase the information content of a headline dramatically, without creating an unreadable block of text.

As I said earlier, most of these examples are from press ads, where the task is a more 'condensed' version of a mailing pack. But even if in a mailing pack you are using only single headlines, please remember that throughout the pack itself you are of course using a dozen or so headlines, and thus you actually have the same technique working for you – it's just not all in the same place.

Again I must confess to outright plagiarism. It is a technique stolen lock, stock and barrel from newspapers and magazines. Very rarely will you see a single headline used in newspapers for complex subjects. They bring to bear an even more impressive armoury – boxed headings, reversed headings, quote boxes, lists…if you need ideas, look in the pages of the daily press and you'll find *plenty*.

HEADLINES THROUGHOUT

In fact, your headlining does not stop at the headline – or at least it shouldn't. The use of sub-heads, for example, is an important part of the headline technique and will allow your reader to continue to absorb information at high speed, until they have reached the point where they have decided to buy, or not buy, or want to know more – which is when they start reading the copy.

In this sense, sub-heads are not merely the bold words that break up the columns of copy. You can have what are in effect additional headlines – near the coupon, for example, to draw attention to a time close – which as far as the reader is concerned become part of the overall headline.

MESSY HEADLINES

You will have by now surmised that this approach leads to a rather messy appearance, with main headlines, overlines, underlines, boxes, sub-heads and bits of headlines over the coupon.

Yes, it does, and this is nothing to be concerned about. In later Chapters I will discuss the way the human eye finds organised chaos more *visually interesting* than the stark and simple. It requires a fine sense of organisation to make it work, of course, otherwise it descends into a hopeless mess. But the fashion in advertising for the clean and simple is not one that commercial reality – measured by the results – finds very attractive. '*Busy-ness*' in a direct marketing promotion is a very desirable attribute, as it is the result of giving a lot of information; clean and simple is not to be encouraged, as it means information has been left out just for the sake of appearances.

HOW DOES MULTIPLE HEADLINING SQUARE WITH THE NEED FOR A SINGLE-MINDED PROPOSITION?

The fact that we should have a single-minded proposition before us in no way detracts from multiple headlining – or giving a great deal more information.

We can use multiple headlining to greatly expand on the proposition, to make it much more exciting, to explore the various shades of meaning surrounding the proposition. For instance, we can choose to develop the benefits surrounding the main product feature: this is usually the most advantageous way to use a multiple headline. Take a mythical example:

"Why waste precious months developing a skill that we can teach you faster than you ever imagined?

LEARN TO PLAY THE PIANO IN 30 DAYS

Revolutionary new technique allows even the complete novice to play well-known melodies without the need for tedious hours of practice."

I have, of course, exaggerated to make the point, but you can see that I use the basic and brief 30 day statement for the headline, and I continue with the proposition in both the overline and the underline, albeit in slightly different ways. I am not adding greatly to the informational quantity, but I am adding greatly to the 'colour' and the force of the proposition. If you believe the proposition to be correct (or, more likely, previous tests show it to be correct) then adding more power to it cannot be but helpful.

I can also use *multiple headlining* in those cases where although I can get a single proposition working in my headline, I think that additional information may also be needed.

"LEARN TO PLAY THE PIANO IN 30 DAYS

And you could win your very own Steinway Concert Grand if you reply within 30 days."

This means, however vital the additional information may be, that you can continue to stick with the simple proposition, rather than getting it watered down by

Fig. 14:
Headlines in mailings.
Headlining techniques in mailings are just the same as for press ads, but with one big difference – you get a lot more space to use a lot more headlines. Here, on a mailing for Age Concern, the headline really starts on the envelope. It continues in an expanded form on the front of the letter, and carries on to the donation form. Really, it's just one headline, with the envelope heading setting up the problem, the letter heading hinting at a solution, and the donation form heading providing the 'time close'. Apart from the main headings, you'll notice many more smaller ones – usually used to emphasise specific points throughout the mailing, such as the action headline above the stamps on the donation form.

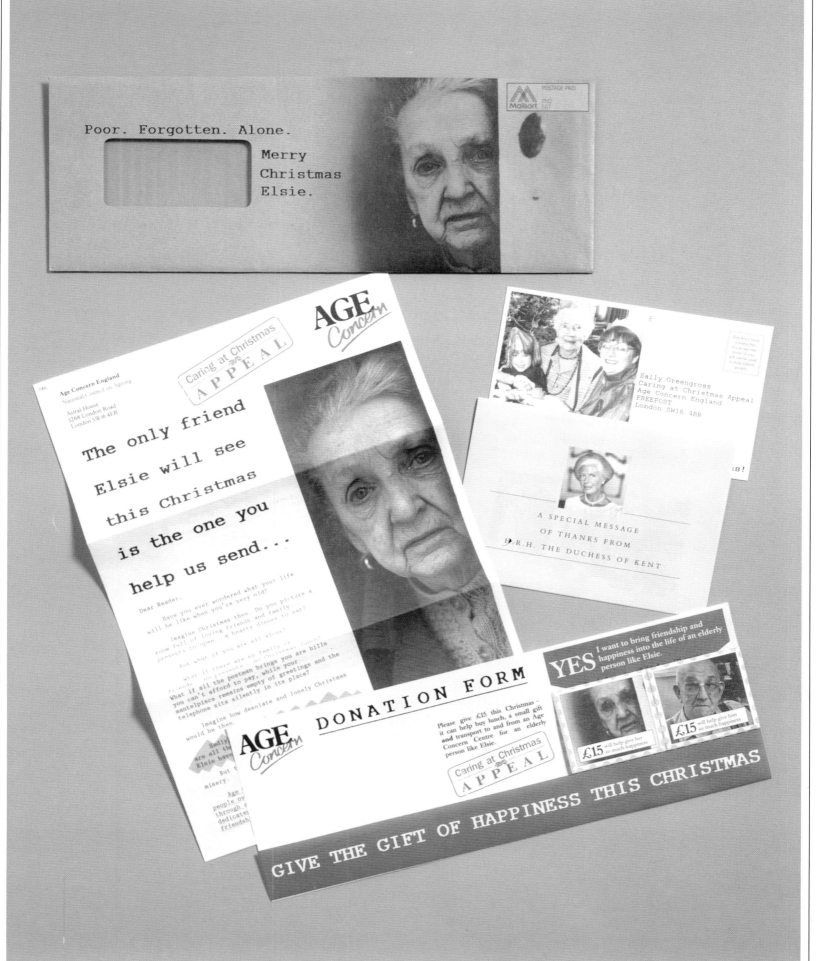

having to add additional information in the main headline itself.

'GUT FEEL'

Sorry about the phrase, but I really don't know another way of describing it. Much as you may follow the guidelines above, and they will undoubtedly produce for you some excellent and hard-working headlines, 'gut feel' remains the final arbiter before the results come in. A good headline, as opposed to a workmanlike headline, always feels 'right'.

A powerful charity headline will, literally, make the hairs on the back of your neck rise. Why? I only wish I could distil the essence of gut feel, but I can't.

How exciting, for instance, is this stark and simple sentence:

> *"At 60 miles an hour the loudest noise in this new Rolls-Royce comes from the electric clock."*

There are no puns, no alliterations, nothing humorous whatsoever. As a piece of written English it is devoid of any pretensions. But for all its simplicity of construction, it remains one of the most *powerful* promises in advertising. The first time you read it, your 'gut feel' tells you it's good: you want to read more, you want to know what the ad is all about, it makes the product sound great.

It is, once again, an example of the simple but often forgotten truth that a great headline is WHAT it says, not HOW it says it.

The penultimate test of what you think is the greatest headline you have ever written is a simple one (the ultimate test being when you run it, of course).

Simply show your headline to a colleague. If their first comment is *"Hey, that's a great headline"*, tear it up and throw it away. If, on the other hand, their reaction is *"That sounds good – can you get me one cheap?"*, you've almost certainly got a winner ■

CHAPTER 3: SUMMARY

The best headlines come through careful preparation; a clear analysis of who you are talking to, combined with a simple proposition.

Write down the proposition longhand – do not attempt to write a headline at this stage. Then polish it until it works. Reduce the number of words, rewrite until it shines. This alone can often give you your headline.

Ensure that your headline is rooted in the product, that it is an expression of what the product does. It may seem dull to you if you're not interested in that particular subject, but it is of consuming interest to somebody who is. Let the product speak.

Make it an 'action' headline ('Give £15 to save a child's life') instead of a 'passive' headline ('Donations needed to save lives').

Consider a benefit-oriented headline. They are currently out of fashion but there is no good reason why they should not work better than a feature-oriented headline.

The more specific you can make your headline, the better. Use specific facts wherever you can.

Use multiple headline techniques – overlines and underlines – to get the full force of your proposition across. There's no need to depend on one single headline: long headlines work better because they convey the maximum information to the most interested people.

Suit the headline you use to the medium you are appearing in. For example, you will need a different type of headline if you're in The Sun than if you're writing a mailing.

Lastly, your headline is probably going to work if it makes your colleagues interested in the product, not in the headline.

EFFECTIVE COPY STRUCTURE

Long copy requires careful organisation to make it work its hardest. To keep your reader's attention while you communicate sufficient information to make the sale is made a great deal more difficult unless you lead the reader stage by stage through your argument. There's a simple formula called AIDCA; but there are other techniques that help you organise your copy, and thus sell more.

W E HAVE talked about theory, propositions and headlines. By now we have got our main ideas well sorted out, and we know what we want to communicate in the body copy.

But before we can physically start writing, in the same way that a proposition gives us a plan, a copywriter will find that producing an organised plan for the body copy gives them a considerably better result, in much less time.

THE FUNCTION OF BODY COPY

Before we go into structure in detail, it's worth just examining what the purpose of body copy is. And no, it's not simply just to 'sell'. If you have followed my argument thus far, you will see that we are working our way down an inverted pyramid:

By use of the headlining techniques described in the earlier Chapter, we have continued this self-selection process.

The multiple headlines will have given a prospect sufficient information to decide either *not to bother* even looking at the ad or mailing in more detail – the product is not for them, or they are not in the market at that moment; or those same headlines will have been sufficient to someone *highly interested* that they are going to buy – you found them just at the right time.

Body copy had no real function to either of those groups. Long or short, it will make no difference to someone who is not going to respond. Someone who is going to respond *anyway* will probably want to read the copy for the sake of reassurance. But its real target, in terms of the above pyramid, are those people in the middle – those who are sufficiently interested by what the headline says to want to know more, and who are prepared to spend some time reading details that will give them reasons to buy.

Fig. 15: AIDCA in action. These ads for stainless steel pans show in a concentrated way just how the AIDCA formula works. The headline is the Attention section, while the opening paragraph takes the Attention and turns it into Interest. Desire is created by paragraphs 2, 3 and 4, which makes the pans sound good. Conviction comes in paragraph 5, which gives the suspicious reader a convincing reason why the price is so low. The rest of paragraph 5 and all of paragraph 6 is devoted to Action – in fact, the Action section takes around 25% of the copy. Whatever the length of copy available, the AIDCA formula can always be followed.

The 'Scotts of Stow' Gourmet Pan Set. German Specification 18/10 Stainless Steel, 5 pans only £49.95

(plus p&p)

Our super value pan set is made from 18/10 stainless steel, the best grade available – pans costing more than twice as much use the same material. '18/10' means basic steel, with 18% chromium to prevent rust and 10% nickel to prevent tarnishing.

The thickness is substantial too. When you feel these pans, you'll be impressed by the weight. Not so heavy as to make lifting them hard work; but heavy enough to give many years of pleasurable cooking.

You'll be equally impressed by the bottoms of the pans. A 3.3mm thick aluminium base is 'sandwiched' between two skins of stainless steel. This spreads the heat virtually eliminating hot spots – whether you use electric, ceramic, hot plates or gas.

And the handles and knobs are made of a special heat-resistant material called Phenolic. They'll take oven temperatures of up to 180°C (365°F) for 1 hour.

So why's the value so good? These pans are made to German specifications, from German tooling – but the factory is in the Far East. So you get quality and value. To order, simply fill in the coupon below and post today; or telephone your order (even on Sundays) on 0793 706111. We gladly accept Access, Visa or MasterCard.

Your order will be sent by secure carrier direct to your door within 21 days. And remember, if you're unhappy with your purchase for any reason, you can return it anytime within 3 months for a full, no-quibble refund.

☎ **Telephone orders – even on Sundays!** Call 0793 706111 to order on your Visa, Access or MasterCard.

SCOTTS of STOW

Admail 222, The Square, Stow-on-the-Wold, Gloucs. GL54 1AF.

The full set:
6" (3pts) with lid;
7" (4pts) with lid;
8" (5pts) with lid;
9½" frying pan;
5½" milk pan (2pts).
(All capacities are approximate.)

A 3.3mm thick 'sandwich' of aluminium between stainless steel evenly distributes the heat.

Scotts of Stow Ltd. Registered Office: The Square, Stow-on-the-Wold, Gloucs., GL54 1AF. Registered No: 2548299 England.

Thus the function of body copy is to take *that* group of people (who are of course by now a small minority of the people who first started looking at the piece) and lead them through a sales argument that will ultimately *convince* them.

This is why long copy works. Of the people who start reading the copy, some are in need of more re-assurance than others. Therefore not everyone who reads the copy will read all of it – they need only enough to convince them. But others will need to read a lot before you have finally achieved the sale.

THE NEED FOR STRUCTURE

The structure of the copy therefore needs to accommodate all needs, from the person who wants to skip-read down to the last die-hards who want *every last item of information* before they finally decide.

Your copy therefore needs to be long; it needs to be packed solid with detail; and because of this, it needs careful organisation to make that amount of detail easily accessible to the reader.

Even if you accept the principle of long copy, simply putting down on paper everything you can is not going to achieve the objective. A legal document is long, contains everything, but defies all but the most patient minds to read and understand it.

And organising your copy is not just for the sake of the reader, though that is the primary need. Thinking out your plan before you start *greatly assists the writer*. It gives a clear picture of what needs to be said, allows the writer to marshal the necessary facts beforehand, and saves time later, often by minimising the need for re-drafts because some vital fact or other was omitted.

In writing copy, there are fortunately some easily-grasped techniques that help this process of organisation. Perhaps the most common copy formula is AIDCA. It stands for:

> *A* ttention
>
> *I* nterest
>
> *D* esire
>
> *C* onviction
>
> *A* ction

The formula is derived from salesmen in America, at the turn of the century, who found that they could achieve higher sales levels if they followed such a formula during their sales visits. It wasn't long before advertising copywriters picked up the formula and adapted it for their own purposes.

Here's how AIDCA works.

First, logically enough, *Attention* has to be gained. This alone is not enough – the prospect's attention has to be geared up a notch, and has to be turned into *Interest*.

Once interest has been achieved, the prospect then needs to be more than just interested – they have to be made to want the product – to *Desire* it.

But the folk down on the farm don't necessarily believe everything they hear from smooth-talking salesmen. So, doubts have to be overcome by assuring the prospect that what is said is true – they need to be *Convinced*.

And finally, most importantly, comes the close – the prospect has to take *Action*, such as signing the order.

To this day, salesmen around the world use more or less the same technique. There is no good reason why copywriters should not continue this tradition, particularly since it works so well.

The AIDCA formula is an excellent way to organise copy:

- The headline will typically gain attention.
- The opening of your copy will then expound the features, creating interest.
- The middle of your copy will turn those features into benefits, creating desire.

Towards the end, you will convince the user that what you say is true – through the use of testimonials for example.

- Last of all, you will then create the required action by asking for the sale.

EDUCATING AIDCA

In the absence of a better scheme, it will certainly assist you in writing copy to simply follow AIDCA, stage by stage, ensuring as you go that you have completed each of the sections before moving onto the next one. It will be a fair and very workmanlike piece of copy – certainly a great deal better than following no system at all. And if you are at the start of your copywriting career, it is an excellent way to learn the craft, to give yourself a discipline to start off with.

However, there are ways in which you can modify the formula, particularly from the direct marketing point of view. You can use AIDCA in more educated fashion.

First of all, the strict 'AIDCA' sequence is not always necessarily the best logic for direct marketing copy. The formula, as I mentioned before, was originated by salesmen, not copywriters. A face-to-face salesman sitting in front of the prospect and 'selling' creates a unique atmosphere. Each stage can be gone through logically and the prospect's reaction judged, so the salesman would know if it was time to move on to the next stage, or keep going. Having those reactions as a 'feedback' is invaluable. You know how well, or how badly, your attempt to sell is going.

Copy does not have that benefit, of course. It has to work from a much *colder* start, there is no feedback other than that which the writer can imagine, and you have no way of adapting your copy to different people: it has to be written for everyone.

One of the greatest drawbacks in this situation is that the reader of copy is much more passive than a person being sold to. If you're reading a brochure about a car, you tend to be passive. You're simply absorbing information and not necessarily expecting to do anything about it. But go up to a salesman in the showroom and the atmosphere *changes*. Both you and he know that you're in a buying mood, even if you come up with the normal 'only looking' put-off. Action is expected. You think you may well part with some money. It adds an entirely different dimension to the situation

CAMERON HOUSE
LOCH LOMOND

Mr R W Postlethwaite
35 Elmsdale Road
Wootton
Bedford
MK43 9JW

A

Please accept my personal invitation to enjoy a luxurious break at our
exclusive country retreat on the banks of Loch Lomond

Dear Mr Postlethwaite,

Have you ever longed to escape from the stress and strain of everyday living? To retreat to a private world of unparalleled luxury, overlooking peaceful blue waters and picturesque woodlands?

If so, it gives me particular pleasure to extend this personal invitation to you and your guest, to spend a leisurely two-day break at the exclusive Cameron House Country Estate, on the banks of beautiful Loch Lomond.

We will fly you both from London, Birmingham or Manchester to Glasgow Airport, where you will find a complimentary car awaiting you, and which is yours for your entire stay. Your room, in the 4-star Cameron House Hotel, will feature every conceivable luxury, and will be reserved in your name for two nights. In the mornings you will enjoy a full Scottish breakfast. You will also be given special complimentary membership of the exclusive Leisure Club with all its excellent sporting facilities at your disposal. And you can enjoy all this from just £199 for two.

Situated in what, to me, is undoubtedly one of the loveliest corners of Scotland, Cameron House has justifiably been called Scotland's premier country leisure retreat. Set in 108 acres of beautiful countryside, it comprises a majestically towered and turreted hotel with two superb restaurants, an exclusive Leisure Club...a challenging 9 hole golf course...and perhaps most breathtaking of all, a 225-boat Marina overlooking beautiful Loch Lomond. All await your discovery...

<u>Discover the special secret of Cameron House Loch Lomond</u>

And if, as I'm certain once you visit here, you find you want to come back again, you may be interested to know that there is a way you can share in this beautiful lochside retreat time after time. For at Cameron House, we have even more to offer you than simply a luxurious Scottish break. We have a special secret that could enrich the quality of your life for many years to come. Allow me to explain...   B

Nestling within the peaceful wooded acres of the Estate stand a selection of beautiful holiday lodges. Aesthetically positioned in small clusters, they have been built with one simple aim in mind – to provide a discerning few with the ultimate luxury retreat. Until you see them for yourself, in fact, it's difficult to conceive just how magnificent they really are.

<u>So, as part of your visit, at a time suitable to you, we will show you around these splendid lodges.
And whilst I must stress there is absolutely no commitment to purchase, I think you will find them
irresistible...</u>

For these are no ordinary holiday homes. They are time-ownership lodges. And because of the special laws in Scotland, you own your own weeks in perpetuity. They are yours to enjoy for the rest of your life, to give to your children, rent to friends, or to sell as you choose. And of course, you buy only the weeks you want to use at a fraction of the cost of buying the whole property. In short, you have your own luxurious retreat at a commendably affordable price.

I really cannot stress the sheer luxury of our lodges strongly enough. The warm sandstone and timber of their country-style exteriors promise you a wealth of comfort and elegance inside. Each is graced with magnificent French windows leading to a private terrace with superb views. From the tasteful prints and tapestries on the walls, to the comfort of the deepest sofas and luxurious carpets, every design feature has been meticulously chosen. The Bang and Olufsen stereo and CD player...satellite television...the latest Gaggenau dishwashers and microwaves...the superb quality chinaware and fine crystal...the opulent Jacuzzi in each lodge. Quite simply, these homes offer the ultimate in luxurious living.

But there are even more exclusive pleasures afforded to lodge owners. As an owner in the Cameron House Estate, you have all the facilities of the luxurious 4-star Hotel, the Leisure Club and Marina at your disposal.

<u>All the waters of Loch Lomond for your personal enjoyment</u>

The magnificent Marina is perhaps the jewel in Cameron House's crown. Set in its own mile of private lochside, it accommodates up to 225 boats. From this colourful setting, sailing enthusiasts have all the peaceful waters of Great Britain's largest inland waterway to explore at their leisure...from Balloch in the South right up to breathtaking Inversnaid in the North. If you have your own boat, we will be happy to make arrangements for its mooring at the Marina...should you not have a boat, we can easily arrange the hire of one for you...and if 'terra firma' holds more appeal, why not simply watch

CAMERON HOUSE TIME-OWNERSHIP
LOCH LOMOND, ALEXANDRIA, DUNBARTONSHIRE G83 8QZ.
TELEPHONE: (0389) 55625, FACSIMILE: (0389) 59906

CRAIGENDARROCH GROUP TIME-OWNERSHIP LIMITED. REGISTERED NO: 134036 REGISTERED OFFICE: 20 QUEENS ROAD, ABERDEEN
DIRECTORS: CJ GORDON C MITCHELL ID PRATT

A MEMBER OF
THE CRAIGENDARROCH
GROUP OF COMPANIES

CHL30   WK01   1800   00710   0000050

Fig. 16:
Structuring a letter.
This letter for up-market time-share operator Cameron House contains the main points of letter structure. The beginning of the letter (A) makes the offer quickly – in this case, a personal invitation. After the offer, a neat link "you may be interested to know that there is a way you can share in this beautiful lochside retreat..." takes the reader into the main argument (B). These are the 'I' and 'D' – the interest and desire – sections. They give real colour to the offer, building 'brick-by-brick' into the reasons why you should buy. This goes on over the page...

the boats sail by from the comfort of the Marina Clubhouse, over lunch or cocktails?

If you are inclined to other watersports, the Estate can arrange expert tuition in sailing, waterskiing and windsurfing - whilst the famous waters of Loch Lomond offer particularly fine sport for fishing enthusiasts. Within the Estate, we have private tennis courts open to all owners, and alongside the Loch runs a challenging 9 hole golf course, designed to make full use of the undulating land.

Furthermore, the outstanding indoor facilities of Scotland's premier Leisure Club are entirely at your disposal. Consider the handsome amenities on offer: two magnificent swimming pools, first-class squash and badminton courts, dance studio, fully-equipped gymnasium, snooker room, games room, sauna, steam room, plunge pool, whirlpool spa bath, and even an exclusive health and beauty suite (including a hair salon). There is even the informal Club Bar and Brasserie to relax in after your exertions!

<u>Relax whilst the children have the time of their lives</u>

We have taken care of the children's entertainment too. For not only are there two children's swimming pools - one a fun pool, complete with stunning water slide, and the other a shallow toddlers' pool - but also a colourful games room. For babies and tiny children, we are happy to provide a fully supervised creche.

With so many tempting recreational activities not far from your lodge, you may be forgiven for never venturing beyond the Estate's great gates. Yet many fascinating places are but a short drive away...from the delightful village of Luss to the cultural city of Glasgow, with its art galleries, theatres, restaurants and shops. And, of course, however you choose to spend your days, there is always the delightful prospect of returning to your own luxurious hideaway home...

But perhaps the most pleasing thought of all is that whenever you desire to leave the privacy of your lodge...to seek out a little like-minded company over cocktails, take the family out for a leisurely lunch...or even do a little shopping...the luxurious Cameron House Hotel is just a short stroll from your door.

With origins dating back to the 13th century, this magnificently restored country house has opened its doors to many distinguished guests during its colourful history, including Dr Johnson, the Empress Eugenie and Winston Churchill. In addition to two first-class restaurants, each with its own unique cuisine prepared by our master chefs, you will find the elegant Drawing Room overlooking the loch, a secluded Library for complete peace and quiet, and even discreet boutiques to browse around. Lodge owners are always welcomed here as our special friends...and greeted warmly whenever they choose to drop in.

If you reflect upon all the outstanding amenities on offer within the Cameron House Estate, you will not be surprised to learn that it was commissioned by the Craigendarroch Group, whose first development - the Craigendarroch Hotel and Country Estate on Royal Deeside - is widely acknowledged as one of the most prestigious leisure estates in Europe. The commitment of such an organisation can only ensure that the levels of excellence at Cameron House will remain outstanding.

<u>Your passport to over two thousand luxurious holidays</u>

There is one more very special advantage to being a lodge owner which I would like to disclose, if I may. Through our association with Resort Condominiums International, you can exchange your week at Cameron House for one of two thousand exotic holiday locations throughout the world...including Florida, the Bahamas and Hong Kong. Indeed, with Scottish holidays always popular amongst foreign travellers, you may even be able to exchange your week at Cameron House for two weeks elsewhere - always secure in the knowledge that you will have your luxurious lochside retreat to return to year after year.

When you consider all the special privileges of being a lodge owner - the exquisite luxury, the outstanding facilities, and not least your very own loch to enjoy - the actual purchasing price may well come as a pleasant surprise. Lodges range from just £4,250 to £22,950, depending on the size and weeks you choose. As an example, a beautiful two bedroom lodge would cost just £12,500 for a week's ownership in August...forever!

If you would like to join us for this special break at Cameron House, simply return the enclosed RSVP to me at your earliest convenience. I would like to stress once again that there is absolutely no obligation to buy. All we ask is that you enjoy the luxury and relaxation of an exclusive Scottish break away from it all...<u>from just £199 for two.</u>

If by chance you have already visited Cameron House under the terms of this special invitation, I very much regret that we are unable to make the offer for a second time. Should you wish to view our lodges again, however, please do not hesitate to contact me on (0389)55625 and I will be delighted to make alternative arrangements for you.

I look forward very much to welcoming you to the Cameron House Country Estate - and to your own, private retreat by the shores of Loch Lomond.

Yours sincerely,

Chris Gordon

Chris Gordon
Director

C

D

<u>**Fig. 17:**</u>
Cameron House
(continued).
...continuing to build up the case for coming to Cameron House. A little over half-way down (C) comes some convic- tion, which is then followed by action (D). If the action section seems a bit weak in this letter, go back to the beginning – the whole opening offer is an invitation to visit, which is of course using Action to lead. Note especially the elegant way in which each 'brick' or selling point is neatly joined to the others; the argument builds up into a highly convincing evocation of a visit to Loch Lomond. (Incidentally, this letter has more copy than most 4 pagers – it's a function of the large format that it's only spread over 2 pages.)

– it has an objective.

POINTS OF DEPARTURE

So one of the first points of departure to consider from the standard AIDCA formula is how you can turn a passive piece of copy, which otherwise could be purely informational, into something much closer to a selling situation. How can you create the expectation that some action will be expected as a result of reading this? *This is, of course, one of the great differences between direct marketing and conventional copywriting.*

Your copy needs to be more than simply *presenting* an idea. It shouldn't just say "Read this because it's interesting". Instead, it should very clearly say, from the earliest possible opportunity, "Read this because I want you to *do* something".

To do this in copy terms, it is often desirable to invert AIDCA, and take Action as the leading point. This immediately creates a sense that something needs to be done as a result of reading this. You can actually start your copy with an action line:

> *"If you reply within 14 days to this remarkable offer, you'll have the opportunity to discover..."*

By using 'action' first, you are immediately creating the desirable atmosphere that this is more than just information - *this is an opportunity to buy.*

As I said earlier, the great difference between conventional and direct marketing is that in our world, *we are also the shop.* Anything we can do to let them know early on that they can actually buy from this advertisement, the better we will do.

USING AIDCA INTELLIGENTLY

There are other variations on the AIDCA theme. Sometimes, for example, you can take Conviction as the leading point. Whiskas cat food has done so uniquely successfully over the years with its "8 out of 10 owners" line. Even the latest variation "Cats would choose Whiskas" is a testimonial, albeit a rather more whimsical one.

Leading with a testimonial approach is, indeed, a very successful way to start an ad or a mailing.

The essential point is that AIDCA is a guide, but not – at least in direct marketing terms – a logical straightjacket. You should use AIDCA with intelligence. But in giving yourself that freedom, you also need to make sure that AIDCA remains your guide. Even if you have played around with the elements themselves, are all the elements present? Miss out one part of the AIDCA formula, and your copy is likely to become that much weaker.

SOME OTHER TECHNIQUES

Besides AIDCA, there are other ways of organising copy and helping you make it more easily digestible. One of the best methods is:

> *Tell them what you're going to tell them, and then tell them, and then tell them you've told them.*

This is of course a basic rule of journalism, but it applies just as well to copywriting and it provides an excellent structural framework which has the desirable effect of making a lengthy piece of copy a great deal easier to read.

Essentially, before you start the main argument in your body copy, you give a *brief résumé* of the story first, taking perhaps the first paragraph or two. Like this:

"LEARN TO PLAY THE PIANO IN 30 DAYS

A new technique of piano playing now lets you learn well-known melodies in less than a month, so you can be playing the piano in much less time than you thought.

No prior skill is needed, and the system doesn't require hours of tedious practice – in fact, just a few pleasurable minutes when you can spare them is all that's needed.

Details of this remarkable new system are available through the post or simply by telephoning; and if you reply within 30 days a superb free gift could be yours.

The new technique is called Miracle Method, and it works like this..."

You can see that the first three paragraphs are a brief *summary* of the whole story, even containing a brief action sequence. You are literally telling the reader what you're going to tell them. After you have told them what you're going to tell them, you then commence the full story, usually through the use of link phrases such as

"it works like this..." "let me explain..." "this new concept means..."

The benefit of this technique is threefold: first, it makes the task of digesting a lot of copy easier for the reader. Second, it makes the task of starting the copy easier for the writer. Third, it adds a subtle 'newsy' flavour which I think benefits the 'action' feeling.

In addition, it also provides a plan in miniature for the copy. At school I was always taught to write an essay by making a little diagram; around a circle in which was written 'essay' were all the points I wanted to make, numbered in the sequence I wanted to make them. Writing the essay became easier because I could take each point, one by one, and expand upon it until I had finished, and then move on to the next.

The summary opening I have discussed here is very similar. Once you have written your summary or precis, then your body copy becomes an *expansion* of the points you have just made. It sets the scene.

And to complete the formula, you would, once you have finished the main copy, then reprise the whole thing – again in precis form – which forms an excellent close, by making sure that you re-iterate your main selling points. The sequence is:

HEADLINE

SUMMARY

COPY

REPRISE

ACTION

This is one of the most usable structures. Almost all good copy tends to follow this sequence, even if only instinctively. By adopting it at the outset you write within a framework that will make your copy work better.

SUB-HEADLINES

If, before you write body copy, you sit down and write the sub-headlines first, this automatically gives you subject headings for each paragraph or two of copy. It's important when you are working out the initial concepts of your ad or mailing to write the sub-heads first anyway; it allows you to ensure that you are covering the details you need to cover.

And, of course, sub-headlining is also by far the easiest way to break up a lot of copy into easily read sections.

This technique, where you write the sub-heads before the copy, is actually very far removed from the newspaper system, where the writer writes the story and the sub-editor simply drops in a few words to break up the column:

'SHOCK'

'SCANDAL'

'SEX'

are typical sub-heads that are single-worders, conveying a great deal of power on their own. Because we are inevitably dealing with rather more mundane subjects, our ability to use sub-heads in the same way is somewhat more limited. I do not think that an insurance ad using similar single-word sub-heads would be quite as powerful:

'ENDOWMENT'

'BONUS'

'ANNUITY'

Clearly a different system is needed. The best method is to use miniature headlines that, in sequence, give the essential gist of the story. The ideal system is a 'feature/benefit' doublet that not only gives the gist of the story but also, importantly, carries the argument further forward, making the idea of reading the copy more attractive:

"ENDOWMENT PLANS MEAN YOUR FAMILY COULD BE WORTH AS MUCH AS £15,000 IN 10 YEARS TIME"

"EACH YEAR YOU EARN BONUSES THAT BECOME PART OF THE GUARANTEED SUM – THEY'RE YOURS FOREVER"

"WHEN YOU RETIRE WE COULD BE HANDING OVER A CHEQUE FOR £200,000 – YOURS TO SPEND EXACTLY AS YOU PLEASE"

Each sub-headline tells a part of the story, but in more detail than the newspaper-type sub-headlines, and besides breaking up the text will actually form a *powerful part* of the selling copy in their own right: the reader should ideally be able to go straight from the headline to the sub-heads and pick up a sufficient amount of the story to convince them to read on.

And, as I pointed out earlier, the use of the system creates for the writer a discipline that means each element of copy under the sub-head has to refer back to that point.

It's much more successful to write your sub-heads before you write your main body copy for exactly that reason: the discipline organises your thoughts and you

Fig. 18:
Breaking up the copy.
In this press ad for home insurance, we have a very complex product story to get across. Using sub-heads and panels is an excellent way of getting the details across in an interesting way. The main copy, on the left hand column, is really just a summary of the product; the panel below – 'The AA Panel concept does the shopping around for you' – gives the main product feature a lot more prominence; and the complex details of the product are then listed on the right-hand column together with little graphics to add some 'colour'. The central panel uses a press cutting to get across even more of the story.

Shocked by rising home insurance costs? *Now, new AA Homequote does for home insurance what we already do for car insurance*

Home Insurance premiums soar!

Home Insurance: AA to the rescue.

New from the AA. The unique 'Homequote' service compares deals from major home insurers in minutes – and finds you our best deal while you wait.

If you're looking for home insurance, did you know that one insurance company could charge *half as much* as another company would for a similar property?

That's why careful shopping around could save you a great deal of money on home insurance. And 'shopping around' is exactly what the new AA Homequote service does for you, via our high speed computer system linked to a panel of Britain's top insurers.

Call us today especially if your renewal date is within 30 days and we'll instantly put your requirements through the system. Then our 'Panel' quotes on a top quality, comprehensive policy for your property and we pass on the best deal to you while you wait. If you want, we can even put you 'on cover' immediately. Only AA Homequote offers you this service.

You don't have to be an AA Member to take advantage of new Homequote, so try it today.

Call into one of our 250 High Street shops or give us a ring (you'll find us in Yellow Pages). And when you ask for our quote, we'll send you a free ballpoint pen.

The AA 'Panel' concept
does the shopping around for you

With 25 years of experience and over 3,000,000 general policyholders, we know what householders really want in an insurance policy.

No one company offered the ideal policy, so we developed our own. Then we went to a number of major insurers, told them what the policy contained, and asked them to 'price' it.

When you call us, we ask a few questions to work out the type of property you have.

We enter these details into our computer system that instantly goes through our 'panel' of companies, looking for the best price for the type of cover you require. Within minutes, we tell you which is the best deal. And if you want, we can put you 'on cover' immediately.

Only AA Homequote offers you this service.

AA checks the cost of insuring your home

THE COST of insuring your home and its contents is likely to soar this year — and many homeowners' home insurance bills have been double the 1991 figure.

The reason for the swingeing increase is that most insurance companies have had to pay out so much in claims that they are raising the premiums to balance their books.

While homeowners have traditionally stayed with the same insurance company, many are now thinking of shopping around to find a more competitive quote.

But this can be very time-consuming. It can also be difficult for the homeowner to compare one quote with another, as most offer different features and benefits.

Now AA Insurance, part of the Automobile Association, has launched a computerised household insurance quotation service for the cost-conscious, which covers both buildings and contents policies.

The AA has lined up a panel of insurance companies including GRE, Commercial Union, Bishopsgate, Minster, and Municipal Mutual — with General Accident and London & Edinburgh planning to join from June 1.

The panel competes to give the best contents and buildings insurance price — and is available by telephone or from 250 AA Insurance shops. The cover is the same in all cases.

Daily Mail
29th April 1992

Free Weekend Breaks

Up to £450 worth of Hotel Accommodation

If you accept our quote, you can claim 3 'Weekend Break' vouchers. Each one entitles you to FREE hotel accommodation for two people for two nights (all you pay for is meals and extras each day of your stay) from over 200 hotels around the country.

Up to £30,000 of cover –
no lengthy valuations needed

Your home contents are covered automatically for up to £30,000 (more if you need it). No need for lengthy valuations; and you reduce the risk of being under-insured.

NEW FOR OLD
We'll give full replacement costs, regardless of age or condition (except household linen, clothing, pedal cycles).

ACCIDENTAL DAMAGE
You're covered against accidental damage to electrical appliances such as washing machines, hi-fi's, and microwaves – even if it's you that causes the accident.

£1 MILLION PERSONAL LIABILITY
These days, you could be sued if you're responsible for an accident. This plan covers you for up to one million pounds personal liability, in or around the home.

24-HR DISASTER LINE
If the worst happens, call us anytime and we'll help you sort the problem out. We'll find local trades people to come round and help.

THEFT
You're covered against your possessions being stolen from your house, even from your garage and garden shed.

FIRE
In the event of fire, we'll cover you for all your possessions that are damaged.

WATER DAMAGE
This plan covers burst pipes and all types of water damage including floods.

STORMS
Damage to your possessions from trees falling on your house is also covered.

£25,000 LEGAL EXPENSES
We'll pay the legal costs (up to £25,000 in appropriate cases) if you have a personal dispute with neighbours, shops, employers – even if the dispute is not directly related to your home.

GARDEN FURNITURE
Garden furniture is expensive – so this policy protects you if your garden furniture is stolen or damaged (other than by storm or floods).

FREEZER FOOD
You're covered up to £300 should a power cut defrost the freezer – or even if it just breaks down.

CREDIT CARDS
You get automatic cover of up to £300 against the fraudulent use of your credit cards.

STOLEN CASH
If up to £300 cash is stolen from your home, you can claim it back under this plan.

24-HR LEGAL HELPLINE
Goods not up to scratch? Nuisance from neighbours? Unsatisfactory workmanship? Our legal helpline gives you free advice any time of the day or night.

BUILDINGS COVER TOO
We also have a policy to cover the structure of your home, against storms, floods, subsidence, and accidents of every type. It can be added to the home contents policy, or we'll cover you separately. Ask us to quote for cover when you call us.

EASY PAYMENTS
Take advantage of our own easy payment terms, or pay your premium by credit card to spread the cost of your insurance.

Visit your local AA shop today for a free quote and claim your Free Pen

Bring this voucher to your local AA shop and claim a FREE ballpoint pen – just for receiving an expert quote! The address of your local AA shop is always in Yellow Pages.

1393

Name	
Address	
	Postcode

AA Homequote

For Insurance, we're all you need to know.

ensure you don't leave any significant points out.

In passing, it's also worth mentioning a bad habit that can arise with sub-heads – the practice of continuing the copy straight from the sub-heading…assuming the reader has read the sub-head first and then, behaving themselves as you would wish them to, moves on to read the copy beneath the sub-head.

WHY IS IT A BAD HABIT?

For the simple reason that I think people usually scan the sub-heads first, then go back to read the copy. The sub-head isn't integral, and the reader will get somewhat confused if you make it a part of the flow of the copy. The best practice is to repeat what you have just said in the sub-headline as though it did not exist. Once the reader has read the sub-heads they go back and read the text leaving out the sub-heads they have just read. Thus, to make real sense, this paragraph should have started:

WHY IS IT A BAD HABIT?

It's a bad habit to follow on from sub-heads for the simple reason that people…

BREAK UP THE TEXT WITH SUMMARIES

It is not sacrosanct that copy should be all one size and neatly run from beginning to end, broken only by sub-headlines. This may work for novels but it doesn't really work for commercial copy where you are trying to communicate a complex idea in the shortest possible time.

It is always advantageous to break up your text with summaries, some types of which are described below. Once again, this technique helps *both* the reader and the writer at the same time. For the reader, it gives easily-digested highlights of the main points, similar to the way that sub-headlines do, helping them to absorb the main arguments quickly.

And, for the writer, by constructing summaries in advance of writing the detailed copy you are being forced to work out the most significant selling features in advance, making the writing of the copy itself an easier and more logical job as you are then obliged to deal with the points you made in your summary. Again, like sub-headlines, just because you've made the point once, you still need to make it again within the main text: the summary will be read first, and then the main copy for further information.

Here are some of the more typical 'summarising' techniques:

■ BOXES Small stories within the main copy to build up a point – often used very successfully for case histories or testimonials.

■ BULLET POINTS An old-fashioned technique but no less successful. It is simply a listing using asterisks or similar typographic tricks. The best ones are actually whole paragraphs rather than just single words – the technique produces such high readership that it's a waste not to use it fully.

■ CAPTIONS Inevitably you will use illustrations if you can to break up the text. You must caption each one: go and look at a newspaper and see how many of their pictures are uncaptioned. They attract the eye and can thus produce *very high* interest – and, again, make them full of detail rather than just an obvious explanation of the picture.

▪ CALL OUTS Similar to captions, but here you use one picture, then refer to highlights of that picture by using captions attached by lines or arrows to the appropriate part of the object in question. This works extremely well for most 'merchandise'. Like captions, make them more than just one or two-word descriptions – make them sell, not simply describe.

These are just the main ones. You can invent your own. Or, if you are as lazy as me, simply sit down with The Sun and cut out all of the 'break-out' techniques they have invented over the years. I particularly like their '20 things you never knew about' approach, and I have used this on more than one occasion with great success.

BUILDING YOUR COPY ARGUMENT BRICK BY BRICK

Most of the techniques referred to above are preliminary to writing the copy itself, though if you use them correctly you will have found that they will have greatly organised the work you have to do.

In writing the actual copy, the most useful technique is the

x has y which means z

formula. Here, *x* is the product, *y* is the feature and *z* is the benefit. I go into the whole subject of feature and benefit copy in the next Chapter; suffice to say that it is the 'building block' of all good copy. The way the formula translates is simple:

> *"This briefcase (x) has combination locks (y), which means no more fumbling around looking for keys (z)."*

But it is the way in which this building block is used that can make writing copy so easy and so much more effective. Taking each point, you simply build them up, one after the other, virtually like a list. It is like building a wall with those building blocks: each one you add makes the wall taller and longer, but leave any one out and the gap *sticks out like a sore thumb*.

Here's a made-up example, but it shows how the feature/benefit listing approach can work with great strength:

> *"This briefcase is made from the finest leather, which gives it an appearance and feel superior to the plastic types common these days. The handle is not simply riveted on, but is secured by four substantial brass screws, set deep into the frame, which means the handle can never come away.*
>
> *And the frame is constructed from solid beech wood, a wood noted for its strength as well as its lightness, so you have a case that's easy to carry yet capable of standing up to the roughest wear and tear.*
>
> *The solid brass combination locks means no more fumbling for lost keys. Your combination is personal to you with over 50,000 settings."*

All this is simply a consecutive listing of feature and benefit…building up the wall brick by brick. You have to add the odd joining words, of course, otherwise it becomes unpleasantly staccato. You need to *vary* the lengths of each paragraph to give the piece rhythm. But these are basic writing skills, and if applied to a listing system like this will result in very powerful copy. With clever writing you can build up the points to a crescendo. And the constant tap-tap-tap of features and benefits on the reader makes them feel that this product has got an awful lot of good things going for it.

COMING TO THE CLOSE; THE IMPORTANCE OF
THE ACTION SECTION

Under the earlier discussion of the AIDCA formula, we looked at how Action was the most important element and how, as far as copy was concerned, it shouldn't really be left until last.

There are some useful structural habits that you should get into in order to create the most powerful action.

The first of these is '*trial closing*'. Again, this is a phrase as well as technique borrowed directly from the salesman. Trial closing is simply asking for action very early in the sales sequence.

In face-to-face selling it works by allowing the salesman to see if the prospect really is interested. In copy we cannot *judge* the reactions of our prospect, but trial closing is nevertheless a valuable technique because it creates the atmosphere of selling that so differentiates a direct marketing piece from any other.

Typically, a sentence like the following would appear at the end of the initial 'precis' or introductory section:

> *"...reply through the post or simply by telephoning; and if*
> *you reply within 30 days a superb free gift could be yours."*

This is not the only place where you can trial close. It is often very powerful to sprinkle it *throughout* the copy itself, whenever an opportunity presents itself.

Let me stress that I do not for one moment suppose these trial closes *in themselves* provoke action. But what they do is add *immeasurably* to the 'active' flavour of the copy: they give the copy a point, and indeed, using such trial closes means that the writer has to constantly bear in mind what the point of the copy is all about.

The real close, logically enough, comes at the end of the copy. It should structurally be the *crescendo*, so far as the internal rhythm of the piece is concerned.

A good copywriter will close naturally: but here's a workmanlike structure for a close that generally works.

First, you would write your sub-head, using something along the lines of 'reply within 30 days' or 'act now'. If you're giving a free gift, it's an excellent idea to use the free gift as the subject of the sub-head.

Then the copy section itself should start with a peremptory 'act now'. Normally this would be along the lines of:

> *"REPLY TODAY*
>
> *Find out more today. Simply clip the coupon or telephone"*

Fig. 19:
Getting the action in.
Perhaps the most important part of copy structure is to get the action strong enough. In this letter for the NSPCC, you can count no less than 4 calls to action (1, 2, 3 and 4) even *before* the main action sequence starts at 5. The action is reprised again in the PS. Putting as many calls to action in as this also creates a powerful sense of urgency in the copy – the whole argument revolves around a need to do something. The 'active' tone is what sets good direct marketing copy clearly apart from the 'passive' tone so typical of much conventional advertising copy.

NSPCC

The National Society
for the Prevention of
Cruelty to Children

67 Saffron Hill
London EC1N 8RS
Telephone 071-242 1626

Will you give £15 this Christmas to help save a child's life?

October 1992

Dear Friend,

That may sound dramatic but, in this country, on average three to four children a week die following abuse or neglect.

And, many, many more are severely injured...seriously neglected...living in daily, hourly fear of abuse...

Children like Jane and Alice...

Their father beat his two daughters so violently that Jane had two black eyes and Alice was badly cut.

After her father brutally kicked her, Jane had to be taken to hospital with bruising on her legs and several fractured ribs.

The NSPCC took immediate and effective action to ensure the two girls were made safe.

If we had not had the funds available to help Jane and Alice - how much worse might the result have been?

£15 could be instrumental in saving a child's life.

Every day of the year abused children, like Jane and Alice, face the most appalling dangers. But somehow, at

Patrons: Her Majesty The Queen, Her Majesty Queen Elizabeth The Queen Mother.
President: Her Royal Highness The Princess Margaret Countess of Snowdon.
Chairman Central Executive Committee: Michael Moore.
Director: Christopher Brown.
Founded 1884. Incorporated by Royal Charter. Charity Registration No. 216401.

Christmas, when the rest of the country is enjoying itself, the plight of these children seems all the more pitiable.

The NSPCC only heard about Paul when he was sixteen. His mother had left home when he was six, leaving him in the charge of his uncle and his uncle's girlfriend. They didn't allow him to make friends. He only left the house to go to school. After tea he was sent straight to bed. Any failure to meet his uncle's or 'aunt's' commands meant a beating.

He pined for his mother and was desperate to know where she was. He mentioned this to a teacher who approached his uncle. As a result Paul was locked in his room for several days.

That is where he spent Christmas Day - without anyone to talk to, and with only basic food and water.

Paul's years of fear and misery have left him scarred. Now he is having psychiatric help.

Just one call to the NSPCC Child Protection Helpline may mean we can prevent at least some of this happening.

Last year we helped many thousands of children in desperate need of protection.

That is why your help means so much. And why, as the season of goodwill approaches, I am asking you to help us carry on answering the many cries for help from children in need.

It enables us not just to protect children who have been abused...but to prevent such situations arising.

It is essential that we carry on being able to respond promptly to the calls for help.

But to do this we need your assistance.

The NSPCC gets very little government money. In fact, nearly 90% of our income comes from people like you, who care very much about the wrongs being done to too many children.

And we spend very little on administration. The greatest possible 'slice' of our income is devoted directly to helping children.

This girl had to be taken to hospital after one of her father's beatings

---

We need your help to provide -

❋ AID TO CHILDREN SUFFERING FROM PHYSICAL INJURY caused by actual physical abuse by their parents or guardians...last year we responded to several thousand children in this frightening situation.

❋ HELP FOR CHILDREN WHO HAVE BEEN SEXUALLY ABUSED. It is hard to express in words just how frightening and traumatic sexual assault is for the children involved.

❋ PROTECTION FOR NEGLECTED CHILDREN. Too often, children are not properly cared for by their parents or guardians - and serious problems can result. Last year, we had many worrying incidents of neglect reported to us.

Without your help we cannot continue to run

❋ THE NSPCC CHILD PROTECTION HELPLINE. Anyone who suspects a child is at risk from abuse can ring one FREE national number 24 hours a day, to ask us for immediate help, which could save a child's life.

❋ CHILD PROTECTION TEAMS, CENTRES AND PROJECTS. These NSPCC services are vital to the protection of children in danger. Every day the NSPCC is working - often in partnership with other professionals like the police, social services and teachers - to help and protect children who have been seriously abused or tragically neglected. It's critical that these services go on being funded.

£15 may not seem a large amount. Yet it can help save a child in danger.

With your help this Christmas we can perhaps make the children as happy - and safe - as they should be.

Can you donate a £15 gift to help save a child's life?

I know Christmas is just about the most expensive time of year. But your gift this Christmas could be critical to a child's safety.

So when you are doing your Christmas shopping, please pretend there's an extra child

Thousands of children need protecting from cruelty every year

---

you have to buy a present for. And it's a gift they'll remember forever...a life free from the fear and misery of cruelty.

I have enclosed a simple form. Please return it as soon as possible. Your gift will be received with more gratitude than I can express.

On behalf of the many children you will be helping, may I thank you very much and wish you both a Happy Christmas and a peaceful New Year.

Yours sincerely,

Fiona Condie

Fiona Condie
NSPCC

P.S. When you remember that, on average, an estimated 3 to 4 children die every week following abuse or neglect, I am sure you will realise just how hard our task is. We need all the help we can get for the children. Please send as much as you can today.

It is impractical for us to check whether you already support the NSPCC in other ways. If so, we'd like to apologise and ask you to pass this letter on to a friend who might be interested in helping the NSPCC too. Thank you.

and note that we are very specific in what we want the reader to do; many otherwise good closes are ruined because the writer has assumed that the prospect is intelligent enough to know what they're supposed to do. They almost certainly are – but they are not reading your copy with much of their mind, and you need to put in these prompts.

Then, you need to state exactly what will be the *result* of them doing what it is you are asking them to do:

> *"We'll then send you full details of this plan/your figurine will be despatched to you within/your donation will immediately go to help..."*

Sometimes the result of their action will be simple. A product will be sent. Sometimes it will be complex – such as a two-stage insurance offer; in the complex cases, you must detail all the stages your prospect will go through. Leave nothing to doubt:

> *"We will send you full policy details for you to look at in comfort. In addition, you'll also receive full payment details – you can use your credit card or take advantage of our direct debit system."*

Then you need to explain how by taking action what your prospect is letting themselves in for. This is the place where you can calm their fears – overcome their objections, in salesmen's parlance:

> *"Remember, you'll be under no obligation/you'll have 30 days to inspect this product in your own home/if you don't like it simply return it for a full refund/no salesmen will call..."*

Lastly, you need to reinforce the offer. You can either take the main proposition and reprise that; or, more typically, you would take the premium offer and reprise that:

> *"And the moment we receive your completed application your free alarm clock radio will be on its way..."*

Finishing off with another hit on the time close:

> *"But remember, we must hear from you by midnight on the 30th July for this offer to remain valid."*

THE TIME CLOSE

You will note that a 'time close' has crept in at the end. Does time closing work? Indeed it does – it is one of the most powerful tools available. But time closing is often misunderstood: it is not because your prospect is genuinely afraid that you will 'run out' of your offer. Instead, it works to promote action NOW – rather than later. In direct marketing, we must understand that our prospect has many other distractions and can turn away from us at any time.

The last thing you want to happen is for a prospect to be completely entranced with your offer, and then (because you have failed to close hard enough) decide that they'll certainly respond...tomorrow. *The moment your ad or mailing is put up on some metaphorical mantelpiece, that's the moment your response goes down.* A time close, quite simply, prevents this happening. I suspect that no time close in the world has ever made more people reply – I think it has, on many occasions, ensured that the people who thought they would reply actually do so on the day, rather than just think about it.

Time closes are particularly effective with follow-up mailings – they give a date which allows you to remind people, or allows you to give them an extension, but only if they apply now.

ONE LAST WORD

If you take nothing else away from this book, please take this one idea: that the initial preparatory work you do in *organising copy* is perhaps the most important thing you can do. It means that you will write the things that are of most importance to the reader – but overriding everything else, it means above all that you have a carefully thought-out plan to write to. It will make your job a great deal easier. It will make your copy a great deal more successful. More than that you cannot ask ■

Chapter 4: Summary

Good copy needs a great deal of information to make it work, which usually means it is long. Only through careful organisation of that copy will you make it easy for the interested reader to skip-read the parts they are interested in, and for the reader requiring more convincing to read through all of the copy.

The basic AIDCA formula provides the internal 'selling' structure. You do not need to follow the structure slavishly, but copy rarely works unless all of the AIDCA elements are present.

The best way to open copy is by writing a short two or three paragraph section that is a summary of the whole story; then go on to tell the story in detail.

Use sub-heads to break up the story; but make the sub-heads themselves tell a story so that the skip-reader can if necessary pick up the whole story from the sub-heads alone. Don't just use single words merely to break up the text.

Use summaries. Break up the copy through the use of boxes, lists, case-histories, call-outs and captions. Like sub-heads, it makes the skip-reading task easier. It also creates a much livelier look to the piece.

Use trial closings throughout the copy to provide a more active feel. These will not in themselves provoke action but simply by adding them you can transform a merely interesting piece of copy into one that has a strong flavour of wanting to sell – and this will produce better results.

Ensure you have a close. And in doing this, make sure you follow a careful structure within the close as well: you must tell people what to do, what will happen when they do it, what won't happen if they do it, when they must do it by and if anything else will happen – such as a free gift. Take great pains to be particularly explicit in this section: your prospect is virtually ready to reply – don't undo it by leaving them with any doubts or by not pushing hard by emphasising the urgency of it all.

COPY STYLE

*Communicating with an audience in order to make them
act is no easy task; apart from formulae and structures,
certain stylistic techniques make communicating easier.
The use of conventional written English is just about the last
style of writing you should employ. Here are some hints
and style guides that should help.*

ENGLISH is not one language but many.

There is the spoken version we employ on a daily basis. Within that alone there are variations; a formal style, for lecturing, for instance; a highly idiomatic style, employed late at night in the pub.

Equally, in written English, there are different styles to suit different occasions. There is the stilted language of an official document; the tortuous prose of a Guardian leader article; the elegant and witty phrasing of a Volvo advertisement; the pungent English of a Sun editorial.

Many of the styles, both spoken and written, are employed to communicate to the hearer or reader not only the content of what is said or written, but also a lot about the prestige or education of the speaker or listener. In other words, much spoken and written English is designed to impress as well as to communicate.

In copywriting, we can use a written style that can take account of this important 'image' effect. But above all we need to use English to communicate as *clearly and effectively* as we can. Our first and main task, that for which we are paid, is to get a message across to our readers, a message that furthermore they will *act* upon.

And not surprisingly, the ease with which we communicate that message has a great deal to do with the type of the language we use.

Does it make a difference? Certainly. It must be remembered that even if our reader falls into the 'very interested' heading that previous Chapters have discussed, we are not generally talking about things of consuming interest in the real world. Our prospects read us with very little of their minds on the task. They are prepared to go along with what we say, but only so long as we make it simple and easy.

Do not fall into the trap of thinking that because of this the reader is dull. This is not the case. But what we have to say ranks low on the reader's scale of importance; and therefore the 'brainpower' the reader employs is generally of a low order. Their minds are usually on other more important things than your insurance plan, your car, your computer or your good cause.

EASY ENGLISH

Given that we need to communicate as effortlessly as possible, we can do this most easily by using English to what I suppose is best called a 'low reading age'. This is the approach of The Sun and The Mirror; and much fun is had by suggesting that the average Sun reader has the mental age of an 8 year old, because the style of English employed is aimed at just that person.

This may or may not be true. I suspect it isn't – I suspect the reason is the same as ours: a need for a basic style that communicates swiftly with the *minimum* effort on the part of the reader.

Having said that, you need to be very careful not to overdo the style lest you begin to alienate your reader, particularly when it comes to certain types of product and service. But more of matching the style to reader a little later.

TO PURCHASE OR TO BUY?

First, let's look at some of the basic techniques behind simple English.

Here are two paragraphs of English:

> *In order to communicate with maximum effect to an audience of purchasers, the requirement is to employ a style of language that is comprehensible to the majority of the individuals who will peruse it.*
>
> *So that we can talk to a group of buyers and get them to do what we want, we need to use the kind of words and phrases that will be understood by most of the people who see them.*

Obviously, it's the same paragraph written in two different styles. The first one sounds more respectable, but I suggest the second one sounds more down-to-earth, and probably easier to understand…certainly, faster to read at any rate.

But the difference goes deeper, and there's a rational explanation as to why the paragraphs say the same thing, but sound so different.

The first one sounds respectable because it employs mainly Romance words – words loaned to English from (mainly) Latin. The second sounds more down-to-earth because it says exactly the same thing, but uses words that are originally Anglo-Saxon (with a few other languages added as well).

English, as we speak it today, is a jumbled mixture of English, or Anglo-Saxon, together with a lot of Latin, French and bits of Welsh and Norse. Up until the Norman invasion in 1066, the language was a fairly pure form of Anglo-Saxon, a Germanic language brought over by the Saxons around 450 AD. The Norse invasions in the ninth and tenth centuries gave this language a few loan-words, but the big change was with the coming of the Normans.

They brought with them Old French, and reintroduced Latin. As conquerors, their language became the *lingua franca*. At court, you spoke Norman French. For written documents, Latin was the general tongue. The Normans rapidly became the ruling class and thus their language, modified a little by borrowing from the natives, became dominant at one level in society.

However, the peasant remained Anglo-Saxon, and continued to speak his native English. Latin was a good go-between language, but was only used by the literate classes, and mainly the Church.

Thus from earliest times two types of English were in existence; spoken, vernacular English, used mainly by the lower orders, and written, court English – really Anglo-Norman – used by the rulers. In time, of course, the gap closed, but it is remarkable to this day that it is possible to use either the Romance word, or the Anglo-Saxon word, to get almost exactly the same meaning but with very different 'image' effects – and also some important comprehensibility effects.

In fact, most people (even educated ones) tend to use a spoken English that is more Anglo-Saxon than Romance. It is more basic and down-to-earth. The vocabulary is easier and shorter. Try speaking using Romance synonyms for Anglo-Saxon words: you will sound like Mr Interlocuter from the days of Music Hall.

But when it comes to writing, most people choose a Romance style. It sounds more educated, with its longer and more flowery words. But professional writers who need to communicate will tend to choose Anglo-Saxon, because it sounds punchier and makes communication easier…unless you happen to be a lawyer in which case the obfuscating tendencies of Romance vocabulary and construction allows you to charge five times more than if you wrote your lease in simple English.

Here are some common Anglo-Saxon/Romance synonyms:

GET/OBTAIN   *BUY/PURCHASE*   *SEE/INSPECT*   *WANT/REQUIRE*
ASK/REQUEST   *CALL/VISIT*   *GIVE/DONATE*   *HELP/ASSIST*
TAKE/REMOVE   *FIND/DISCOVER*   *LIKE/ENJOY*   *PICK/SELECT*

In most cases, common verbs of a Romance origin have an exact synonym with an Anglo-Saxon root. Wherever possible, go for the Anglo-Saxon word. It is more quickly understood. More people will know what you are talking about, and they will need less effort to reach that understanding.

STYLE AND IMAGE

Having said all of that, I shall now go back upon myself. One of the more subtle techniques available to the skilled copywriter is *tailoring the style* of the copy to the subject. It would be highly inappropriate to use a punchy, Anglo-Saxon style for a product in, say, the investment area, where you are looking to create an educated, confident effect.

Here is where you can use writing style to create an image or a feeling about your product, over and above simply the things you say about it.

A charity mailing will require a gentle, concerned but determined tone, for example. You cannot write:

> *"Send money today! Your cash will be rushed off to the kids so they don't get beaten up. And don't worry – we don't spend a brass farthing more than we need to on running things. Every penny goes to the kids…"*

and expect anyone to take you seriously. Instead, you need to write:

> *"Please give what you can, and as soon as you can. Your generous donation will be used quickly to help those children in the greatest need, those who need our help and protection immediately. And rest*

assured, we spend as little as we can on administration: the great majority of your donation will be used directly to help those who need it most."

You will see that in some cases, in order to achieve the style, I have abandoned the Anglo-Saxon and used the Romance. This is the most common way to add 'respectability' to copy when it needs it – but be careful not to overdo it, otherwise it ends up sounding like a legal document.

Indeed, some bad copywriters adopt a high-flown style for everything they write, trying presumably to impress either fellow writers, or themselves. Forget your own intellectual superiority and put yourself in the reader's shoes.

I mentioned investment products. Many financial products require a different, more up-market style, and this can be achieved in much the same way. An educated style is going to give certain products the aura of respectability that they need. Compare

> *"This plan puts your cash into shares and gives you a profit*
> *at the end"*

with

> *"This scheme invests your premiums in equities in order to*
> *achieve the maximum dividend at the end of the period."*

If you're writing a fulfilment pack where sheer *understandability* is important, you would probably opt for the first case. But where you are trying to convince the public that their money is safe in your hands, you would probably go for the latter. The way you choose your words will depend entirely on the effect you are looking to achieve.

Incidentally 'Fog' indices and other mathematical ways of 'calculating' readability are great fun but of no great use to the working copywriter – they might tell you if what you wrote *was* readable, but they don't tell you *how* to write it for readability in the first place, unless you want to spend as much time counting long words as writing them. The Romance/Anglo Saxon effect described above achieves the same end, and is actually a lot easier to work with.

CONTRACTIONS

The use of contractions is a surprisingly large contributor to style. Put contractions in and you have a vernacular style:

> *"It shouldn't be forgotten that it's important to create the right flavour*
> *for copy; it isn't right if the style doesn't fit the subject."*

Take them out and you go up several notches in respectability at once:

> *"It should not be forgotten that it is important to create the right*
> *flavour for copy; it is not right if the style does not fit the subject."*

It slows the pace down, but it gives a more ponderous, weighty flavour which may be appropriate in some cases. Some people, I know, dislike contractions and remove them on principle. This can be counterproductive in that the extra readability conferred by contractions is usually a positive benefit for most forms of copywriting.

Fig. 20:
Does it sound as though
you mean it?
An important part of copy tone is enthusiasm – does it sound as though the writer is full of enthusiasm about the product or service? Is it dry and mechanical – or does the copy bubble over with infectious commitment to the idea? Here's a very angry letter for the RSPB – angry literally because the writer was personally highly involved in the cause, and this involvement comes out clearly. A good writer can (and, indeed, must) have the skill to get worked up about any cause, product or service that they are asked to write about, and must have the writing skill to use that enthusiasm without it taking over.

THE ROYAL SOCIETY FOR THE PROTECTION OF BIRDS

THE LODGE · SANDY · BEDFORDSHIRE · SG19 2DL · TEL: 0767 680551 · TELEX: 82469 RSPB · FAX: 0767 692365

RED ALERT for UK Birds of Prey

Dear Member,

...40 golden eagles, from a population of just 424 adult pairs...24 red kites - out of a total of 60 pairs...65 peregrines...68 kestrels...57 hen harriers...39 goshawks...71 owls...367 buzzards...plus white-tailed eagles...merlins....marsh harriers...and dozens of sparrowhawks. Altogether a devastating total of 814 birds of prey killed <u>illegally</u> in the UK from 1979-1989. The statistics, shocking though they are, do not come near to telling the whole appalling story.

THEY ARE MERELY THE TIP OF AN UNACCEPTABLE ICEBERG

An iceberg on which the conservation of some of our rarest birds could founder. Unless we act now.

Already this year the RSPB Task Force has recorded over 200 alleged incidents of wild bird persecution. That's why we are calling urgently for a red alert for the UK's birds of prey. And asking for your help.

Let me make one thing quite clear. <u>All</u> birds of prey are protected by law. It is illegal to kill them and the people who do so are criminals. They break laws designed to protect the wildlife heritage of our country. They put internationally as well as nationally <u>endangered</u> species at risk.

A GLOBAL RESPONSIBILITY

The red kite, for example, is one of three UK birds identified in the <u>World Checklist of Threatened Birds</u> as being globally endangered. Over the past three years the RSPB and the Joint Nature Conservation Committee have been undertaking a programme to re-introduce a small number of red kites from the Continent into the UK. **Already at least four of those birds have been poisoned.** Continuation of this project can only be justified if persecution levels do not jeopardise their success.

And these are just the reported cases, the ones we have found out about, the tip of the iceberg. We know that the <u>true</u> mortality figures are much higher because anyone deliberately killing a protected species is going to make sure they get rid of the evidence. Many birds may suffer a lingering, unseen death in remote areas where no one is likely to find the corpses.

HOW DOES IT HAPPEN?

Many birds of prey are killed <u>deliberately</u>, simply because of the belief that they threaten populations of game birds or lambs. Others are <u>accidental</u> victims; they inadvertently eat poisoned bait put out illegally for foxes and crows. And they can suffer through the <u>careless</u> or negligent use of poisons allowed for other purposes. Eggs are also removed from nests, for illegal collections and to supply the falconry trade.

Poison and traps are also <u>indiscriminate</u> killers. Owls are common victims of the illegal pole trap, dying cruel and lingering deaths. Poison, illegal though it is, may be laid for one species but claim the lives of many others such as badgers and hedgehogs.

Even family pets are at risk - 435 dogs and 276 cats were killed by poison during 1979-1989.

WHAT CAN WE DO?

We can put more pressure on the Government to introduce stricter <u>controls</u> on the availability of certain poisons and pesticides. We can <u>educate</u> people to show that birds of prey, rather than the 'pests' they are still seen as in some areas, are a truly magnificent part of our heritage. We can fight for fines and sentences that reflect the seriousness of the offences. We have recently called successfully for existing legislation to be strengthened to make landowners more <u>accountable</u> for birds killed on their land. We can

BIRDS OF PREY	POISONED	SHOT OR TRAPPED	TOTAL KILLED	NESTS DESTROYED
RED KITE	24		24	
SPARROW-HAWK	12	38	50	
BUZZARD	228	139	367	
GOLDEN EAGLE	27	13	40	7
OSPREY		4	4	
KESTREL	28	40	68	2
PEREGRINE	10	55	65	24
OWLS	6	65	71	4

Pole-mounted spring traps have been illegal since 1904 but they are still used today. Owls are often the victims because of their habit of hunting from perches. Trapped by the feet, this bird died a cruel and lingering death.

Registered charity no. 207076

Patron **Her Majesty the Queen** President **Ian Prestt** Chairman of Council **Adrian Darby** Chief Executive **Barbara Young**

▼ DETACH HERE ▼

STOP the illegal killing of our birds of prey

We really need your help

AN RSPB DETECTIVE AT WORK

RECYCLED PAPER

YES. I want to help the RSPB Task Force succeed in stopping the bird killers.

HERE IS MY GIFT OF				Every gift is welcome whatever the amount
☐ £15 ☐ £25 ☐ £50 ☐ £100 ☐ £600* ☐ £_____ (other)				

☐ I enclose my cheque payable to the RSPB
☐ I wish to donate £ _____ by RSPB Visa/Access/other Visa   (please delete as appropriate)

My credit card number is

☐☐☐☐ ☐☐☐☐ ☐☐☐☐ ☐☐☐☐

Expiry date

Cardholder's signature _____   Date _____

If you would like details of covenanting please tick this box ☐
*If you can donate £600, please tick this box. We will then send you a GIFT AID form with which we can claim an extra 33% tax rebate immediately. ☐

Indeed, it's natural to speak in contractions – just try talking sensibly without them!

(Incidentally, please be very careful in not mistaking the apostrophe used for a contraction, representing a missing letter or letters, with the possessive apostrophe – or, indeed, giving plural forms the apostrophe.)

The misuse of language and grammar by copywriters is counterproductive. Anything that is confusing, even to only a part of the reading population, is working against the fullest and easiest understanding of your copy.

CREATING TONE

Each product or service will benefit from having the copy tailored closely to the *image* you wish to portray. This does demand from the writer an ability to imitate styles of writing, or 'tone', and this is something that comes through practice.

In the same way that there are different styles of English, there are within the style you choose sub-groups which give you 'tone' – and the tone you choose gives a subtle but important picture of the type of organisation or product that you are. You can be high-quality, exciting, friendly, down-to-earth, innovative, intellectual – all of these things can be achieved through 'tone' alone.

Here's a short list of some of the writing styles, or tones, that are regularly employed. There are very many more. But all of them use simple, straightforward English that would be easily and rapidly understood by most readers:

- A Daily Mirror Editorial
- A Sun Page 3 Girl Caption
- A BBC Nine O'Clock News Story
- A Reader's Digest Prize Draw Letter
- A Money Mail reply to a reader's financial query
- A Government Minister's statement
- A Party Political Broadcast
- A Les Dawson story
- A Scientific American article

Each one has a completely different tone, and often the tone suits what people would expect. You expect a certain tone from the BBC, for instance, which would be inappropriate language to tell a joke in.

In order to develop your ability to write in different tones to suit the product or service you are selling, you should read as many newspapers as you can, as many magazines as you can, and you should generally acquire truly catholic reading habits in order to discover new styles that will help you.

It is not possible to exploit the full range of the English language unless you have a reasonable acquaintance with written English in all its forms. This is only achieved by reading – and reading *anything*, good or bad, interesting or dull.

Creating tone is essentially the art of parody. If you can write parodies of well-known styles, then creating tone in your copy is not going to be difficult.

But because style is such a personal thing, it is very difficult to pin down how 'tone' comes about. But I often find that imagining a 'voice' as I write is one of the best ways to achieve tones. You can imagine a warm and sincere voice. Or an aggressive voice. Or an enthusiastic voice.

One of the creative directors at WWAV, Maria Phillips, actually uses a photograph; she finds a picture representing the person she's writing to and sticks it in front of her when she's writing the copy. Having this sort of visual aid can help you find the right tone.

Choose the 'voice' most appropriate to your product, or choose a well-known style that suits, and then write your copy in that style. It makes a surprising difference.

Lastly, the *worst* thing a copywriter can have is a style of their own. If everything you write comes out sounding the same, you are going to have a very limited range and you will need to work hard on your style to make it more transparent.

PARAGRAPHS

Paragraphing is another major contributor to style and tone. Going back to the example of a legal document, if you ever trouble to read one, you will see that lawyers have never heard of paragraphs. But if you read a Daily Mirror editorial, they have fallen in love with them.

Clearly, short paragraphs are easier for the reader to absorb than long ones. As far as writing sensible copy is concerned, the basic rule is always to keep paragraphs short, and typically start a new paragraph when you start a new thought.

There was a school of copywriting current in the sixties and seventies.

I suppose it could be called the VW School.

(Because VW advertisements prepared by DDB were among the first to use the style.)

It used extremely short paragraphs.

Each sentence became a paragraph.

Sentences became shorter.

Until it happened.

A paragraph became a single word.

Just one word.

One.

This New York style was very popular for some time, but reached a point where it became pointless. It began to be written for the sake of fashion more than anything else, and apart from the staccato effect which became difficult to read, the amount of selling information you could communicate in this fashion was very limited. Style overtook content.

But a reasonably short paragraph will enable you to make the point you want to make, and then move easily on to your next point leaving your copy looking open and accessible.

Paragraphs in advertising copy should ideally contain *no more than three sentences*, and the paragraph should be devoted to one single thought at a time. Don't, of course, then proceed to make every paragraph just three sentences long. You will need to vary paragraph lengths as you go – some points will, in any event, need more

NSPCC

The National Society
for the Prevention of
Cruelty to Children

67 Saffron Hill
London EC1N 8RS
Telephone 071-242 1626

Will you give £15 this Christmas to help save a child's life?

October 1992

Dear Friend,

You've already shown how deeply you care about the safety of defenceless children through your support of the NSPCC.

And nothing would give me greater happiness now, in thanking you for your past generosity, than to say you are no longer needed to help protect these children from the horrors of abuse.

But the frightening truth is that today your support is needed more than ever. Because, in this country, on average three to four children a week die following abuse or neglect.

That is why I must ask you, once again, if you can help us save a child's life.

And the problem doesn't end there. As well as these desperate children whose very lives are threatened, there are many, many more who are severely injured...seriously neglected...living in daily, hourly fear of abuse...

Children like Jane and Alice...

Their father beat his two daughters so violently that Jane had two black eyes and Alice was badly cut.

After her father brutally kicked her, Jane had to be taken to hospital with bruising on her legs and several fractured ribs.

The NSPCC took immediate and effective action to ensure the

Patrons: Her Majesty The Queen, Her Majesty Queen Elizabeth The Queen Mother.
President: Her Royal Highness The Princess Margaret Countess of Snowdon.
Chairman Central Executive Committee: Michael Moore.
Director: Christopher Brown.
Founded 1884. Incorporated by Royal Charter. Charity Registration No. 216401.

NATIONAL SOCIETY FOR THE PREVENTION OF CRUELTY TO CHILDREN

PATRONS – HER MAJESTY THE QUEEN – HER MAJESTY QUEEN ELIZABETH THE QUEEN MOTHER.
PRESIDENT – H.R.H. THE PRINCESS MARGARET, COUNTESS OF SNOWDON
CHAIRMAN CENTRAL EXECUTIVE COMMITTEE – LADY HOLLAND-MARTIN, D.B.E, D.L.

Headquarters

67 SAFFRON HILL – LONDON – EC1N 8RS

TELEPHONE 01-242-1626

DIRECTOR Dr ALAN GILMOUR, C.B.E.

Dear Friend,

As Director of the NSPCC, I always view the approach of Christmas with somewhat mixed feelings. It is never far from my thoughts, nor from those of my many dedicated colleagues, that while we may enjoy the festive season, there will be many children and families for whom Christmas is a time of misery.

The fact is, festive season or not, there will be innocent children who will be subjected to neglect, abuse and even physical assault right through the holiday. The importance of our work in preventing such terrible treatment seems to take on new dimensions at Christmas.

Because, of course, we will maintain our caring service even on Christmas Day. Should the need arise, an Inspector will leave his own family on Christmas Day to attend a call for our help.

Last December, for example, we were called in to help 1,914 children. Naturally I hope these figures will fall this December, but whatever the demands on our time and our services, we will be as willing to help as we have been for the last 101 years.

And without the support of 'Friends of the NSPCC' this work would be far more difficult than it is already. The financial help you have given us in the past genuinely makes a real contribution to our abilities to answer those cries for help.

As a charity, we depend greatly on the income we receive from our many Friends.

Thus as Christmas approaches, I feel sure you will understand my writing to you to seek your financial support too.

From our supporters, this December, I hope to be able to raise the sum of £30,000, and I do hope that you will be able to help us towards that target.

You will, naturally, wish to know what £30,000 will buy these days. I think you will be surprised. If as many children need our help this Christmas as they did a year ago, it could cost £30,000 just to protect them for the same two week period.

We calculate that on average to provide protection for one child for one month could cost £30.96. So a donation of, for example, £15.48, can enable us to protect a child for two weeks.

A Christmas donation will help us provide a child with immediate protection.

Founded 1884. Incorporated by Royal Charter. Charity Registration Number 216401

Fig. 21:
Two different styles to the same donor.

Here are the front pages of 2 NSPCC letters, both addressed to the donor file. The first letter is the 'normal' one, signed by the fundraiser, where the tone and style are bright, direct and aimed at getting your money.

The second letter has the same aim (getting your money) but this time it's from the Director. Clearly the Director would write in a very different way. You'll notice the language is more circumspect, the sentences are longer, the approach more oblique, the pace slower and more gentle. It would grate on the 'ear' of the reader if there was a hard appeal from the Director, and probably would then lack the believability to work. Both worked well, in fact, and both were written by professional copywriters who could have easily interchanged styles.

BARCLAYS BANK PLC
Customer Services Centre
PO Box 111, Gloucester GL4 7RP.

Mr A B Sample
123 Any Street
Anytown
Anyshire
AB1 2BC

X007695945   00188

October 1992

Dear Mr Sample,

Help protect yourself with up to £90,000 tax-free if a serious accident happened to you.

If an accident suddenly prevented you from ever returning to gainful employment again, how well prepared would you be **financially**?

Think about it for a moment. You may well be faced with all the additional expenses that a serious injury can often involve - like special equipment or adaptations to your home or car. All at a time when your regular income may be uncertain.

You may already have life assurance - and even private health care. But if you suffer a permanently disabling accident, the chances are that <u>neither</u> of these will protect you adequately.

The fact is, you could well need additional financial help. Which is precisely why Barclays Insurance Services Company Limited, the insurance broking subsidiary of Barclays PLC, would like to recommend the Barclays Personal Accident Plan.

<u>A Plan designed by Sun Alliance - one
of Britain's leading insurance companies</u>

Sun Alliance were chosen to develop a simple, comprehensive and value for money Plan. As one of the

:SABILITY. If an accident
 you could receive a
£90,000, free of income tax
 julations, to spend as you
 the money for your future
: specially adapted or even
:e...the choice would be

for a range of permanent
 /ou lost a limb, you could
  £45,000. You'll find
 leaflet.

(OU SPEND IN HOSPITAL.
 as an in-patient after an
 .ccident Plan will pay you
 :h day - up to a maximum of

 paid to you <u>in addition</u>
 a may receive under the Plan
 / way you choose.

. If you are unfortunate
 an accident, a cash sum of
 state. However, if both you
 ar the same Policy, the
 e <u>doubled</u> to £90,000 each
 the same accident - a total
 estate.

 the whole family

 benefit from the protection
 it Plan. You can insure
 iren if eligible, at a very
 or any one of your family
 disabling accident, the
 . And as cover for your
 than £15 a month, it's a
 isiderable peace of mind.

 and premiums increase
  original amount each year,
 to help maintain the value of the Plan in the future.

As you become older, the chances of having an accident with serious consequences become greater. So, rather than increase premiums, the benefits have been halved for people aged 65 or over, except for permanent total disablement from all gainful employment cover, which ceases.

<u>Two simple ways to pay</u>

You can pay the monthly premiums by direct debit from your Bank current account or, if you prefer, you can

Barclays Bank PLC. Registered in London, England. No. 1026167. Registered Office: 54 Lombard Street, London EC3P 3AH.
00188/0000007
4/5247AC

Fig. 22:
Setting the right financial tone.

This letter is from Barclays to its customers, suggesting that they consider a Personal Accident Plan. You'll notice the careful style adopted here...understated, serious, helpful. It never presumes to *sell* anything, simply to point out the usefulness of this type of product ... 'you could well need additional financial help'. Writing this type of copy demands an understanding not only of the sensitivity of the customer about a plan that only pays out in the event of a pretty serious injury, but also demands an understanding of the sensitivity of banks writing to their customer files. Yet, for all its sensitivity of tone, this never gets in the way of it being a hard-working mailing letter which follows all of the classical direct mail rules. It just doesn't *sound* as though it does, which is of course the whole point.

copy than others.

But by varying paragraph length around the mean of three sentences, you will be able to create a variety that will be more attractive to the reader.

CREATING THE SENSE OF BENEFIT

Given a vernacular style and short paragraphs, together with the appropriate structures discussed in the previous Chapter, you should by now have a reasonably good grip on a copy style. I also spoke previously about adding trial closes in order to give your copy a sense of urgency. A similar technique, but one more to do with style than structure, is the feature/benefit technique.

First, we need to distinguish between a product feature and a product benefit.

A *feature* is something that belongs to a product or service. A *benefit* is what happens to the purchaser of that product or service as a result of the feature.

I may buy a word-processor because it has a large memory. This is a *feature*. What *benefit* does that confer upon the user? Perhaps it means it works faster, so I have to wait less time, so my work can be faster and more accurate.

Almost any feature brings a benefit with it. Fast is a feature – takes you less time is a benefit. Cheap is a feature – you can make your money go further is a benefit. Made of aluminium is a feature – doesn't rust and lasts you a lifetime is a benefit.

Why is this important? Simply because people don't really want things for the features they get, but for the benefits those features confer. The benefit is the point of the purchase, and this is what lets us turn Interest into Desire.

Using a feature/benefit 'doublet' in copy gives it an altogether *different* flavour, even though the difference is subtle. From what can be a rather dry iteration of product features, suddenly the whole piece becomes livelier, more active, and I assure you will work a great deal better.

The doublet is based on a simple formula which has been introduced earlier:

$$x \text{ has } y, \text{ which means } z$$

x being the product or service, y being the feature, and z being the benefit that this feature will confer upon the buyer. In writing terms, every feature should be coupled to its benefit, and you should see it as an inseparable doublet. One should always be attached to the other.

THE FEATURE/BENEFIT DOUBLET IN ACTION

Look at this:

> *"This alarm clock radio has a memory chip that stores a host of functions. There's a snooze button, a two-time alarm, a sleep function and you can even programme it to turn on the radio at a pre-set time."*

This is simply a list of product features, and the result is that this particular clock radio sounds rather ordinary.

Let's introduce the feature/benefit doublet and see what happens. All I will do is take each feature in turn and make a benefit from it.

> *"This alarm clock radio has a powerful memory chip that*

stores a host of different functions, making each feature simple and fuss-free to use. There's a snooze button, so you can give yourself an extra few minutes of dozing, safe in the knowledge that you won't miss the alarm again. There's a two-time alarm, so you can programme an evening or a morning alarm. There's a sleep function, meaning you can drift off gently to the music of your favourite radio station – knowing it will turn itself off automatically.

And you can programme it to turn itself back on again at the same time as the alarm – so you can wake up in comfort".

Each feature has been dramatised and made a great deal more important by the extraction of an appropriate benefit. Yes, the copy is a great deal longer – but by now we should be happy to see this effect. But more importantly, I think the flavour of the piece is improved. Now, *this* clock radio sounds a great deal more exciting than an *ordinary* clock radio. Rather than just listing the features, each one has been sold, by coupling it to a benefit.

FEATURES AND BENEFITS APPLY TO EVERYTHING

The feature/benefit technique can be used in every type of copy. It certainly requires a reasonable amount of hard work on the part of the writer to achieve some of them, but this is what distinguishes good copywriters from mediocre ones.

Hard merchandise is of course the easiest type of product to create the feature/benefit doublet for, simply because features are easy to grasp and the benefits clear.

Life becomes a little more complex with insurance and financial products, but it's remarkable just how much you can turn a dull list of features into something that sounds like a million pounds when you apply this technique. *Take each feature of the insurance plan, derive a benefit from that feature, list them all together, and you will have a very effective piece of selling copy.*

The same technique can even be used for fundraising copy, even though with some differences:

"By completing your covenant form now, you'll be giving us an income we can rely on, meaning we can start to make plans to help those children who today we simply cannot reach."

Here, of course, the benefit is inverted. The benefit…meaning we can start to make plans…' is actually a benefit to the organisation and the people it will help, rather than to the reader directly – although, of course, the reader is gaining the benefit of 'being of help', one of the fundamental benefits of all fundraising appeals.

From the point of view of pure technique, the simple link phrases:

"Meaning that…"   *"So that…"*   *"Which means…"*

"Enabling you…"   *"Giving you…"*   *"Providing you…"*

give you easy ways to join the feature to the benefit.

You will do better if you stretch the benefit as much as is reasonable. Rather than a terse statement:

"a snooze button, so that you can wake up again"

it's more effective to extract as much from the feature as you can, so long as you have the space to do it:

> *"a snooze button, so that you can gently drift back to sleep to catch those few extra minutes, safe in the idea that come what may you'll be called again. No matter how sleepy you are, this clock radio simply won't let you oversleep."*

This becomes much more powerful. As I said earlier, the ability to create strong benefits from features is what makes a good copywriter. I almost always look for this ability – and this ability alone – in looking at a copywriter's work. *Almost everything else can be taught, eventually, but this ability to turn features into benefits, almost automatically, is a salesman's instinct that only the very best copywriters possess.*

YOU AND US

A big difference to copy style and tone can be made through the use of 'you' and 'yours', instead of 'us' and 'ours'. Here's what I mean:

> *"We would like to announce that we have developed a new type of computer that is years ahead of the others. Our best scientists have spent many years researching the subject, and we are confident that we have developed the finest machine in the world."*

You can find examples of copy like this everywhere. It is totally self-centred. It is only concerned with itself, not with what it can do for the consumer.

There are two 'technical' faults with it. First, it fails to turn any of the features it mentions into benefits for the consumer; the fault is then compounded by the use of 'we' and 'us', all the way through. Copy like this cannot be saved merely by adding a few benefits. The whole standpoint from which it is written needs to be changed before it can hope to make any kind of positive appeal to the reader. Something like this would be an improvement:

> *"This new product is the best machine in the world. It took years of development: developments that bring significant advantages in terms of speed, cost and ease of use."*

This actually says much the same, but the *attitude* of the writer is different. Now the writer wants to stress what can be done for the reader, rather than extolling the glories of the company.

But it still lacks the reader-oriented attitude that the use of 'you' would give it. Adding a few 'yous' makes an almost magical difference to tone:

> *"If you're looking for the best machine in the world, you can now find one that's so advanced, it took years of development: developments that bring you significant advantages in terms of speed, cost and ease of use."*

It is a simple enough change. In fact, it is one of the ways in which you can often turn a rather dull piece of copy into something a lot more vivid, simply by adding a few

Fig. 23:
Hitting the emotional chord.
This Compton and Woodhouse ad shows how copy can become much more emotional when the subject warrants it. The product here is a Mother and Baby figurine, and clearly the appeal is highly sentimental. A dry description of the figurine would hardly convey the right emotion, so here the copy deliberately goes for the sentimental jugular. Note phrases such as 'celebrated here for eternity'…'a poignant highlight'… 'bear witness to the excellence of Royal Worcester'…these are deliberate archaisms which say little in substance but which add hugely to the emotional flavour. The tone of hushed reverence is copied from an imaginary Richard Dimbleby commentary on some imaginary royal occasion – just to give the flavour!

'Sweet Dreams' is the first charming figurine in the 'Mother's Love' collection. It is available only by direct subscription to Compton & Woodhouse. Each figure stands 8¼" high.

ROYAL WORCESTER
ENGLISH FINE BONE CHINA

The tenderness of a mother and her sleeping child
brought touchingly to life with exquisite detail in
Royal Worcester English fine bone china

'Sweet Dreams'

A serene child stilled and sleeping in its mother's arms…a fleeting, precious moment of tender love celebrated here for eternity in *'Sweet Dreams'.*

This unique figurine is handcrafted in cream glazed Wallbody fine bone china from Royal Worcester. Indeed, *'Sweet Dreams'* is the first in a special series of four figurines called *'Mother's Love'* – each one portraying a poignant highlight in a child's early years.

In *'First Steps'* the mother leans protectively over her lively little toddler …In *'Once Upon a Time',* the little girl listens enraptured to a bedtime story…And in *'New Arrival',* the first-born meets her new baby brother for the first time.

It is details such as these which portray the supreme skill of the sculptor, and bear witness to the

The other enchanting figures in the 'Mother's Love' collection.

excellence of Royal Worcester. Both make *'Mother's Love'* an enchanting collection you will be proud to display in your home.

Despite the high level of detail which has gone into creating these Royal Worcester masterpieces, each figurine is available in affordable monthly instalments with absolutely no obligation.

Compton & Woodhouse
Specialists in English fine bone china
Registered Office: Arundel House, 80 Lawrence Road, London N15 4TR.

'yous' in the appropriate places.

Better still is to start off by writing 'you' rather than 'we': if you make this your tone from the outset, you find that inevitably you are drawn into writing copy *from the reader's point of view*. This ensures that whenever a feature is mentioned, you are almost *forced* into relating that feature's benefit to the reader ■

CHAPTER 5: SUMMARY

Long copy requires the use of a language that is easy to understand. Use words of Anglo-Saxon origin where possible, instead of words with a Latin root. They are more easily comprehended, and are shorter. They are more like the spoken language.

But it is also necessary to suit the tone and style of the copy to the product and the audience; sometimes it can benefit you from the tone point of view to use the longer words.

There is a wide variety of tones of copy that you can use. Read as much as you can to discover the different tones of written English that are available: develop the ability to parody well-known styles to give your writing greater flexibility.

Contractions make snappier copy; but leave them out if you wish to convey respectability.

Use short paragraphs, and attempt to give yourself one paragraph per thought, and rarely more than 3 sentences per paragraph. But don't go for excessively short paragraphs.

Try reading your copy out loud; if you stumble over it, you can be sure your reader will face similar problems when reading it.

When writing copy don't just use a list of features: always turn the features into benefits using the feature/benefit doublet. Remember your reader is ultimately more interested in the benefit than the feature, and by using benefits you make your copy sound a lot more exciting.

Always uses the word 'you': it disciplines you into writing copy oriented towards the reader's interests and helps you avoid the sin of corporate self-centredness. People are far more interested in what's in it for them, a great deal less interested in what you have done.

OPENING THE COPY

Starting copy is one of the most difficult arts; failing to start copy properly results in the reader drifting quickly away. You will have failed to catch their interest and thus all the rest of your work is wasted. But there are specific techniques that enable you to create better, sharper openings to your copy which catch the reader quickly.

WHY, when you read an ad or a mailing that you've just spent days sweating over, are you uncomfortable with the piece? Why doesn't it feel quite right? Why does it lack strength – what's missing even when all the 'rules' I have been expounding have been so carefully followed?

The usual reason why copy fails to 'grab' is almost certainly that the *beginning* of the copy is poor. The start is slow. It doesn't get to the point quickly enough, and therefore fails to capture the reader's attention.

Like the opening page of a novel, an ad or a mailing has to win the reader's interest *immediately*. But unlike the opening pages of a novel, advertising copy is rarely read for enjoyment and warrants only minimal attention from the reader – and therefore you have to win your reader's interest within seconds. You certainly don't have the luxury of a page or two to get things warmed up.

So, even though you have captured attention through the headlines, you still have a major task in getting the reader to continue reading your copy argument. Unless you can create and sustain interest at the very beginning, your chances of getting the reader to work through the rest of the copy are very slim. No matter how much work you have done throughout the rest of the ad or the mailing, none of it is going to be much use unless you can get your reader *started*.

The prospect is not, of course, going to read the headline, then start at the beginning of the copy, and then work their way carefully through to the end. They will 'skip-read' all round the piece (hence the importance of sub-headlines) until they have absorbed sufficient information to allow them to reach a decision as to whether they want to read more or not. Yet because it is the beginning, it assumes an importance in the reader's mind even if they ignore the strict logic of reading.

The physical start of the copy – the opening paragraphs of a press ad or the first few lines of a mailing letter – will be an important part of the 'skip-reading' process, ranking behind the headline (and about equal to a PS if it's a letter) and therefore retaining as much importance as if the reader really did 'start at the beginning'.

The failure to open copy well is one of the most common failings of any copy. Yet it is one of the things that is most easily put right; and sometimes with the stroke of an editor's pen you can transform a rather limp piece of copy into a powerful, high-

Fig. 24:
Off to a fast start.
This letter was for some years the unbeatable control for recruiting TSB Trustcard holders. It has one of the fastest starts of any mailing letters. Built around a 'nomination' proposition, note the way the letter begins *immediately* with the invitation. Before any mention of the product is made, it goes straight into the application form, demands action within 7 days, offers you a free gift – and only then starts to talk about the product, with a very neat transition line: 'But first, let me point out some of the most significant benefits to be gained from possessing a Trustcard'. Starting letters like this takes courage, given the abrupt nature of the start, but as far as the reader is concerned it helps them greatly, mainly because it gets to the point quickly.

TRUSTCARD

Head Office
Trustcard House
Gloucester Place
Brighton BN1 4BE

Our Ref: CI23

Mr Setty
113 117 Faringdon Road
LONDON EC1

A FREE GIFT WITH OUR COMPLIMENTS IF YOU REPLY WITHIN 7 DAYS

If you accept this nomination and return the enclosed application form within 7 days, we will present you with this elegant Trustcard Travel Alarm Clock, once your application is approved and your card issued. Please see enclosed leaflet.

Dear Mr Setty,

I am pleased to be able to inform you that you have been nominated to receive this invitation to apply for a personal Trustcard.

I have therefore enclosed your nomination form, together with the application form, both made out in your name. The nomination form is valid for one month <u>only</u>, and you should, therefore, return your application as soon as possible.

If you act quickly, and return the form within the next 7 days, you will <u>also</u> qualify to receive a free gift with our compliments upon acceptance of your application ... the stylish 'Alarm Card' shown above.

But first, let me point out some of the most significant benefits to be gained from possessing a Trustcard.

You may well be surprised to learn that Trustcard is one of the <u>most widely accepted</u> cards in the world. Because Trustcard has the worldwide VISA network behind it, <u>no other card</u> is more widely welcomed.

MORE THAN 5 MILLION OUTLETS WORLDWIDE

Your Trustcard will be accepted for the payment of goods and services at <u>any</u> shop, garage, restaurant, airline or other outlet displaying the VISA sign. In the UK alone, there are over 240,000 places where you can use your Trustcard, from your local Tesco supermarket to London's finest restaurants.

MORE THAN JUST A CREDIT CARD

You can also get cash with your Trustcard. All of us, no matter how well organised we are, run out of cash ... usually at the times we need it most! With your Trustcard, you can draw <u>any amount</u> of cash you want within your credit limit (there is no £50 limit as with cheques), at <u>any</u>

performance piece that will work well.

WHY DOES COPY START SLOWLY?

One of the most striking differences between direct marketing copy written in the US and copy written in Britain is the relative slowness of the start. Copy written in America, or by an American, will almost always strike you as much 'harder', more powerful, more pungent. Copy on the same subject in this country tends to be much slower, more circumspect. Should you read copy in French, German or Italian, I suspect you would find the same problem.

The problem lies in the difference of the American approach to selling, and the British (and probably European). Selling in this country remains a not altogether respectable occupation. Selling in America seems to suit the brash, up-front style of the Americans more so than here. I do not hold a brief for American direct marketing practice in many areas, but in this one the cultural difference has a *marked* effect.

Thus when an American writer commences copy, there is no need for polite introductions to the subject. They go straight in. In British copy, by contrast, we seem to feel a need to slowly develop our argument…to go in gently. It seems, after all, a little *rude* just to go straight in. We tend to apologise a little, nerving ourselves to suggest that you might be interested in this product…

The result is woolly, uncertain copy that takes several paragraphs to wind itself up to the point where it starts to sell. If you have managed to capture the reader's attention with the headline, *they really do want to know more*. The opening of the copy is a *key* place for them to go: and if you waste their time then they won't stay with you for long.

Good copy requires a sharp and interesting start. The opening *line* of copy should be compelling, let alone the first paragraph. It must take the attention and interest you have created in your headline and sub-heads, and lead the reader quickly on.

WHERE TO START?

Having said that, the starting point for copy is not always that obvious. Even if you wished to dive 'straight in', where exactly is that?

Let's take a brief look through a starting sequence of an imaginary piece of copy and see how it works in practice. The task is to generate subscriptions to a magazine that reviews 'best buys' in computers.

Now, in creating a promotion for such a product, you will have a huge choice of propositions open to you, some based on the product itself, others based on stronger and stronger forms of incentivisation. For now, I'll leave out any particularly strong forms of incentivisation – not because they'd be wrong, but because I devote a whole chapter to that subject later on, where there will be more time to go through the complexities of using incentives.

BEST COMPUTER

Here's what we might do if we were asked to produce an advertisement for 'Best Computer' magazine. Having reviewed propositions along the lines of my earlier

Chapter, we decide upon the following proposition:

> *"Buying 'Best Computer' will save your organisation money, because when you buy a computer you know it's not about to become obsolete tomorrow."*

Clearly, saving money is the main proposition; avoiding obsolescence a handy and desirable subsidiary benefit – a version of the feature/benefit doublet. This means that our headline simply has to be a condensed version of the proposition. To get as much of the story in as possible, we might have an overline that says:

> *"Fed up with finding new computers obsolete the day they're delivered? New 'Best Computer' magazine helps you make the right decision"*

followed by a main headline saying:

> *"NEW 'BEST COMPUTER' MAGAZINE WILL ALMOST CERTAINLY SAVE YOUR COMPANY OVER £2,000 THE FIRST DAY YOU READ IT"*

to which we could add a boxed paragraph just beneath the main heading:

> *"Why waste money on buying a £2,000 PC that may already be out-of-date? The trouble is, few businesses have the time to really 'shop around': 'Best Computer' magazine can help you do a week's shopping around in half an hour."*

STARTING THE COPY THE SLOW WAY

Our task is now to start the copy. You have seen that all of the headlines have concentrated upon cost-saving in one form or another. That was our original proposition and all of the headlines you have read above take that central thought and express it in different ways.

Our reader is now either looking somewhere else in the magazine or newspaper, because they are not interested in cost-saving (another proposition may catch them), or else they are keenly interested in what we have to say. They are *extremely* interested in the idea of saving money. We can be sure of this because that's all our headlines have said. We have snared our reader on that single proposition: that is the bait we have dangled before them and they are going for it.

Now, in starting the copy, would you be tempted to write something along these lines? Most writers would:

> *"Every day, as technology progresses, new developments are announced in computers: new developments that mean bigger memories, faster processing, more facilities, greater ease of use. And with hundreds of computer manufacturers around the world competing for business, new ideas can sometimes be almost 'hidden away' – ideas that could mean the computer you're about to place an order for is already superseded by a faster, better model.*
>
> *New 'Best Computer' magazine is devoted to helping you avoid just such a problem. By keeping a constant, expert eye*

on the whole world of computing, our writers will let you know what's happening, when, and where: so the next time you spend £2,000 on a computer, you're assured that it's the best you'll be able to lay your hands on."

It's not such a bad bit of copy. But its problem is that it fails to get IMMEDIATELY to the point that the reader has started on with us.

We enticed the reader into our lair with promises of saving money. Now, instead of telling them about that, we talk about 'developments'...we tell them how we do it...we tell them what we do. *It's a classic case of talking about 'me' when what I should be talking about is 'you'.* In other words, I should be telling them about what's in it for their business.

It's the 'British' disease, I think, causing the problem, rather than any lack of wanting to get to the point. The 'point', such as it is, starts to make its hesitant way into the argument right at the end of the second paragraph.

In writing this copy, I have felt the need to *justify* the proposition, to introduce it to my reader, so that having 'set the scene' I can then get down to business.

IRRITATING THE READER

'Setting the scene' might make me, the writer, feel happier and more polite. But in fact it can be very irritating to the reader.

"You said you could save me money. I'm prepared to listen. But I don't have that much time. Get to the point, for heaven's sake" you can almost hear the reader plead – or at least, I hope you can.

Let's try again, this time not bothering to be polite. We'll try to jump straight in, and not worry about setting the scene.

> *"When you read new 'Best Computer' magazine, your business will benefit from day one. You'll be discovering machines with bigger memories...while your competitors are paying over the odds for smaller systems. Now you'll be getting the fastest processors available...while your competitors are still shelling out for slower machines. Now you can be sure...in fact, absolutely certain...that the machine you're about to spend money on is the best you'll find in the market. Taking the right decisions like these in buying computers can save you thousands...even hundreds of thousands of pounds: but you need new 'Best Computer' magazine to help you.*
>
> *No business can afford to spend all its time looking through endless catalogues. With hundreds of computer makers all over the world, it's been impossible up until now to know that you're getting the best deal. 'Best Computer', with its network of resources around the world, reports every month on the latest developments, keeping you in the forefront of technology, making sure you know what the best buys are, making sure your business doesn't end up making a costly computer mistake."*

RSPB

THE ROYAL SOCIETY FOR THE PROTECTION OF BIRDS

THE LODGE · SANDY · BEDFORDSHIRE · SG19 2DL · TEL: 0767 680551 · TELEX: 82469 RSPB · FAX: 0767 692365

DE483

Mrs S Bassett
3 Meadowbank
Worle
Weston Super Mare
Avon
BS22 9NR

Join the RSPB today and receive the official RSPB 96-page 'BIRDS' magazine absolutely free – 4 times per year...

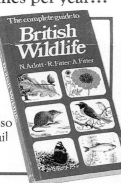

1   Receive 'BIRDS' magazine 4 times per year – FREE

2   Gain free entry to over 100 beautiful RSPB nature reserves around the country, <u>at no extra cost</u>

3   You'll also be sent your FREE car sticker

4   And if you REPLY BEFORE THE CLOSE DATE you'll also receive 'The Complete Guide to British Wildlife' FREE (retail £7.99), a 287-page pocket guide to Britain's natural history

Dear Mrs Bassett,

Do you <u>really</u> care about birds and wildlife? Good! Because I'd like to invite you to become a member of The Royal Society for the Protection of Birds.

I'd also like to offer you the superb Collins 'Complete Guide to British Wildlife', a 287-page colour guide to virtually <u>all</u> our wildlife. Published at £7.99, it's yours absolutely free - but only if you reply before 26th February 1993.

Why am I making these offers? Quite simply, because the threats facing birds today are greater than ever, and the RSPB <u>needs</u> your support right now...and offers like these are a marvellous way of prompting people who <u>really</u> care to act now. And <u>you</u> get important benefits too:

    * Your RSPB membership card gives you <u>FREE admittance to over</u>

> **YOURS *FREE*
> IF YOU REPLY BY
> 26 FEBRUARY 1993**

Registered charity no. 207076

Patron **Her Majesty the Queen**   President **Ian Prestt**   Chairman of Council **Adrian Darby**   Chief Executive **Barbara Young**

0000141

Fig. 25:
Going for the offer.

In this RSPB mailing we decided to try a strongly incentivised approach to recruiting new members. You can see from the first page of the letter that a boxed section enumerates the offers clearly. But notice how the letter itself starts – going quickly into an invitation to join in the very first paragraph. It then goes on to make an offer of a free book linked to a time close – and only then does it discuss the other benefits of membership. If you decide to go for an incentivised approach, it pays to ensure that you start the copy with the incentives that you're offering.

The second version was actually much more difficult to write than the first. You have to have a steely nerve to commence with quite such strong statements, and it takes *ruthless* editing to get the first few lines as strong as they could be. You also need to discipline yourself to stay faithful to the original proposition until you (and your reader) are quite satisfied that you have developed your point as strongly as you can.

The copy goes straight in. It starts at the point that the headline captured the reader with, and then moves quickly on to develop that attention into interest. Unlike the first piece of copy, it does not deviate from the central proposition; and, importantly, it constantly reiterates benefits FOR THE READER, right from line one.

Certainly, I hope just by reading the two pieces that you can 'feel' a difference in pace and strength. I think the second version has 'pace', while the first feels 'lazy'. Would the harder approach work better? Almost certainly. And I would certainly feel much happier about running the second version than the first if my livelihood depended on it.

THE 'STARTING-HALFWAY-DOWN-PAGE-ONE' TRICK

Given the problem I mentioned earlier where writers have difficulty in getting to the point, it is not at all unusual that once all of the 'introductory' copy is got out of the way, there is a very reasonable starting point to the copy hidden further down in the text.

The 'starting point' normally occurs about *half way down* the first page; the writer has done the scene-setting and eventually they work their way round to a sentence or paragraph that says something of true interest to the reader. If all of the 'introductory' copy can be got rid of and the copy started at *that* point, then you have a much stronger opening. Simply cross out the first half of page 1, and you get off to a much better start.

Let me return to 'Best Computer' magazine with a slightly different proposition this time, in order to demonstrate the point. Here's the same opening copy as previously recommended, but towards the end of the copy we introduce the concept of a 3 Month Free Trial.

> *"Now you'll be buying machines with bigger memories when your competitors are paying over the odds for smaller systems. Now you'll be getting the fastest processors available while your competitors are still shelling out for slower machines. Now you can be sure...in fact, absolutely certain...that the machine you're about to spend money on is the best you'll find in the world. Taking the right decisions like these in buying computers can save you thousands...even hundreds of thousands of pounds: but you need 'Best Computer' magazine to help you.*
>
> *'Best Computer', with its network of resources around the world, reports every month on the latest developments, keeping you in the forefront of technology, making sure you*

know what the best buys are, making sure your business doesn't end up making a costly computer mistake.

In fact, we're so convinced that 'Best Computer' will save you money that you can take the next three issues entirely free and without obligation: if you're not convinced that 'Best Computer' really can save you money, it won't have cost you a penny to find out."

BRINGING THE OFFER UP FRONT

Which is the strongest way to open the copy now? Having introduced a strong incentive offer, such as a 3 Month Free Trial, it's much better to use a *hard* offer as your opening: in every case where some form of incentive is available, *starting off your copy with the incentive is stronger* than starting off your copy even with product benefits.

But in the example above, the copy starts on product benefits and leaves the meaty offer to last. What happens if we bring the offer forward?

Here's how it would read if we edit away all of the copy and start straight in with the offer:

"We're so convinced that 'Best Computer' will save you money that you can take the next three issues entirely free and without obligation: if you're not convinced that 'Best Computer' really can save you money, it won't have cost you a penny to find out.

This free trial offer is your chance to discover how, with 'Best Computer', you'll be buying machines with bigger memories when your competitors are paying over the odds for smaller systems. You'll be getting the fastest processors available while your competitors are still shelling out for slower machines. You'll be sure...in fact, absolutely certain...that the machine you're about to spend money on is the best you'll find in the world."

What we've done here is simple. We've taken the hard offer, the free trial, and made that the start of the copy, leaving the product benefits to come second.

We've edited out half-a-page of text and got to the main offer, hidden as usual half-way down the first page.

If you want to truly impress a copywriter, simply get the first page of their copy, take out the first half, re-write small bits to get the flow back again, and you will almost certainly have a *stronger, punchier, more persuasive* piece of copy than you started with.

This trick works almost every time. After some years you eventually learn to discard the introductory stuff mentally, and start writing at the point of most interest to your reader. But even then, you still find yourself sometimes not getting to the point fast enough and hard enough, which is where the editing pencil needs to come out.

This system works for press ad copy and inserts, but works particularly well with mailing letters, where with 4 pages to play with and the personal 'feel' of a letter, few writers seem prepared to dive in without four or five paragraphs of 'introduction' before reaching the main offer or proposition. Take those 'introductory' paragraphs out

The Natural History Museum announces the first ever publication of a Franz Bauer collection

THE KEW BOTANICAL FLOWER ILLUSTRATIONS
—— OF FRANZ BAUER ——

A limited edition from the Natural History Museum Archives

Paeonia sp. *(Peony)*
Shown here is smaller than actual size of 22" by 17½". Each print is fully framed and measures 12¼" by 8¼" inside mount. No money is required with your reservation.

Detail of Rosa multiflora Thunb. showing the high degree of fine detail that Bauer has captured in each illustration. NOTE: the quality of reproduction here is clearly inferior to that of the actual print.

A selected collection of four fully framed prints from the hitherto unpublished work of Franz Bauer (1758-1840), held by the Botany Library of the Natural History Museum.

Issued in a strictly limited edition of 5000, each print bearing the edition number on a Certificate of Origin authorised by the Natural History Museum. The Museum will not authorise a further publication of this Collection.

The first print in the series will be sent without obligation for subscribers to inspect at home. There is no subsequent obligation to purchase all four prints. Payment may be made in instalments. No payment is required when you apply.

This Limited Edition Collection is available only from the official Publishing Agent by direct application. The Collection will never be available from any other source.

Hidden away within the archives of the Botany Library of the Natural History Museum in South Kensington, is a superb treasure house of early 19th century botanical illustrations.

It represents the magnificent work of many artists in this field, but of them all, the work of Franz Bauer is outstanding. And now, for the first time ever, the Natural History Museum has authorised publication of a collection of his work in a strictly limited edition.

Furthermore, once the collection limit has been reached, the printing plates will be destroyed, and the Natural History Museum will not authorise this collection to be re-published.

FRANZ BAUER AT KEW

Franz Bauer was born in 1758 in Austria, and over the years he learned, and perfected, the painstaking attention to detail that distinguishes the true botanical illustration from mere paintings of flowers.

In 1788 he arrived in England where he joined the Royal Botanical Gardens at Kew, as an outstanding botanical artist.

Apart from the sheer aesthetic value of Bauer's works, it is this connection with the Royal Botanical Gardens at Kew that gives his paintings a unique value.

EXTRAORDINARY DETAIL

Looking at Bauer's work, the degree of detail is extraordinary.

In the hands of an artist of less delicate sensitivity, the illustrations would be superb scientific diagrams. Yet with Bauer, as you stand back and look at the entire painting, it is elevated to a work of art in its own right.

FINE FRAMING

To produce this edition, each original Bauer painting was carefully photographed and high quality plates were then made. The actual print-

making was carried out by a specialist fine art printer to render faithfully the fine detail and delicate colours of Bauer.

Each print in the collection is mounted and hand-framed in a classical burr walnut veneer frame, chosen so as to allow Bauer's work to be displayed with understated elegance.

On the reverse of each frame will be pasted the signed Certificate of Origin, bearing the Natural History Museum edition number and the plant's name and scientific Latin name, as well as details of the plant's history and habitat. In addition, each print is numbered on the Certificate, with a statement of the limits of the edition.

There are 4 prints in the series: *Paeonia* sp., originally a type of Rose, *Rosa multiflora* Thunb., a variety from Japan; a *Gladiolus cardinalis* Curtis, a member of the Iris family from Africa, and a *Gardenia* named after Dr L.E., a correspondent of Linnaeus from South Carolina. Collectors of all 4 prints have the *same number* on each print, making a complete set.

SUBSCRIPTION / WITHOUT OBLIGATION

These framed prints are available directly from the Museum's Publishing Agent. They are not available from any other source. You may order by Freepost coupon, or by telephone.

Do not send any money with your reservation. Your first print will be sent for you to inspect at home. You may return it within 28 days, or you will be under no further obligation if you decide to collect the series. The first print in convenient instalments of £25. The framed, numbered prints in the series will be sent to you on a trial basis, and again convenient instalments without obligation to complete the set.

From receipt of your order, please allow 4 – 6 weeks for delivery, as the printing and framing process is time-consuming and cannot be hurried.

The Natural History Museum announces the first ever publication of a Franz Bauer collection

THE KEW BOTANICAL FLOWER ILLUSTRATIONS
OF FRANZ BAUER

A limited edition from the Natural History Museum Archives

Fig. 26:
Say what you're going to say.

One of the most effective ways of starting ad copy is by using the journalistic technique of 'say what you're going to say,' then say it'. This is essentially a precis of the whole copy right at the beginning, and allows the reader to absorb the key elements before getting into the detail. In this ad for Design

Marketing, note how the copy quickly introduces the artist, mentions the publication by the Natural History Museum, mentions the limited edition, says it will not be re-published...and then, in the 4th paragraph beneath the first sub-head, reverts back to talking about the artist again. The rest of the copy is an expanded version of this precis opening.

Craigendarroch Time Ownership, Braemar Road, Ballater, Royal Deeside AB35 5XA, Scotland. Telephone: (03397) 55558

```
            Mr P J Bowers
            12 Millers Gardens
            Wells
            Somerset
            BA5 2TW
```

```
Dear Mr Bowers,

    Imagine a Highland haven far away from the hustle and bustle of
the city...a private world where you can pamper yourself in
unparalleled luxury...and relax in surroundings of timeless beauty.

    This is Craigendarroch...one of the most exclusive holiday
retreats in the world.

    And it gives me great pleasure to personally invite you and your
guest, to spend a luxurious weekend on the Craigendarroch Country
Estate, just a few miles from Balmoral in the heart of Royal
Deeside.

    We will fly you both from London, Birmingham or Manchester
to Aberdeen, where you will find a complimentary car waiting
for you, and which is yours for the entire weekend.  Your
room in the 4 Star Craigendarroch Hotel will feature every
conceivable luxury, and will be reserved in your name for
two nights.  In the mornings, you can look forward to a
full Scottish Highland breakfast.  You will also be given
weekend membership of the exclusive Country Club with its
numerous facilities.

    And you can enjoy it all from just £199 for two.

    I think you'll find my invitation difficult to resist.  Not just
because of the extraordinary value it represents, but because of
the unique qualities our auspicious holiday retreat has to offer.

    Indeed, so diverse are the pleasures awaiting you at
Craigendarroch, I feel a letter alone cannot do justice to them...

    That's why I've taken the liberty of preparing and enclosing a
suggested Personal Itinerary, which incorporates an abundance of
ways you might enjoy your stay with us...
```

Fig. 27:
An easy way to instantly improve mailing letters.

Here's the mailing letter for a very successful Craigendarroch pack. The proposition of the mailing is an invitation to come up and see the facilities. The letter above, though, doesn't get to the point as quickly as it could. Note how paragraph 1 and 2 are 'introductory'...the copywriter feels nervous about plunging in straight away. An instant improvement to this letter would be to simply cut out paras 1 and 2, and start the letter at para 3, eliminating the initial 'And'. Thus the letter would start: 'Dear Mr Bowers, It gives me great pleasure to personally invite you and your guest...' Almost all letters, and much other copy, benefit from this pruning where you take out the initial 'introductory' copy to get right to the point of the letter. You need to ask what your letter is *really* trying to say – and then ensure that's how it starts.

and you will have a much better letter for it.

Read through the copy until you find the first mention of the main offer, or proposition. Once you get to it, then you can afford to delete the paragraphs ahead of it.

This offer-led approach works across all areas of direct marketing, including fund-raising, where the temptation to have a soft opening is often greatest, presumably because the writer feels guilty about asking for money. Imagine how much a street-collector would raise if they didn't rattle the collecting tin under people's noses; your opening copy must do the same.

TELL THEM WHAT YOU'RE GOING TO TELL THEM...

In Chapter 4 on Copy Structure, I referred to some of the journalistic techniques available to copywriters. One of the best ways of getting a start to copy is adopt the

'Tell them what you're going to tell them, tell them, then tell them
what you've just told them'

system. It demands an introduction, followed by the story, ending with a reprise or summary.

Whatever newspaper you read, once you start looking for the technique it's surprising how often it turns up. At random, I picked up a copy of a Daily Mirror. Here's the start of the lead story:

> *"FREED hostages Jackie Mann and John McCarthy*
> *yesterday savoured the joy they had yearned for – back at*
> *home in Britain with the women they loved.*
>
> *Jackie, 77, flew in after 865 days in captivity..."*

The first paragraph gives the gist of the story; and then it moves on with the second and subsequent paragraphs being essentially elaborations of the story, containing more details.

Here's the same technique, taken from a lead story in the FT:

> *"ANGLO UNITED, owner of the Coalite smokeless fuel*
> *business, has proposed that it buy British Coal, the coal*
> *producer which the UK government plans to privatise*
> *should it win the next general election.*
>
> *The offer, which is being examined by the..."*

Again, the first paragraph summarises the story, and the second paragraph begins the detail. You'll read more about this technique on page 50, in the Copy Structure Chapter.

SIGNPOSTS

Using that initial summary technique provides clear signposts for the reader; in a newspaper it allows the reader to skip around articles and decide which ones are the most interesting. In copy terms, it provides our reader with exactly the same benefit – if we go back to our 'most interested' reader theory, it allows the person who is most interested in the product to pick up the gist immediately, which means of course that you have to say something of immediate interest to *that* reader.

Here's an example to show how the technique works. It simply copies the same technique from the newspaper examples quoted above.

> *"Now, exclusively from Wonder Widgets, here's a new type of widget that outperforms every other widget in its class, thanks to five powerful new features. It's available only by mail order, and you can order direct by ringing 0800 090909 today.*
>
> *The new Wonder Widget was invented in Cleethorpes where..."*

You can see that the first paragraph is a highly concentrated version of the whole story.

It starts by saying what it is, then says what's special about it, then says how you can buy it. The rest of the copy will then be an *expansion* of that single paragraph, going into much more detail.

Our readers can decide for themselves if they're interested.

If not, they haven't wasted time with us. If they are, we've given them plenty of 'tasters' and signposts to bring them in with us, giving them the whole story early on, not making them read through a lot of copy to discover what the main features are.

QUESTION OPENINGS

Asking a question can be a good way to start copy, too.

> *"Have you ever wished..."*
>
> *"Do you wonder why..."*
>
> *"Wouldn't it be nice if..."*
>
> *"Which would you choose..."*
>
> *"What would you do if..."*

are all good ways into your subject. There is one simple rule to remember if you use a question opening, however. Never ask 'just' a question – turn the question into a benefit. So, instead of asking:

> *"Have you ever considered investing in a savings plan?"*

you would turn it into a *benefit* by asking:

> *"Have you tried to find a savings plan that combines a high rate of interest with easy access to your money? Now you can invest in..."*

A multiple question technique can also be used, but this needs some care. If you ask too many questions you never get to the point, so the best approach is to use no more than two, and at the very most three (if they are short) questions:

> *"Are you looking for good rates of interest? Do you need immediate access to your money? Now, here's a plan..."*

YOU AND NOW

The last two thoughts I will leave you with in starting copy are simple ones.

First, I referred in the previous Chapter to the necessity for using 'you' and 'yours' rather than 'us' and 'ours' in writing copy – a discipline for ensuring you talk about the benefits and advantages *to the reader,* rather than to *you.*

The same technique can be helpful in starting copy. If you make the very first word of your copy 'You', you immediately start your copy in a more active way. 'You can…' 'You will…' 'You'll like…' or as a slight variation, the question version 'Do you…?'

Opening your copy in this way demands that you start your copy with something of immediate interest to your reader. Opening with 'You' makes you write 'straight at' the reader.

Second: there are few words that have more power than 'Now', with all the implications of newness that it carries. You can start almost any copy with 'Now', and copy greatly benefits from it.

In fact, there are few better ways of starting copy than by combining 'You' and 'Now':

"Now you can…" or *"You can now…"*

This is a very straightforward way of adding a little extra punch at the start of your copy, and of course it can be easily added after you've written the piece. If what you have written sounds a little flat, or needs a bit of beefing up, try putting a 'Now' or 'You' in as the first word of the copy and see the effect it can have.

Depending on the way you have chosen to start your copy, it's not always possible to get an immediate 'You' or 'Now' start. This isn't necessarily critical; but where it is appropriate, do use it ▪

CHAPTER 6: SUMMARY

Copy usually suffers from not having a good beginning. It is the greatest fault in most forms of copy, yet it is very easily cured. A few moments spent in altering the start of copy is probably worth hours of re-writing.

Once the proposition is identified, the copy should commence by talking immediately about the proposition contained in the headline. Avoid the temptation to start at a different point. The reader was brought in by that proposition and that's what they want to read about.

If the proposition is an offer, the copy should start by talking about the offer, even before the product features and benefits. The offer always takes priority over anything else in your copy.

Copywriters normally take little time to warm to their subject. Often, the best starting point for copy is half way down the first page, after the writer has got the 'introductory' paragraphs out of the way. By cutting out those paragraphs, you can usually get a much better beginning.

First paragraphs of copy should follow as far as possible the method used by journalists: it should always be a summary paragraph, giving the reader a brief outline of the 'pitch' you are about to make. This actually helps your committed reader to get into your story, without frightening them off with too much detail too early.

Try to make the words 'You' or 'Now' the very first words you use.

ART DIRECTION FOR RESPONSE

The old adage 'copy is king' in direct marketing isn't wholly correct. Art direction has a much greater role to play than many people suppose. It is not simply to make an ad or mailing look good: there are specific design techniques that will make a major difference to response. However, you have to look beyond simplistic fashions in art direction, and view it in the widest possible context – that of creating the best environment in which to achieve the sale.

ART direction makes its main contribution (but not its only one) to creating better responses essentially by creating the right kind of 'environment' – a visual environment that encourages the prospect to buy.

A prospect can be encouraged to respond simply through a visual look so long as that visual look is aimed at 'conditioning' certain reactions in people. Visual stimuli are powerful, at least at a basic, emotional level. We react strongly (and surprisingly similarly) to a whole range of such stimuli. At a sublime level, the Sistine Chapel ceiling evokes extraordinary feelings in people, for what is after all 'only' a splash of colour. On a more mundane level but for our purposes a more practical example is a case that I saw in a presentation about art direction. The speaker held up two advertising slogans. One said

"Fresh farm milk for sale"

and the other said

"Dental practice – reasonable fees".

Then he held up the milk slogan again, this time lettered in a computer-style typeface. Then he held up the dental practice slogan, lettered as though done by a farmhand, crudely drawn on a plank of wood.

The point was made tellingly; and of course was duly re-inforced by inverting the style of lettering, where the more *appropriate* typeface was correctly matched to the slogan.

This simple example shows how much can be achieved through visual signals to help our prospect along his way to buying. Art direction is no substitute for copy – it is, however, a good ally and will add to your argument if carefully and appropriately used.

An integral part of art direction, as far as direct mail is concerned, is also the format. But this is a subject of sufficient importance and complexity to warrant its own Chapter (the next one), and this section can therefore concern itself wholly with the design aspects of art direction.

THE PROBLEM WITH IMAGE

Before we consider the positive aspects of art direction, it has become sadly necessary to first of all tackle the great problem of art direction, at least as far as direct marketing is concerned.

Conventionally, the process of creating a visual environment for the purposes of marketing is referred to as 'image'. The trouble starts when this is taken to be synonymous with 'quality'; in other words, the art director's task is sometimes seen as creating a *quality* visual image or environment, where beautiful photography and fine illustration is the only point of the exercise.

There are certainly times when this approach is correct. There are many products where, by creating a high quality image through the use of visual techniques, you can quite dramatically improve the performance of an ad or a mailing.

The problem comes, however, if this process of creating a *quality* image is seen as the one and *only* object of the art director.

THE MOST APPROPRIATE LOOK, NOT THE PRETTIEST

Serious direct marketers should not have such a narrow view of what art direction can achieve. At least in terms of direct marketing, the great battle for everyone to win is in looking at art direction as a tool that should concern itself with creating the *most appropriate* visual environment, the environment which is most likely to produce the desired response; and this is not always by any means the prettiest look – the 'Fresh farm milk for sale' sign gained its greatest impact when crudely lettered in a barely literate hand.

Let's look at some practical examples.

Selling a £150 fine bone china figurine clearly demands some high 'production values' – good typography, good photography – in order to justify (albeit subtly) the price to the prospective purchaser.

Conversely, if you were a discount shop, where you wanted people to feel they were getting a bargain, then clearly the visual environment of an advertisement promoting that shop has to work equally hard to create the required image – except the image in this case would be a deliberately cheap and cheerful one. Attempting to make it look expensive and up-market will clearly militate against the image you are trying to create.

This effect is seen strongly in direct response work for charities. It is a sad fact that the beautiful ads that win awards for charities rarely work in response terms. One of the reasons is that they look, in fact, too good. It was established many years ago that ads and mailings that look crude and amateurish produce significantly better results than the glossy ones.

'LATE AT NIGHT ON THE KITCHEN TABLE'

Harold Sumption, who brought up a whole generation of fund raisers, said it best:

> *"Your ad or mailing should look as though it was put together late at night on the kitchen table by a couple of dedicated old ladies."*

Clearly, while the judges in advertising awards respond almost exclusively to

Fig 28:
Ugly works.

This advertisement for Book Club Associates is highly successful, and the main reason is because of the excellent art direction – not excellent from a traditional point of view in that the ad would be regarded by most art directors as truly hideous, but excellent from the functional point of view. Given that what is being sold is value and choice, this 'flash bang wallop' style works superbly. Would a more elegant, up-

market approach work better? No, it's been tried on many occasions and it comes nowhere near the results this style achieves. But to get this look is demanding – it's actually harder to achieve this style than the conventional style and do it

genuinely rather than as a parody. As with fig. 30 further on, the art director (Derek Way) can just as easily turn his hand to superb typography and layout in the traditional way.

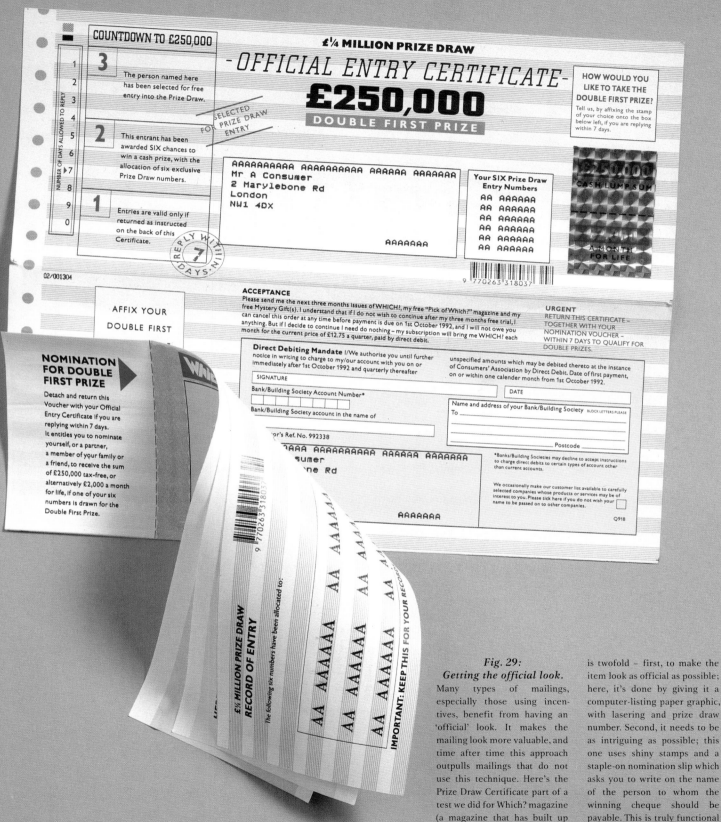

Fig. 29:
Getting the official look.

Many types of mailings, especially those using incentives, benefit from having an 'official' look. It makes the mailing look more valuable, and time after time this approach outpulls mailings that do not use this technique. Here's the Prize Draw Certificate part of a test we did for Which? magazine (a magazine that has built up one of the largest circulations in the UK *exclusively* through using prize draw mailings). Here, art direction is *the* key element. Usually the copy fits in around the design. The art is twofold – first, to make the item look as official as possible; here, it's done by giving it a computer-listing paper graphic, with lasering and prize draw number. Second, it needs to be as intriguing as possible; this one uses shiny stamps and a staple-on nomination slip which asks you to write on the name of the person to whom the winning cheque should be payable. This is truly functional art direction – art direction that is dictated by purpose rather than by fashion. Incidentally, this style is perhaps the hardest of all for art directors to get right.

high-quality visuals, the giving public actually resents the expense of such works and respond better to communications that look as though the charity *really* needs the money.

This is using art direction to create the *right* visual environment, the one most likely to get money out of people's pockets given the special nature of the product being 'offered'. The visual signals being given to the prospective donor are in tune with his or her expectations; the look is appropriate, even if it is not to the taste of people like you and I.

It has to be said that most art directors find this degree of visual flexibility a very difficult process to come to terms with. After years at art school where they had visual quality drummed into them, to be suddenly confronted with someone like me saying 'make it look crude' is, not surprisingly, difficult to take.

THE RETAIL ANALOGY

The closest analogy to this process must be in retail, where the design of the shop itself is a crucial part of the marketing effort. Retailers have for many years understood the need to give the appropriate visual stimuli to the shopper, to create the right kind of atmosphere in which the purchase decision is made easier.

There are very obvious cases, such as Next or Harrods, where up-market or trendy design works very well. But there are very many other cases of retail design, aimed at different niches, where the design of the shop does not necessarily delight a designer but which does its job with signal efficiency. Marks and Spencer must be a case in point, with the carefully understated look. Woolworths has its bargain feel. Kwik Save leaves the merchandise in the packing carton to emphasise low price. Hamleys piles up toys in profusion to assault the visual senses.

In fact, very few successful retailers are wholly designed to please the average art director. Thus the direct marketing art director must also learn the value of designing for the marketplace, not for him or herself. And clients, too, must stop looking at design in a personal way and ask themselves "Does this appeal to the marketplace most likely to buy my product?"

FITNESS FOR PURPOSE

Indeed, the most common mistake *inexperienced* people in direct marketing make is wanting things to look pretty, quite often as an instinctive reaction to the 'junk mail' feelings they may have about the medium. People new to direct marketing often want to attempt to get away from that image by having the mailing designed purely to look good – an approach that can be very dangerous as we shall see later.

If all it does is look good, then they're happy. Unfortunately, the process of art direction in direct marketing is far more complex than that. While those folk are worrying about relatively minor details such as background colours and styles of illustration, cleverer people than they are looking instead at the *functionality* of the design, asking if the visual 'works' to make the sale…and then going on to reap the business rewards afterwards, probably while others are still worrying about the background colour.

Thus fitness for purpose is the very core of direct response art direction. Every ad or mailing must be designed to achieve the objective set for it – and not designed simply to look good. There are some notable examples of how certain visual approaches work well, but which do not satisfy aesthetic criteria.

Book Club ads, for example, are far from the most beautiful ads in the world. With the books crammed in, the hard offer headline shouting out in strong type and typically a bright yellow background colour, they are examples of the kind of advertising that gives many art directors nightmares.

Yet the fact is that they work much better than clean, tidy and discreet versions of the same thing.

Why? Because the soul of a Book Club ad is 'bargain' – you are offering three books for £1 (or variations on the theme) and clearly the most appropriate visual message has to be one where that 'bargain' element is reinforced. They are visual equivalents of "pile 'em high and sell 'em cheap". The visual style is cunningly crafted to reinforce strongly that image in the reader's mind. It is not that the art director of such ads is a lousy art director!

UGLY WORKS

But surely they would work even better if the ads projected a more up-market image? After all, wouldn't more people be inclined to go for the offer if they felt the ads came from an organisation that was concerned about 'quality'…quality that could be so easily portrayed if the whole style of the ad was much more elegant and up-market?

This has been tried. And it doesn't actually appear to work. Book Club Associates have tried the 'clean and tidy' approach in the past in an effort to go 'up-market'. The problem is that a clean and tidy looking ad doesn't give the right visual 'bargain' signals, and such ad styles almost inevitably fail.

This is proved more strongly by looking at what happened when the existing bargain style was developed even more strongly, in a series of ads for the video club.

Derek Way, then Head of Art at WWAV, clearly understood that the bargain flavour was critically important, and in designing a new ad style exploited this flavour even more strongly. The ads themselves were not, by any measure, pretty ads. But they were brilliantly crafted *of their type* with the result that the ad series was highly successful.

(This example, incidentally, also proves that copy isn't king – the changes made were wholly on the art direction side, with some excellent results accompanying them.)

Ugly, in that particular case, worked.

NAKED LADIES

Another successful approach worth mentioning was when Book Club Associates took a whole page ad in The Sun, featuring a scantily-clad female posing next to a pile of books. Stan Remington, then chief exectuive of BCA, and one of the brightest brains in the business, had a fit – and Stan Remington having a fit is an experience not to be forgotten! The ad, not surprisingly, never ran again, though I believe it worked.

DULL AND BORING

Another example of how the most *appropriate* design works is seen in many financial products. If a Book Club sells on bargain, many financial products are sold on 'trustworthiness', and in those cases it has been demonstrated that quite literally a dull design works better than a bright one.

In looking for the good place to invest your money, you are hardly likely to invest it with a glamorous-looking outfit who seem to spend lavishly on colour brochures. Instead, you would go for the conservative type of organisation, one that seems safe if a little dull. If you walked into a bank and met a member of staff clad in an Armani suit, sporting a gold Rolex and Gucci loafers, you would rightly worry about where your investment really was going to end up. You would feel happier with a soberly-dressed individual of rather more modest tastes. A colleague remarked at how disgusted she felt when she found out that the Pope wears a gold Rolex.

The same effect works with financial direct mail. Flashy, gimmicky packs, loaded with colour, actually do *significantly* less well than dull 'financial-looking' packs.

This will come as a sad shock to those people in financial direct marketing who think financial direct mail is already too dull. The truth is, most of it is simply not dull enough.

SLABS OF GREY TEXT

Slabs of grey text, the sparing use of colour (and what little colour is used should be muddy colour, not bright colour), complex charts and diagrams, and lots of numbers…heresy to most art directors and product managers, but for the direct marketer who seriously wants to make their financial direct mail succeed these are techniques that are, in some quarters, employed with great skill.

Clearly, the underlying needs of good communication, such as readability, have to play their part. In the hands of a skilled direct marketing art director, slabs of grey text can actually be very readable. Good art direction creates the dull, conservative, safe atmosphere without affecting readability and efficient communication.

Bear in mind that the recipient to such a mailing will end up receiving the official policy documentation, and too brash an approach up front will make the policy document, when it eventually arrives, a bad let-down.

ESTABLISHING THE VISUAL PROPOSITION

In starting to think about the design of the piece, the first task the art director has to face is determining what is the correct visual atmosphere for the product or service being advertised.

It is helpful to think about this atmosphere as a visual 'proposition' in exactly the same way that the headline of the ad or mailing will be determined by the marketing proposition. In other words, what do you want your reader to think or feel as a result of reading this communication?

For a copywriter to work from a proposition statement is in some ways easier because it is almost always purely logical. The art director's task is more difficult. The visual proposition can sometimes be a very subtle thing; and only skilled art directors

Fig. 30:
Two styles, same hand.
Here are two ads for completely different products, showing how art direction needs to adapt itself to the taste and expectations of the audience, not the art director. The bottom example is a DPS for Compton and Woodhouse. Aimed at an older, female market, it takes its art direction stance from the nature of the product. The use of a 'flowery' typeface, vignettes and a round-ended caption panel adds subtle feminine touches to the ad which goes comfortably with the product. A deliberately old-fashioned look, in other words, but a genuine one rather than simply an art director trying to be clever. The ad above, on the other hand, is aimed at an entirely different audience with a high-fashion product. Here, the art direction is just as deliberate, but this time aims to reflect the fashion values in the product. Interestingly, both ads were produced by the same art director, Chris Albert.

can see the ways in which the use of graphic techniques can create different visual atmospheres.

The starting point is, of course, to ask what visual environment is most likely to affect sales? We're back to the milk for sale and the dentist sign – which is the most appropriate signal to give?

POSITIVE AND NEGATIVE VISUAL PROPOSITIONS

As discussed above, if you are a financial institution, then you need to clearly identify what flavour you wish to impart. Simply saying, for example, "I want to appeal to young people" isn't enough – it misses the point of attempting to identify the visual environment that will make someone respond. Even if you are after young people, it is the case that even they will be most likely to invest their money in an institution that they can *trust*. Thus employing fancy, high-fashion graphics with a presumed 'young' feel may be quite the wrong thing to do, even though marketing logic will suggest otherwise.

From the response point of view, the right method is try to find the right visual proposition to help the reader respond. There could be any number of these propositions, depending on the product and the market you're trying to reach.

Some visual propositions are 'negative' ones, in that you use visual techniques to overcome problems. Let's say, for instance, that we are asked to design a mailing for a high-risk property bond. Clearly, while the copy only goes so far to reinforce a 'trustworthy' message, the visual side can help greatly. You would want to impart a feeling of solid, conservative reassurance. This point was not lost on the Victorians who were as big a bunch of financial rogues as ever seen – but who designed their banks using solid granite with impressive Greek pillars to lure investors into a sometimes quite unwarranted sense of security.

Even in these more regulated days, the same need for security can be felt. Instead of granite and pillars, the art director can use styles of illustration, design and typography to create that same Victorian solid feeling.

But let's imagine a financial product that was dull and boring…a safe investment but one that gives a low return. Here, the art director's task may well be the *reverse* of one just described. In order to make the product look attractive, it may well be more appropriate to come up with images of excitement – perhaps more lively typefaces, illustrations of exciting investments, a more 'sparky' graphic approach.

These visual signals are designed to overcome negatives. Equally, art directors can reinforce positives. A health care product can have an 'ethical' look, for instance. A unit trust specialising in overseas investment can be designed to have an international flavour.

Exactly what visual flavour you choose to give your work must depend on a clear identification of the marketing proposition – not on passing visual fashion.

POTS AND PANS

Another clear example is from the world of mail order – in this case, Scotcade, one of the pioneers of 'up-market' mail order. The essence of Scotcade at the beginning was in bringing bargain offers before a group of purchasers who didn't normally go for mail order bargains – the trendy middle-class colour supplement reader.

The first Scotcade ad was for a set of pots and pans at an excellent price. Bob Scott, the founder, used a classical 'above the line' agency (BMP as it then was) because that was the kind of agency he was used to. The result was an ad that offered a bargain so far as the headline and the proposition was concerned – but an ad that was designed to the high visual standards of that time. Bargain pots and pans ads there were many…mostly crude efforts in the postal bargain section of the newspapers.

But the first Scotcade ad, aimed at that trendy reader, looked extremely high class – and as a result made the pots and pans look better than they probably were. With classical typography and superb photography, all subsequent Scotcade ads followed the same formula, much to the founder's great benefit.

This is an example of art direction adding a great deal to the marketing argument. Frankly, the formula was originally discovered by chance…but Bob Scott had the great good sense to seize the idea and maintain it. In those ads, art direction *overcame the negatives* of bargain offers at least as far as that particular market was concerned, and added to the perceived value of the goods on offer through using high-quality photography that made almost anything look good.

THE LOGIC OF ART DIRECTION

For that marketplace – the colour supplement reader that you could easily argue was highly visually sophisticated (I suspect the majority of them at the time were actually art directors working in advertising!) this approach clearly worked.

But as I cannot emphasise too strongly, this is not the *only* approach that will work. The Scotcade era introduced high quality art direction to mail order, and many people tried to copy it. It worked if your market was the same market. It did not work at all if the market was different. This must be the fundamental lesson: 'high quality' is *not* the only visual approach you can take. To the professional direct marketer, it is just one way of designing the 'shop', sometimes right, sometimes wrong. Identify the market first, the proposition second, and then the right style of art direction will logically follow.

TECHNIQUES OF ART DIRECTION

It is not the purpose of this book, nor my area of competence, to instruct anyone in the finer points of art direction – good designers have the necessary skills to do this for themselves. It is, however, worth looking at some of the basic techniques if only to explain to people who have the task of approving and judging creative work some of the underlying processes.

As discussed earlier in this Chapter, the starting point in deciding which look to give the piece must be through an understanding of the proposition, and thence through a process of identifying the market.

This checklist may well be useful:

1 Understand the proposition
2 Identify the market (use the shop analogy…which type of shop will

most appeal to the market you are looking for)

3 Are there negatives to overcome?

4 Are the positives to accentuate?

Following this checklist, you should then be able to describe quite clearly the visual look you should be taking strictly from the point of view of what is *most likely* to create an environment calculated to help response.

How you achieve this look then requires a great deal of talent. Only a good designer is able to design with sufficient flexibility to make a success of this business. One day you will be designing a trendy look, the next day will be a postal bargain, the day after will be a deliberately dull financial piece. All have to be done with great skill – and few art directors possess this *range* of talents.

BORROW FREELY

One of the best ways to achieve the look you need is to borrow one. By this I mean that simply by looking around you can find endless examples of different visual atmospheres – and by studying them you can use them for your own purposes.

Look at the design of the sports pages of the Daily Mirror for strong, punchy, down-market graphics. Look at the design of Vogue if you need a fashion look.

Get hold of a Sotheby's sale catalogue to see how up-market art treasures are best portrayed. A life insurance policy or an official bank document will give you the right flavour of dullness for some financial products. Viz magazine will help you get a feel for graphics to appeal to a young audience. What the local printer produces for a charity fete can guide you towards the right look for fundraising.

All of these have the benefit of being familiar to the public, and thus they can act as shorthand for the designer to help them get the look across with less effort.

MAIN ELEMENTS OF DESIGN

The main elements that make up design are generally as follows:

1. The Grid

The grid is basically the number of columns of type on the sheet – seen clearly in newspaper design, where typically eight columns are used. Type is best arranged in columns because short measures are more easily readable than long measures.

By using a classical grid of narrow columns and sticking to it, a very traditional, editorial look can be easily achieved. All the elements of the design must be based on the grid module...pictures will run across a multiple of the column, for instance. On narrow measure grids of eight columns, pictures can take just one column, with inevitably a very short depth – giving you pictures that become subsidiary to the text.

Moving further away from a narrow measure grid, you tend to move the design more towards a 'graphic' approach. When you reach just two or even one column, you are in the territory of brochure design. Wide columns are more difficult to read and therefore tend to be used for shorter copy and more illustrative purposes...pictures are again used on a multiple of the measure but on wide measures the pictures are naturally large – hence this style is ideal for the brochure look.

Thus even as simple a choice as the number of columns can profoundly change

Fig. 31:
The colour of money.
With mailings for financial products, you need to take care to make sure you don't make your product too glamorous – potential investors distrust flashy bankers! These two mailings show the difference. The first is an investment product from Homeowners Friendly Society, a successful and cautious organisation. Note how the art director has deliberately kept the whole pack restrained. Little colour is used, and where it is used, it's sparing. The feeling that comes across is solidity and trust-worthiness. The Marks and Spencer pack, on the other hand, uses colour and images much more strongly, even on the outer envelope. Partially this is because it's a loan product and therefore dull respectability is not so important; but also because as Marks and Spencer it really doesn't have an image problem, so the art director can afford to liven the whole pack up.

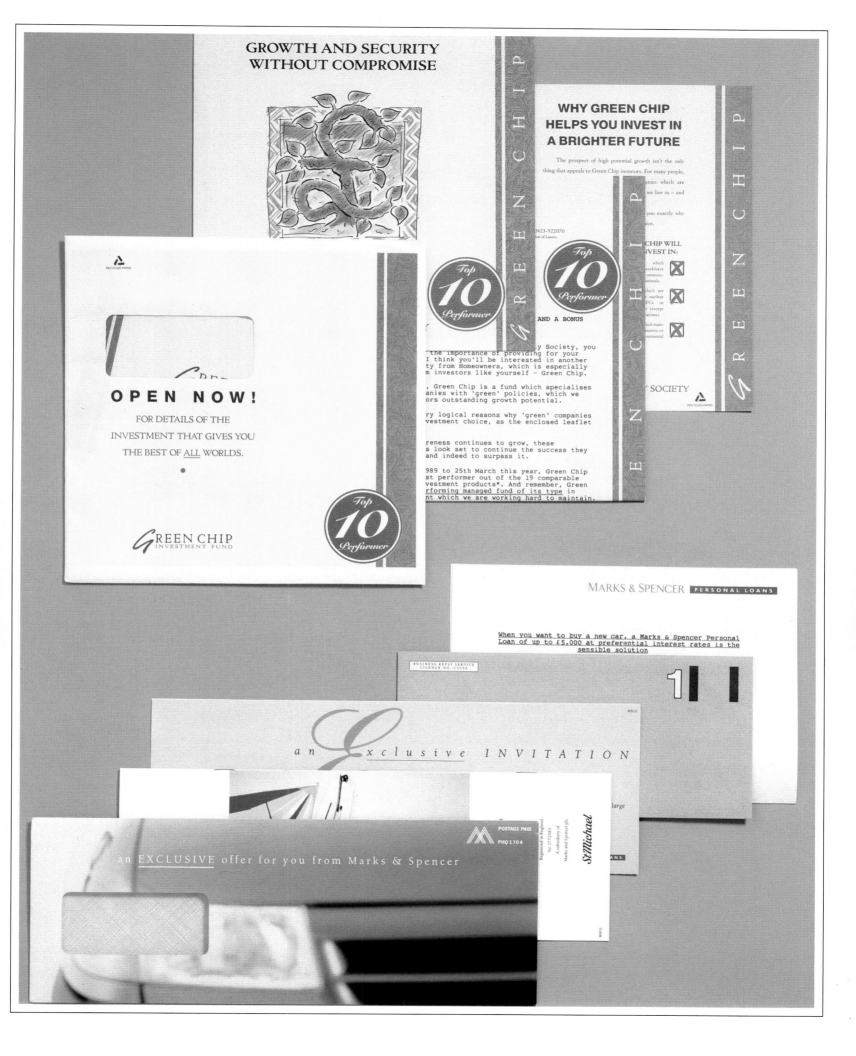

the visual character of the piece. For copy-intensive, hard-working direct response material, multiple narrow columns are clearly most useful – you will get that editorial feel very easily. Three columns tends to be the norm for classical 'above the line' ads – and if that is the right look for your purposes then you will find it makes some very elegant ads. Two columns and one column take you away from editorial and into books and brochures – again, this may be the right look for the job you have in hand.

2. The Type

After the choice of grid, then the next most significant factor in affecting the visual look is the typestyle that you choose.

Typefaces come in an extraordinary range. On modern photo-typesetting equipment, over 2,000 separate typefaces are commonly available; this does not count variants within the typeface, such as condensed, expanded and otherwise distorted versions of the basic face. You can even use handwriting where appropriate.

This vast choice allows the art director to use type to achieve his or her ends with some ease. Normally, choice of type is based on pure fashion – at the time of writing the current fashion is sans-serif type set on its side, à la First Direct.

As I hope I have argued with some persuasiveness, mere fashion is not the basic motivation for direct marketing art direction, and thus the choice of type will be made from a marketing perspective, and not a fashion one.

I referred earlier to the 'grey' look that some financial products may require. The choice of a classical serif face with an old-fashioned look (such as Caslon) will greatly help. Or I might be trying to achieve a strong bargain look, in which case a thick black type such as Franklin or Helvetica could be appropriate.

Perhaps the need is for a soft, feminine look. There are hundreds of scripts available which will achieve just this look.

Classical typography practice will tell you not to mix typefaces – it creates a mess. Sometimes you will want a clean, elegant look that sticking with a single typeface will give you…but at other times that 'mess' may be just what you need, particularly if you are trying to get a bargain offer look.

I believe that generally too little attention is paid to typography in direct marketing. This is a mistake, not from the artistic point of view but from the marketer's point of view. The right use of type can create an atmosphere that I am convinced is *fundamentally* part of achieving higher response. How much difference type makes, on a percentage of response basis, is hard to define because little if any testing has been done. But as I mention elsewhere in this book, a mailing letter that looks as though it has been typed, as opposed to typeset, will usually work better – if that can make a difference, then I see no reason why other variations in type cannot make *equal* differences. Incidentally, it's possible for bad typography to ruin good copy: set the copy in capital letters, for instance, and the effect is so unreadable as to make the whole thing a waste – yet you see examples of this every day.

3. The Picture

The illustration that you use is the third and final significant element of design.

Most direct marketing communications benefit from an illustration of some sort – obviously in merchandise the picture is critical; but even in mailings or ads that do not feature hard merchandise, such as charity or financial work, illustration makes a big difference.

One of the fundamentals of illustration is that, for most purposes, a photograph is to be preferred to a drawing. This is for reasons of realism: many of our mailings and ads need the Conviction element of the AIDCA formula to be reinforced, and 'an actual un-retouched photograph' is an excellent way of doing this. It is naturally mandatory for merchandise. You want to see exactly what it is you are buying. But with charities it can work equally powerfully – the photograph of the dead horse hung up on a hook in an ad for the RSPCA was so strong that the ASA banned it. Black and white shots can be exceptionally powerful.

The quality of the photograph is usually the subject of much debate. For merchandise, it must be worth hiring the best photographer in town to make your very ordinary set of pots and pans look superb. Remember, this photography is the equivalent of a shop – the only opportunity your reader will get to see and 'examine' the merchandise, so it clearly pays to use the best techniques available. The danger, though, is to allow the lighting and the propping to overwhelm the subject. A simple, straightforward shot, clearly lit, is preferable to some of the more lavish efforts that art directors and photographers can dream up between them. The point is to take a picture of the subject; not to turn the photograph into a work of art.

Even cropping is important. There have been fashion ads where the art director has cropped above the hemline, so no-one could see how long the dresses were.

Drawings in direct marketing are rarely successful for the reasons of credibility mentioned above. 'Artist's impression' must be one of the must damaging phrases ever written. But the use of what is termed 'information graphics' is a good idea. The advent of software packages that turn the most mundane numerical information into colourful charts gives us a good lead – information graphics is essentially a method of doing the same thing. Graphs, pie charts, diagrams…all of these can help you get complex information across. The type of visual approach used by Dorling Kindersley, one of the must successful publishers in recent years, is pure information graphics – it helps hugely in financial products or anywhere else where numbers are part of the argument, although this approach is by no means limited to numbers.

QUALITY OF REPRODUCTION

Quality of reproduction also becomes an issue as far as illustration is concerned. The trouble is, poor quality of reproduction isn't actually the problem people think it. Look at a black and white photograph in a newspaper – you will never think that the quality of reproduction is poor. Firstly, you are far more interested in the subject matter to worry about whether the page has been overinked. Secondly, because everything is printed to the same 'poor' standard within that paper, your eye automatically compensates for the quality.

In fact, look at a halftone with a crude 65 screen in a paper and you won't see the screen at all. Put that same photograph next to one in a magazine with a 120 screen and the 65 screen picture will look fuzzy and indistinct. It's the same process at work as in the cinema, where the eye translates a succession of still pictures into motion by 'filling in the gaps'. Your eye does the same for the crude black and white picture in the paper – it actually fills in details that are not there.

The best example of this effect was an ad for a plate series. After much effort to photograph the plates clearly, the ad duly appeared one Sunday – and to our horror the register of the colour printing was so far out that the picture appeared to us to be nothing more than a fuzzy mess of reds and yellows. First thing on Monday we were on the phone to the publication demanding huge compensation for what was clearly going to be a failure. The trouble was, by that same Friday, the results were pouring in, and it became a *massive* success.

Most of the copies printed were out of register. But such is the power of people's visual sense that their eyes compensated for it, and saw what was not actually there. Most people just didn't realise it was out of register.

TRACKING OR 'PACE'

A last word on art direction concerns 'tracking' or 'pace', particularly applied to mailings or inserts. 'Tracking' means the way in which the designer of the mailing, through the use of format, folds, and even colours, can help (or even make) the reader 'track' through the mailing, in order to create greater interest or drama. This technique implies thinking about the *whole* mailing, and the way the pieces relate to each other, rather than just looking at individual items. One of the great benefits of direct mail is the 'tactile' element…you feel a mailing as much as you read it…and this can be turned to good effect. An example of this is the case of broadsheets – large 'posters' of paper folded down to an intriguing size, that the reader has to unfold. Few elements of a mailing are more involving than a DL sized leaflet that opens and opens, fold after fold, to reveal a huge A2 sized colour sheet, showing the product in all its glory. Art directors should always look at tracking as an important design element. Use it to create extra drama and involvement, and your results will be enhanced by it.

BRAND IMAGE

You'll notice that throughout this Chapter I have said very little about brand image. It seems to me, when this comment comes up in creative arguments, that people 'doth protest too much'. It's always struck me as extremely obvious that whatever you design, it has to be designed *within* the brand image. Thus, if you designed a mailing for IBM looking as though it came from Dixons, it really wouldn't make any sense. Good direct marketing art direction will work – *within* the brand image, and make the most of it. But please, never let brand image overwhelm the practical realities of good direct marketing. If your brand image calls for lots of white space and no headlines, you're really not going to find that direct marketing will work for you. Combine the best of both and you will always get much better results than just concentrating on one or the other ■

CHAPTER 7: SUMMARY

Like a shop, a great deal of attention should be given to creating the right atmosphere in your ad or mailing, an atmosphere that helps the prospect buy. Art direction makes its main contribution to generating higher responses by creating this atmosphere.

You must avoid at all costs the temptation to see the visual look of a piece purely in terms of quality. A quality look is sometimes right, but can equally be quite wrong.

Identify the market you are going to, and then devise a visual approach that is more likely to appeal to the market, given the product or service you are selling.

Art direction can create visual atmospheres that can help overcome negatives or accentuate positives, or both at the same time.

Avoid the use of graphic fashions unless you wish, for purely marketing reasons, to be seen as fashionable. Use graphics that are fit for the purpose – any number of atmospheres can be created through the use of good art direction...you need to devise the visual proposition before you start.

Borrow freely from other sources to create the look you need; these looks are familiar to your reader and act as shorthand to help you get your visual message across faster.

Careful selection of the right grid will help you to get the look you want – narrow, multiple columns for the editorial look, one or two columns for the highly illustrative look.

Use type to get your message across, rather than just following the latest typographical fashion. Cunning typography is one of the most important parts of getting the visual look right.

Wherever possible use photography for the sake of realism, and don't worry too much about quality of reproduction – it actually isn't that important from the point of view of response.

Pay attention to 'tracking' – the way the mailing is designed can force it to be opened and read in a certain way. This adds to the drama and involvement.

Making Formats Work

One of the starting points for creating successful direct mail packages is the choice of format; this is rarely as simple as an envelope containing a letter, a brochure and a reply form. Intelligent choice of format reinforces the proposition and gives you an uplift on response beyond that which the copy alone can achieve.

O NE OF the areas of creativity in direct mail that only a handful of professionals understand is that of the format. By understand I do not mean a technical understanding of print and production process, but rather an appreciation of the difference the format *alone* can make to responses.

Format, in this sense, means both the physical shape and nature of the piece, and also the way in which the design turns the mailing into something special.

A Reader's Digest mailing is a good case in point. Designers at Digest spend a great deal of time thinking of new formats: the basic proposition of a prize draw remains the same, and it is then almost a pure design function to find new and unusual ways of presenting that proposition – by using *physically different* formats as well as finding ways of making those formats unusual.

DOUBLING AND TRIPLING RESPONSE

The differences in response are marked. Simply changing one format for another (but leaving the basic proposition alone) can have the effect of doubling and even tripling response. It is this extraordinary feature of formats that few people appreciate: testing formats is highly expensive, after all, and few companies mail in the quantities that Digest do, thus opportunities for testing for many people are limited.

Nevertheless, the fact remains. Indeed, one of the more exotic ways of improving responses to a mailing is not to tackle the copy end, but simply change the format.

Some years ago Consumers' Association, publishers of Which? magazine, had developed a control package using prize draws. One of the problems with such packages is that once the proposition is right – such as 'Win £100,000' – the copy or proposition cannot go very much further. What can you do to improve results beyond that stage?

RAFFLE TICKETS

The answer was in formats. Bob Seabright, easily one of the most talented designers of such mailings in the UK, took the basic prize draw which featured a certificate with multiple entry numbers (one of the more successful variants of prize draws, by the way). He designed not only a physically different format, but also turned the mailing away from a simple certificate and into a 'Raffle Ticket' format.

Instead of a basic certificate, a bunch of different coloured 'raffle tickets' met your eye, each one representing a chance to win the big prize. This was tested against the old control and proved so successful as to become the new control package – it still is, even today.

Having proved successful, further development of that format could then take place, using either physical changes or design changes, but still leaving the basic raffle ticket idea in place.

To finally illustrate the strength of the concept, WWAV was asked to look at insert versions of the raffle ticket format: it had proved successful in mail and equally so in press inserts. The brief was simple – leave the copy and proposition virtually unchanged, but *find new and interesting formats*. That change alone was sufficient to justify a whole new development process.

WHY ARE FORMATS SO IMPORTANT?

The question needs to be asked why what appears to be only a superficial change can have such powerful effects on response rates, particularly bearing in mind what I have written before about the importance of propositions and copy.

The answer is in two parts. First, dramatisation. Second, change of pace.

DRAMATISATION

Whether you are Reader's Digest or Sun Alliance, it clearly makes sense to ensure that your mailing communicates your proposition in the *strongest* possible way. In a press ad you have only limited ability to use different formats to reinforce your proposition. But with direct mail you are in complete control of the printing process, and you can therefore use this control to shape the mailing around the message you wish to communicate.

This means that your format can dramatise the proposition, making it that much more effective. Instead of a simple letter and brochure, you can employ a range of shapes and sizes of paper to make your proposition both clearer and more exciting. I shall go on to show how this works in practice.

The second reason why formats are important is what is called 'change of pace'.

CHANGE OF PACE

Change of pace is a concept used originally by Lynne Pearson of WWAV, in relation to direct mail. The point of change of pace is simple: with any mass mailer (by mass you should assume 1m per season upwards) using a control package, there comes a point where the average person will have seen that control package *too many times*. How many times is too many? Quite simply, it's when the results from that control begin to tire…in the case of very heavy mailers, it could be in just two seasons; lighter mass mailers will have a longer life.

Thus 'change of pace' is required: a new pack based on exactly the same proposition as the control, using (typically) exactly the same copy as the control. All that changes is the design – and this is done mainly by changing the format, although sometimes just copy and visual changes are just as effective. On several occasions mailings which are slowly declining resurrect themselves purely through 'change of

POSTAGE PAID
1
PHQ 567

'CHEQUE' ENCLOSED

BOSTON
A SUBSIDIARY OF THE BANK OF BOSTON

Boston Trust & Savings Limited, Boston House, Lower Dagnall Street, St Albans, Herts AL3 4PG

30th July 19 84   40-40-01

SPECIMEN

Pay___ MR/MRS PETER JOHNSTON _____or order

Two thousand, five hundred and twenty four pounds

| MR/MRS PETER JOHNSTON
5 TANSEY CRES
STONEY STANTON
LEICESTER   LE9 6BT | and 65 pence. | £ 2524.65 |

FOR AND ON BEHALF OF
BOSTON TRUST & SAVINGS

⑆256746⑆ 30⑆9487⑈ 0254578⑈

CUSTOMER MEMORANDUM   BOSTON

ACCOUNT NO.   01 130 7236
OUR REFERENCE   123/000020

TO: MR/MRS PETER JOHNSTON

FROM:
Ian P. Reeves, Manager,
Boston Money Services,
27 Belgrave Gate,
Leicester
Telephone Leicester 538046

FOR JUST £11.03 MORE THAN YOUR PRESENT PAYMENTS PER MONTH, A CHEQUE FOR THE ABOVE AMOUNT COULD BE YOURS...

Good news from Boston. I am now in a position to invite you, as a valued customer, to have 'More Money' ... with only a <u>modest</u> change to your present repayments.

At the moment you are repaying £50.08 per month which allowed you credit of £932 originally .

However, you could shortly be repaying just £61.11 PER MONTH ... AND WE'LL BE giving you a further cheque for £2,524.65!

HOW? It's quite simple. You see our records show that you are a homeowner. So you can use the equity in your home to secure a larger loan at a much lower rate of interest and have <u>up to 7 years</u> to repay. In other words, while your repayments will go up only modestly, you can have a great deal <u>More Money</u>.

I have worked a few examples for you. The attached Quotation shows several different levels of monthly repayments and the amount of loan each represents. I have then shown the amount of money available to you, after the balance of your old loan has been deducted.

All these figures are calculated at the current, low interest rate of 11% per annum <u>(APR 19.6%)</u> and this I will be happy to guarantee until the 13th August 1984.

<u>As you'll see, by combining a lower interest rate and a repayment period of 7 years, you can have a substantial amount more money for very little extra each month.</u>

Q&A

BOSTON

HELPS YOU...

...AS) – which means

...only a slight increase

...this Quotation.
...at happens to interest

1784

Fig. 32:
The cheque format.
When your mailing involves giving, loaning or winning money, the format itself can be used to dramatise this proposition. Here, in this mailing to Boston Trust customers (now Nationwide Trust) an offer of a further loan is made. The outer envelope indicates the presence of a 'cheque', and when opened the first thing that comes out is a specimen cheque for several thousand pounds. A great deal of care needs to go into this type of mailing: the lasering, for instance, is vital to give the idea believability. Notice, too, how the cheque sits on top of the main letter, giving it a great deal of prominence. The format does the communicating here – very few headlines are used, for example; the cheque speaks for itself.

Fig. 33:
You have been nominated.

This pack was highly successful in recruiting Trustcard enquiries from cold lists. We identified that one of the main reasons for people not applying was fear of rejection (particularly from the better quality customers) and thus we devised this 'nomination' pack. The idea was that you had been specially nominated to get this mailing because you were a potentially good customer. The right choice of format was critical to get the idea working dramatically. Besides the normal letter and application, we used a Nomination Form with your name lasered on it. We wanted the sprocket holes and the OCR reading marks left on to give it a feeling of being genuine – in fact, only one side of the form had sprocket holes the way it was printed, and we had to have the holes in the other side specially punched. Little details like this make a big difference to making formats come alive.

pace' – given that the only change is to the format, this alone would suggest that the format is a *key* element in the creative mix.

Major mailers should look to have 2 'control' packs anyway – the greater the mailing or broadcast volume, the earlier the control pack will tire out, and having 2 controls means you can rotate the creative treatment.

Whether dramatisation or change of pace is the motivation in a particular case, it is clear that by working as hard on the format as on the proposition or copy, significant improvement in results can be gained.

CHOOSING YOUR FORMAT

Given the importance of the format, it is therefore logical to say that the first thing you should do when creating a direct mail pack is choose the format you are going to use.

In other words, it will be more productive if you *don't worry about writing headlines or designing elements of the mailing until you have got your format fixed firmly in mind.*

Critically, you should have already agreed on your proposition. You should have a very clear idea of what proposition you are going to use on your target market. This is not just the marketing proposition, but also the 'visual proposition' that I referred to in the previous Chapter on Art Direction.

The format should then grow *naturally* from the proposition. The right format will reinforce that proposition and make it work better…this is the dramatisation effect at work. Choosing formats is thus not an arbitrary, 'creative' process, but fixed firmly in the objectives you are trying to achieve.

As many serious mailers have discovered, and as Graeme McCorkell said, direct mail is a 'tactile' medium. You have more than just words and pictures to play with – you have pieces of paper that with imagination can be turned into devices that can help you create the right dramatic effects.

And not only does this help the response, it also greatly simplifies the process of designing a direct mail package. Few tasks are more forbidding than sitting down with a blank sheet of paper and trying to start on a package. Unless you have a *clear idea of the format* you want, you can waste very many hours groping in the dark. Once the format is clear, then designing and writing the elements that make up that format is a relatively simple process.

A MOTTO FOR CREATIVE PEOPLE

From all points of view, then, choosing the format before commencing the design and copy gives you a much greater chance of success. The sequence should be engraved upon your heart, or word processor, or layout pad:

First – MARKETING PROPOSITION

Second – VISUAL PROPOSITION

Third – FORMAT

Last – DESIGN AND COPY

It can be hard to reduce the creative process to such logical steps. Yet when you think back over the packages you have created that you were most pleased with (and those that worked well!), you will find it is that process that you went through. Following that 'formula' will not only improve results – but it will make life *easier* as well.

FORMAT CASE HISTORY 1: TSB TRUSTCARD

Let's look at some real case histories that will, I hope, demonstrate the importance of getting formats right.

First, a TSB Trustcard Mailing.

When WWAV started working on TSB Trustcard, we had already found a variety of mailings worked reasonably well for them – including a prize draw. A new mailing was required to see if we could beat the existing pack, which was a fairly plain DL envelope, letter and reply device.

Following the formula I mentioned earlier, the first job was to work out the proposition.

We were mailing cold lists. We knew from previous experience that fear of rejection was one of the most common reasons why people didn't take up offers of credit.

By a process of discussion and elimination it seemed to us that this would be the best proposition, albeit a sort of negative one: in fact, there was so much credit card marketing activity at the time that there was little in the way of a more positive proposition that we could use, apart from a prize draw. Ours was a Visa card like everyone else's, and therefore a proposition built around acceptance was one of the few left.

'YOU HAVE BEEN NOMINATED'

Could we turn a *negative* proposition into a *positive* one? Clearly, we could hardly use a proposition such as "You will be accepted" (although by using pre-scoring we could have got close to this – but in those days the risks were too high). What we needed was something that implied acceptance, rather than stating it overtly.

We ended up with a simple enough phrase:

"You have been nominated..."

which carried with it a strong suggestion of acceptance. In fact, this is nothing more than a variant of the famous "If the list upon which I found your name..." opening, coined by Ed McLean.

It sounds more respectable, of course – more financial, in other words. And the obvious flattery aspect is by no means unimportant. Trustcard always was a downmarket card (in spite of subsequent efforts to make it upmarket), and I think it certainly appealed to such a group to be 'nominated'.

Thus we had our proposition.

What I think was then critical to the success of this package was that we decided to go for a format that lived up to this proposition. I do not think this package would have worked half as well had the format not accorded so closely with the 'nomination' idea.

THE NOMINATION FORM

We could only exercise our creativity on the format to a certain extent. Much of the package was already dictated. The application form was standardised for the processing people; a weighty copy of the terms and conditions had to be included under the Consumer Credit Act; these pieces were a standard size and thus a DL envelope was the most logical. A brochure could be included, as could a letter. What else?

Given the 'nomination' theme, what more obvious than a nomination form? Almost anything in a direct mail package that looks like an official document will work, particularly if you get the recipient's name on it. Thus the Nomination Form was born. (Interestingly, when we tested the word 'invitation' on the same format it failed – the format matched the 'nomination' proposition and nothing else.)

But the *execution* of the form itself was critical. In my previous Chapter on Art Direction I referred to the necessity for creating the right atmosphere. For this Nomination Form we decided to make it look like a computer-generated piece.

In order to give it the maximum authenticity, we wanted two sets of sprocket holes down the sides. In fact, the piece of paper had only one set – it came from the same piece of continuous stationery as the lasered application form. Instead of slitting off the sprocket holes in the finishing process, we actually wanted this piece to go back to have an *extra* set of holes punched in it! You can see this pack illustrated in figure 33.

This may seem finicky, but small details like that make formats work. The more realistic you make your format – particularly if you choose the official document approach – the greater the chance you will have of success.

The copy itself simply stated that the person named above had been Nominated to apply for the Trustcard. The design of the form went along with its official nature.

The result of all this effort was that for some years this package ran unchanged and was responsible for recruiting something like 250,000 new Trustcard holders. Under Martin Salter and John Loring, who at that time were the heads of marketing at TSB Trustcard, TSB Trustcard adopted one of the most aggressive direct mail strategies in the country, and experienced one of the highest growth rates all of the card issuers.

COMPUTER-GENERATED

Why the 'computer' feel to the Nomination Form?

Oddly enough, what appear to be computer-generated documents in direct mail packages seem to work very well. One of the best I ever saw was an insurance offer using an old IBM punch-card, which the pack asked you to return. There is a fascination in such things that few people can resist. Not only that, but people are so used to getting computer-generated material from banks, credit card companies and other financial institutions that it probably seems perfectly natural.

A TELEGRAM FROM LABOUR

As my second example, a telegram format has been used successfully for a number of clients: in this case, The Labour Party, for whom WWAV has worked for a number of years on the fundraising front.

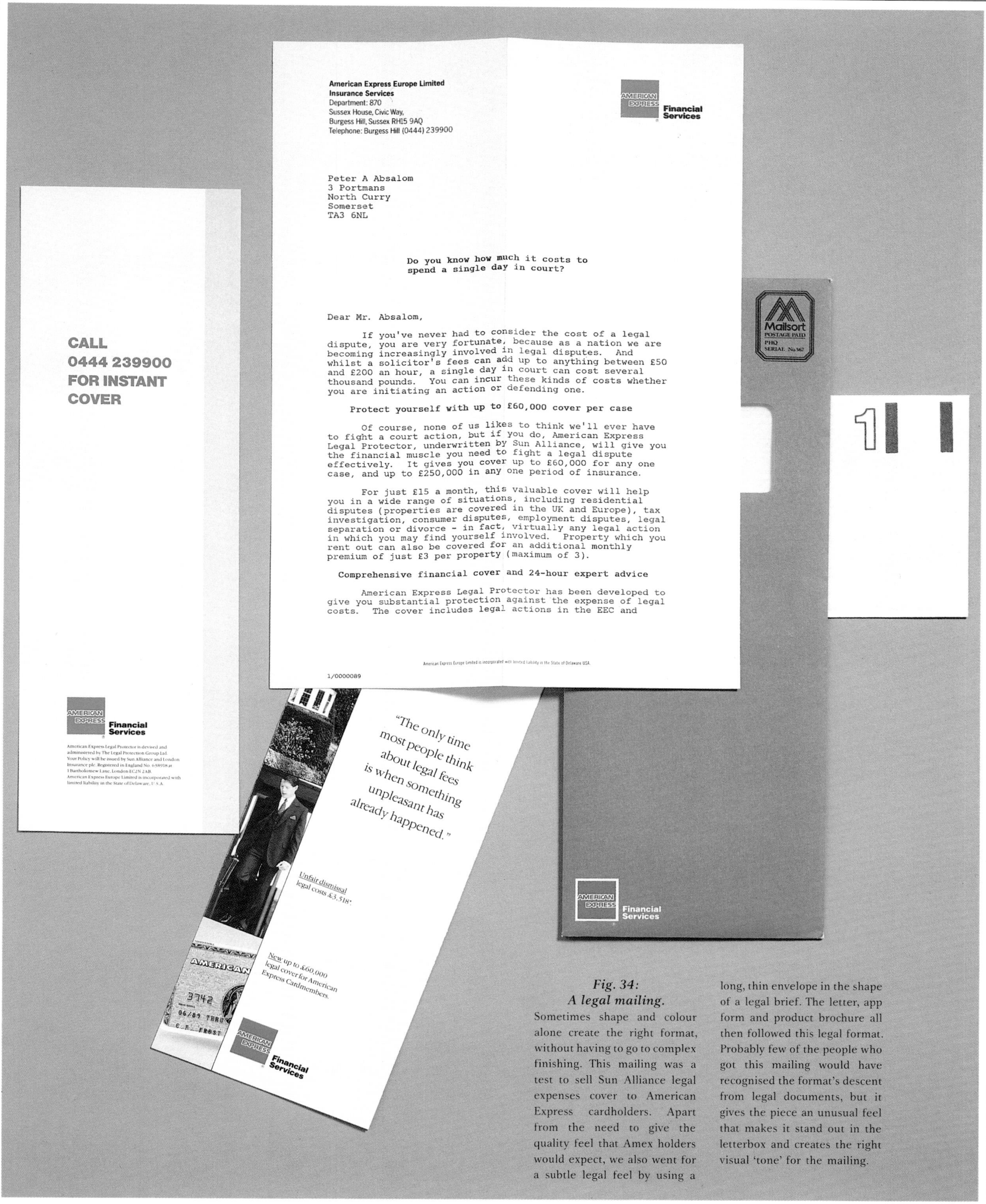

American Express Europe Limited
Insurance Services
Department: 870
Sussex House, Civic Way,
Burgess Hill, Sussex RH15 9AQ
Telephone: Burgess Hill (0444) 239900

AMERICAN EXPRESS **Financial Services**

Peter A Absalom
3 Portmans
North Curry
Somerset
TA3 6NL

Do you know how much it costs to
spend a single day in court?

Dear Mr. Absalom,

If you've never had to consider the cost of a legal
dispute, you are very fortunate, because as a nation we are
becoming increasingly involved in legal disputes. And
whilst a solicitor's fees can add up to anything between £50
and £200 an hour, a single day in court can cost several
thousand pounds. You can incur these kinds of costs whether
you are initiating an action or defending one.

Protect yourself with up to £60,000 cover per case

Of course, none of us likes to think we'll ever have
to fight a court action, but if you do, American Express
Legal Protector, underwritten by Sun Alliance, will give you
the financial muscle you need to fight a legal dispute
effectively. It gives you cover up to £60,000 for any one
case, and up to £250,000 in any one period of insurance.

For just £15 a month, this valuable cover will help
you in a wide range of situations, including residential
disputes (properties are covered in the UK and Europe), tax
investigation, consumer disputes, employment disputes, legal
separation or divorce - in fact, virtually any legal action
in which you may find yourself involved. Property which you
rent out can also be covered for an additional monthly
premium of just £3 per property (maximum of 3).

Comprehensive financial cover and 24-hour expert advice

American Express Legal Protector has been developed to
give you substantial protection against the expense of legal
costs. The cover includes legal actions in the EEC and

American Express Europe Limited is incorporated with limited liability in the State of Delaware USA

1/0000089

CALL
0444 239900
FOR INSTANT
COVER

AMERICAN EXPRESS **Financial Services**

American Express Legal Protector is devised and
administered by The Legal Protection Group Ltd.
Your Policy will be issued by Sun Alliance and London
Insurance plc. Registered in England No. 618918 at
1 Bartholomew Lane, London EC2N 2AB.
American Express Europe Limited is incorporated with
limited liability in the State of Delaware, U.S.A.

"The only time
most people think
about legal fees
is when something
unpleasant has
already happened."

Unfair dismissal
legal costs £3,518*

New up to £60,000
legal cover for American
Express Cardmembers.

AMERICAN EXPRESS **Financial Services**

Mailsort
POSTAGE PAID
PHQ
SERIAL No 867

AMERICAN EXPRESS **Financial Services**

Fig. 34:
A legal mailing.

Sometimes shape and colour alone create the right format, without having to go to complex finishing. This mailing was a test to sell Sun Alliance legal expenses cover to American Express cardholders. Apart from the need to give the quality feel that Amex holders would expect, we also went for a subtle legal feel by using a long, thin envelope in the shape of a legal brief. The letter, app form and product brochure all then followed this legal format. Probably few of the people who got this mailing would have recognised the format's descent from legal documents, but it gives the piece an unusual feel that makes it stand out in the letterbox and creates the right visual 'tone' for the mailing.

This is a totally format-driven creative treatment. Once you decide on this format, the rest of the package writes and designs itself.

Again, though, as with Trustcard, the first task was to create a clear proposition. In this case, a by-election was coming up and the opinion polls suggested that Labour would do well. In the event of a victory, the newspapers would feature it heavily and the average Labour Party supporter would feel quite positive. Over the years we had already developed a file of Labour Party donors, almost exclusively generated through direct marketing, and previous testing showed that we would raise a fair amount of money if we mailed them immediately after the result was announced.

Speed was the essence. We knew that the hoped-for victory would only feature in the papers for the next day. After then it would be cold news.

There was no point in going through the process of mailing a normal package, which would take at least two or three weeks. Good news as it was expected to be, even the most dedicated Labour Party supporter would have forgotten about it by then.

But speed was only one part of the story; sheer drama was equally important. Here was a headline-hitting event, full of urgency and excitement. Only a mailing that carried the same enthusiasm and excitement would work well.

Our proposition was therefore: "Celebrate a great Labour victory by giving now, so that we can forge ahead for the General Election". Urgency was all.

The format by now becomes obvious (and it's remarkable just how obvious a format will become once you have done the spadework with the proposition). The telegram was thus created. Not only did it carry urgency in its own right, but it was a fast and simple format to mail into the bargain, once all the tapework had been done.

Of course, we anticipated various results, from victory to defeat, and had texts set up accordingly. The material was printed and the lasers held ready until the result was known first thing in the morning. The lasers were turned on, and by late afternoon they had all been printed, burst and trimmed and enclosed, ready to post that night by first class mail. Most of the supporters received their telegram the morning after the great victory, and not surprisingly the results were excellent.

Much of the success of the package again lies in the attention to detail. The bright yellow envelope, stolen with grateful thanks from BT 'telemessages'. The telegraphic language. The highly personal flavour.

This pack is shown in figure 35.

A CHEQUE FROM BOSTON

Here are two more brief examples of how the right format plays an important part in your mailing.

First, a mailing to a file of existing borrowers of Boston Trust (see fig. 32). The product is a secured loan, which when offered to unsecured customers, implies a lower interest rate and therefore lower repayments per £1,000 borrowed – the customer could borrow much more money for a little extra on the repayments.

The proposition focused on the cash that was 'available' to you. Thus the format chosen featured a cheque, lasered with the recipient's name together with the amount of money we were prepared to lend. In its first 'outing', this mailing created over £2 million of business from just 6,000 customers. The format of the mailing was constructed wholly around the cheque…a different proposition would, of course, demand a different format to exploit the proposition as much as possible.

Second, an example from Touche Remnant (see fig. 36). Here the task was to invite financial intermediaries to the launch of a new investment fund.

The proposition and the format could hardly be simpler. The proposition was the invitation – and the format could only be, of course, an invitation.

But it is attention to detail that makes this kind of pack work: the invitation really does look like a real one, even down to the handwriting of the invitee's name (handwriting can be employed on surprisingly large quantities) and the real postage stamp. The separate card, printed on thick stock, is also part of the format, and an important one.

The invitation is one of my favourite formats. It has all of the attributes of a good pack: personal, action-oriented and simple.

But if you use this approach, you must ensure absolute accuracy. I have seen many invitational packs fail because they do not include the invitation card, for instance, or because the mailer has not gone to the trouble of personalising the piece.

'OFFICIAL' DOCUMENTS

'Official' documents form one of the bedrocks of format ideas. This is a very common theme throughout direct mail packages; the three examples I have quoted above all use 'official' documents – a Notification of Nomination, a Telegram, a Cheque. While this is by no means the *only* way of choosing formats, it provides an excellent creative shorthand and allows the designer to work within a known format rather than having to be totally inventive.

'Official' documents also have a powerful impact upon the reader. I do not for one minute think that anyone is 'fooled' into thinking that they are real documents. They work, I think, by making the package more noticeable than just, say, a printed letter or brochure can, and thus they attract *greater* attention.

In the same way that Copywriters should study various different styles of writing in order to widen their stylistic repertoire, so should Art Directors and Designers study various official forms to gain an equal insight into the types of style available to them:

BILLS	*SHARE CERTIFICATES*	*BANK NOTES*
LICENCES	*LOG BOOKS*	*TREASURY BILLS*
RAFFLE TICKETS	*INVITATIONS*	*REGISTRATIONS*
CHEQUES	*BANK DRAFTS*	*LETTER OF CREDIT*
PROXY FORMS	*EXAM CERTIFICATES*	*COURT SUMMONS*

and so on. Some of these documents are quite hard to lay your hands on, and Finance Departments can be a useful source of material. Another excellent source is what is called 'printed ephemera', a class of antique that appeals to some collectors. Old share certificates and bank notes often feature in such collections, and should you come

||||||||||||||||||||||| **URGENT VICTORY SPECIAL** |||||||||||||||||||||||

```
URGENT:
FROM LARRY WHITTY, GENERAL SECRETARY, THE LABOUR PARTY

TO:


MR M WARD
17 BROAD ROAD                              23RD MARCH 1990
BLACKHALL, HARTLEPOOL
CLEVELAND
TS27 4BB



DEAR MR WARD,

UNFORGETTABLE!

SYLVIA HEAL'S MOMENTOUS VICTORY AT MID-STAFFORDSHIRE WILL GO DOWN IN
THE HISTORY BOOKS.

LABOUR CRUSHED A TORY MAJORITY WITH THE KIND OF SWING THAT WOULD MEAN
VICTORY AT THE NEXT GENERAL ELECTION.  WE'RE ON OUR WAY - BUT FOR ONE
MAJOR PROBLEM.

WHILE WE HAVE A CLEAR LEAD OVER THE TORIES IN THE POLLS, THEY HAVE A
MASSIVE LEAD OVER US IN RESOURCES.  THEY WON'T FORGIVE THE DEFEAT
WE'VE INFLICTED ON THEM EASILY.  WITH MILLIONS OF POUNDS OF CORPORATE
DONATIONS BEHIND THEM, WHAT THEY LACK IN POPULAR SUPPORT THEY MAKE UP
FOR IN SHEER CASH.

DON'T LET THEM BUY VICTORY.  I AM APPEALING TO YOU TO HELP US WITH A
CASH DONATION NOW, OR EVEN BETTER A BANKER'S ORDER TO GIVE US INCOME
WE CAN RELY ON.

THE LOCAL ELECTIONS COMING IN MAY WILL BE THE NEXT BATTLE GROUND.
ALREADY OUR SLIM RESOURCES ARE UNDER STRAIN.

PLEASE HELP IF YOU CAN.  MID-STAFFS IS JUST THE BEGINNING.  HELP THE
PARTY SEIZE THIS MAGNIFCENT OPPORTUNITY NOW.  WE NEED YOUR SUPPORT
MORE THAN EVER BEFORE.
```

- - - ✂ -

```
FROM:  MR M WARD, 17 BROAD ROAD, BLACKHALL, HARTLEPOOL, CLEVELAND,
       TS27 4BB.
TO: LARRY WHITTY, RM 313, THE LABOUR PARTY, FREEPOST, LONDON SE17 1BR

YES, I'LL GIVE A MONTHLY SUM TO HELP FINANCE A LABOUR VICTORY AT
THE NEXT GENERAL ELECTION.

  ☐ £25    ☐ £15    ☐ £10    ☐ £5    ☐ £3    ☐ £2    OTHER £_____

NAME AND ADDRESS OF BANK _____


_____

CURRENT ACCOUNT NO. ☐☐☐☐☐☐☐☐    SORT CODE ☐☐-☐☐-☐☐

SIGNATURE_____    DATE_____

BANK INSTRUCTIONS:  PLEASE PAY THE ABOVE AMOUNT ON THE 21ST OF EVERY
MONTH TO UNITY TRUST BANK (08-60-01) FOR THE ACCOUNT OF THE LABOUR
PARTY (A/C NO. 58118588).

  ☐  I WOULD PREFER TO GIVE A SINGLE DONATION OF £_____ AND ENCLOSE A
CHEQUE MADE PAYABLE TO THE LABOUR PARTY.

000194                          DFD1                          5213186
```

Fig. 35:
How formats can
dominate.

It is always vital to get the format right – so much so that when the format is right you should allow it to dominate the other creative 'rules' of direct mail. Here is a telegram style of mailing used for The Labour Party following a spectacular by-election win in 1990. Urgency was not only a desirable feeling to create – given that we only had about 48 hours to prepare this mailing there wasn't much option. The copy is short, there isn't much in the envelope – but the format itself does all the work anyway. The use of bright yellow for the outer as well as the telegram itself is part of the realism, as is the use of the capital letters on the telegram – capitals are harder to read than upper and lower but it creates a more realistic telegram feel. Again, attention to small details is important to make formats like this believable.

John Smith

Smith Investments

1 Smith Street

Smithtown

Smithshire

exposé

Fig. 36:
The invitation format.
One of the most successful formats for business-to-business mailings is the invitation, here used to the ultimate degree in this mailing for Société Générale Touche Remnant Unit Trusts, inviting intermediaries to a presentation of a new product. But invitations only work well if they're done properly. This one uses a handwritten outer envelope, a personal salutation also written by hand, and has the invitee's name handwritten on the card – note that it's a proper, thick invitation card, too, not a cheap slip of paper. Mailings like this only work because the format is brought to life by the use of handwriting, for instance. The same thing done without the handwriting would fall flat on its face. Technically, by the way, it's easy to produce mailings like this in surprisingly large quantities, although a few hundred to a few thousand is a more normal level.

SOCIETE GENERALE TOUCHE REMNANT UNIT TRUSTS

Dear Mr Smith,

     I'd like to invite you to one of our special Société Générale Touche Remnant Roadshows.

     I very much hope that you will be able to attend. We aim to make these Roadshows both informative and enjoyable.

     For us, it will be an excellent opportunity to meet with key opinion-formers in the financial industry like yourself, and introduce you to the new face of SGTR.

     Even if you know Touche Remnant quite well, I think you might be surprised by how much we are changing. Changes in personnel and the link-up with Société Générale have made us extremely well-positioned to take advantage of investment opportunities in the years ahead.

futur
expla
month

indus
with

and f
the s

PO BOX 598 MERMAID HO

The Chairman and Directors of
Société Générale Touche Remnant Unit Trust Management Ltd
request the pleasure of the company of

JOHN SMITH

at the SGTR Roadshow and lunch

On: Monday 14th October 1991
At: Smeatons Vault, The Brewery,
Chiswell Street, London EC1 4SD.

11.30 for 12.00 noon

RSVP Mags Little
071 634 0297

across an auction of such material it's worth going in and buying a few pieces.

SHARE CERTIFICATES

I suspect that Digest would not have got quite as far as they did unless somebody, somewhere, latched on to the 'Share Certificate' format. Not only does the Share Certificate in itself suggest great wealth (and the proposition behind a Digest pack is simply the chance of winning great wealth) but the very *design* of them allows the designer to create a piece that I think few people could resist.

Particularly old share certificates, and especially American ones, are covered with engraved lettering, swashes, curlicues, repeat backgrounds, seals, and almost every other device you can imagine. Based on the principle that a forger would find it hard to replicate such documents, they go to extremes that even bank notes resist.

In looking at Digest packs, the sheer attention to detail is remarkable. The use of advanced printing and finishing methods is generally in evidence, and such techniques as foil blocking, fifth colours (especially metallic gold) and hand-finishing are not cheap. This surely must suggest to all but the most prejudiced that such techniques pay their way.

DANGEROUS GLAMOUR

If your proposition suggests the use of a format using 'official' documents, I have already laid stress on the need to be absolutely accurate to the official document you are 'copying'. Clearly, there are limits to accuracy – some imposed by legal means!

But sometimes you will find that the official document you are using is only a base for the idea, and needs considerable modification to make it work for your needs.

In doing this, the *greatest* danger is to over-glamorise, or to 'improve' the original. Art Directors spend 3 years in art school learning how to be original, and it can come as something of a culture shock when the need is to 'copy'. The temptation is to exercise one's own artistic skills: this very rarely works unless you were a bank note or share certificate designer in a previous life. *Accuracy and attention to detail based on the original is far more critical than any need to be original.*

THE OFFICIAL LOOK

I mentioned above that there are various types of official document. In studying any of them you will see that certain elements, used carefully, go to create this 'look':

SIZE Most official documents are peculiar sizes. Certainly few are A4 or DL in shape. Using unusual sizing often helps you create interesting and unusual envelopes as well as formats – the long thin 'legal' envelope being one of the best.

TYPOGRAPHY Official documents fall into two styles. There is the lavish, engraved style of share certificates, and great fun to work with. But there is also the 'untypographed' style where the local printer has set the type in something like Grot 9 with a primitive lack of attention to things like letter spacing. Centring, use of capitals and other crude typographic techniques are usually in evidence.

COLOUR Colour is either non-existent (it's remarkable how much impact can be gained from a black and white piece in the midst of a colour pack) or uses washes and tints. Black type with red capitals or red underlining is particularly effective.

LANGUAGE The language of official documents is highly stilted, full of 'wherefores', 'notwithstandings' and 'hereinafters'. Sentences are mercilessly long and paragraphs almost unheard of. Bear in mind what I say in Chapter 5 on copy style – sometimes the use of high-flown language can help you create the right 'image'.

EMBOSSING Embossing is popular. Even today certain company documents have to be 'sealed', with a hand-embosser over a red stick-on seal. These look very good, but can work out to be expensive.

PAPER Last but not least, paper stock can also play a part. Valuable documents, such as prize draw certificates, can be usefully printed on 'antique' papers or similar heavy stocks. But it's also worth thinking about unusually flimsy papers as well.

In looking at these aspects of official documents, you will get some sense of how far you need to go in order to get the right look – like the sprocket holes on the Nomination Form mentioned earlier.

ONE-PIECE FORMATS

No discussion about formats is complete without mention of one-piece formats.

It has been for many years the tradition of direct mail that mailing packs consist of multiple items enclosed in an envelope: a tradition that arose quite simply because that is what works best.

This, however, is expensive. Some years ago, enterprising printers in the US and Germany began to design machines that would produce the whole piece 'in-line'…a web (or roll) of paper would enter at one end, get printed, then in the same continuous run would be perforated, cut, folded and enveloped – even the addressing could be carried out in the same in-line operation through attaching high speed ink-jet printers or laser printers. This made the production of such packages much faster, cut out a lot of handling and therefore reduced the costs.

You had to accept one small compromise, though. The mailing was one piece – you had to pull on a 'tear here' strip to separate the items, and even then some of the items were attached to each other.

This seemed like a small price to pay. The dramatic reductions in costs and timings were more than enough to tempt many people to try this new technology.

The sheer variety of sizes and styles open to the designer was also a considerable influence. So for quite some time the direct mail world was full of one-piece ideas.

The idea ultimately failed, or at least did so in the majority of cases. The problem was – and still is – a simple one. The grand old tradition of making direct mail full of odd pieces of paper still worked better – the way in which multi-part mailings can separate different benefits and dramatise them proved unbeatable.

In fact, in several tests of one-piece v conventional multiple packs that I am aware of, the multiple packs outperformed the one-piecers – and by outperformed I mean in cost-efficiency terms. Thus even the lower costs of one-piece mailers were insufficient to outweigh their lack of responsiveness. Probably the only area when one-piecers might work better is for generating enquiries, rather than sales: proceed with caution before you get seduced by low costs and technology.

THE RESULT IS THAT FOR MOST PURPOSES, A ONE-PIECE MAILER SHOULD NOT BE CONSIDERED AND A CONVENTIONAL MULTIPLE PACK USED INSTEAD.

Of course there are times when one-piece mailers can be used; inserts, with their restrictive weight considerations, often need to be one-piece. But even when used, the closer you can get to a conventional multiple pack, the better the result you will tend to get. Try if at all possible to design a pack that doesn't need 'tear-off' strips to separate the pieces.

PERSONALISATION

The excitement of personalisation is long gone. Nowadays modern data manipulation techniques and high speed, high quality laser printers allow most personalisation techniques to be freely employed. However, the basic themes of personalisation have not really changed.

With laser printers than can virtually replicate print quality, you now have the opportunity to put people's names in type, rather than just typewriting. And for the vast majority of the population, the effect of *seeing* their name 'in print' is extraordinarily strong.

This is a technique that allied to your choice of format can give you some exciting packages. In addition, the use of *other* data where appropriate can add greatly to the impact: this is something that has worked well in loan mailings, where we use, for example, the exact amount of repayment that individual would need to make to clear an existing loan and take out a new one.

LUMPY BITS YOU CAN FEEL THROUGH THE ENVELOPE

Creating a mailing where you can feel lumps through the envelope can often prove very successful. All sorts of extra bits can be added to the basic format – plastic cards, rub-offs, pens, address labels, the most famous is probably Digest's 5p piece (which started life as a shilling). Most of these techniques work, but remember that they will add hugely to the cost of the pack, and therefore you need to modify your whole format to make the most of such a device. Digest's 5p piece mailing is designed *around* the coin – the coin is not an after-thought – and thus the idea will work a great deal better.

MAKE MORE OF YOUR MAILING

These are just some of the possibilities open to you when you take a careful look at formats. It is one of the most truly creative aspects of the direct mail designer's job, and it is an area where a little thought can make a profound difference to responses.

There is never an excuse for making a mailing that is just a plain DL envelope with a letter and the reply form inside, unless you have reached such heights of database skill that the letter is so personalised as to be in effect a real 'one-to-one' letter. Few mailings even remotely approach that level of expertise, and thus you should be using your format ideas to make opening and reading a mailing a rather more exciting experience for your prospect than just opening and reading another dull letter ■

Chapter 8: Summary

The format is one of the most critical decisions in creating a direct mail package. Changes to format alone can result in considerable changes to response rates.

Before beginning to write or design a mailing, you must have a clear proposition to work with, but you must also have worked out your format too.

The best formats are born from the proposition. The two should be inextricably linked. A proposition should also automatically give rise to a format that can best communicate it.

Typically, formats based around 'official documents' do best: cheques, share certificates, invitations. But these only work well if great attention to detail is used. In order to make an imitation official document work, you need to study real official documents and copy the styles they use.

One-piece mailers rarely work as well as conventional multiple formats, and should not be used unless there are compelling reasons to do so – possibly weight restrictions on inserts.

Personalisation should work hand-in-hand with the format. A good direct mail format will employ personalisation not just for name and address but also for other personal data as well. But remember, people still love seeing their names 'in print'.

CREATIVITY AND COST

*In approaching the creation of a direct mail package, insert
or broadcast ad, a crucial factor needs to be taken into
account: the 'allowable' cost of promotion. Around this hinges
the basic approach you can take. It is not just a matter of
creating a low cost pack when the allowable is slim; equally
important is identifying when the allowable is high, thus
enabling the creation of a stronger pack.*

Y OU will probably have heard the often-quoted story of the creative team who started every commercial they wrote with: "Open on a deserted palm-fringed beach with the blue sea lapping in the background…", be the commercial for toilet rolls or tea bags!

The world of the direct marketing creative team may not provide quite so many opportunities for such glamour, but it does provide opportunities for creative people to more intelligently exploit the possibilities of direct marketing if they take the trouble to understand the financial side.

By understanding the underlying financial mechanics of direct marketing, creative people can approach the task of creation with a greater chance of success. Clearly, there will be many times when keeping the costs down to a certain acceptable level will mean that the pack simply has to work *less hard* in order to succeed. More challengingly, making that pack even cheaper may significantly improve the performance of the piece – and there can be as much creativity in reducing the pack cost as in redesigning a whole new one.

But as I shall go on to demonstrate, *simply reducing costs is not by any means the only route to success*. In fact, the case for actually spending *more* money on creativity is often compelling. Few people appreciate this simple fact, yet once understood it can provide as strong a way of actually improving cost-per-response as in cutting costs. This may sound like financial suicide to the more conservative direct marketer, yet there are very many cases where this approach has worked.

Let's look at the financial structure of direct mail in more detail, in order to understand these points.

DIRECT MAIL COSTS MONEY

Direct Mail is certainly the most expensive advertising medium available, in terms of 'cost-per-target' type calculations. Discount postage charges for a mailing are around £122 per thousand people. In contrast, a 30 second TV commercial going out during the daytime will cost around £3.40 per thousand viewers; and a whole page press ad in a national newspaper will be reaching those same 1,000 people for just £2.90; in other words, the media cost of direct mail is some 3,400% more than TV.

These numbers may help to put direct mail into context. However, in the world of the direct marketer, it is not 'opportunities-to-see' that is important, but 'cost-per-response' that is critical. In other words, how much is it costing me to generate a reply? Unless it costs less than the immediate or short-term profit that reply generates, the whole exercise is going to be a financial waste.

Although on an 'opportunity-to-see' basis direct mail is expensive, once you look at it on a cost-per-reply basis, it becomes a great deal more attractive, mainly because it is more targeted – the people seeing it are more likely to buy from direct mail than from press or TV, and thus cost-efficiency is greater.

In fact, direct mail has very much higher cost-efficiency than most other media. Only press approaches it for cost-efficiency…but press cannot compete with direct mail for sheer *volume* of replies. In some cases, inserts can be as good – both in cost and volume.

ALLOWABLE

Given the revenue potential of a marketing exercise – the amount of profit needed to break-even on a direct promotion – it then becomes easy to follow the concept of the 'allowable' – direct marketing jargon for 'allowable cost per reply'. *The allowable is quite simply the amount of money you think you can afford to spend to generate a reply* – and from this number, the whole creative side *has* to follow.

In every campaign, an 'allowable' is easily worked out. This is mainly the expected gross revenue generated, less the required profit, giving you net revenue; the cost of the promotion must therefore be equal to or less than this figure.

If you exceed this sum, you cannot hope to succeed. However good your creative is, you will never be able to generate sufficient numbers of replies in order to pay the costs of the piece. Your response would have to be impossibly high simply to break-even.

A FATAL FLAW

But as I said earlier, simply reducing cost-per-thousand is not always the best way to improve cost-efficiency. The logic has a fatal flaw.

The flaw is that *increasing* the costs of package does not always *worsen* the cost-per-reply: it only does so if you make the misleading assumption that the response rate *remains exactly the same*. This is the problem – sometimes increasing the costs of package provides so much *extra* marketing leverage that in fact the response rate rises faster than the cost, thus (sometimes) dramatically improving cost-efficiency.

Let's look at a case:

■ A pack costing £500 per thousand mailed to 100,000 people at a response rate of 1% gives a cost per reply of £50. (1% of 100,000 = 1,000, total cost £500 times 100 = £50,000, therefore cost per reply 1,000 into £50,000 = £50.)

We will assume that £50 is the allowable cost per reply, and no more can be permitted. So what happens if the pack is more expensive?

■ A pack costing £600 per thousand mailed to 100,000 people at a response rate of 1% gives a cost per reply of £60.

Fig. 37:
More margin can mean more space to sell.

Products with high margins are usually expensive; this means that to sell them you need maximum marketing 'leverage' – which you can afford given that the margin is high…a sort of virtuous circle. This Compton and Woodhouse figurine sells for £138. Tried in a single page version and a double page spread, the DPS works considerably better than the single page. The main reason is that the DPS isn't just a blown-up version of the single page. It contains a lot more copy and a lot more illustrations, adding more marketing leverage. Few people in direct marketing think that making things more expensive is a good idea – yet when the margin can take it, it can often make a big difference. Incidentally, using a DPS means you get more sales per 'hit' – you can't repeat ads all that often, so DPSs generate higher overall volumes.

cretly buys Ferranti bombs

quipment be withheld, although the deal has been approved by Whitehall and Washington, according to sources in the defence industry.

Approaches were first made to Abu Dhabi in the early 1980s by James Guerin, then head of International Signal and Control, a Pennsylvania-based company. They were taken up by Ferranti after the British company took over ISC in 1987.

The Hakim missile, Arabic for "the Wise One", is guided on to its target by data fed into a kind of television camera on its nose.

There have been reports of difficulties attaching the bomb to the UAE air force's French-made Mirage 2000s. The system is currently being tested on American F-16 aircraft in the United States. But sources insisted yesterday that the contract was not in trouble, that it was running to schedule, and was operating satisfactorily.

In an oblique reference to the project last December, Eugene Anderson, the chairman of Ferranti, told shareholders the company's aerospace division was making good progress in its missile business. "Deliveries are scheduled ahead of contractual requirements," he said.

Allegedly outstanding contracts raised the purchase price of ISC, but, when these appeared non-existent after the takeover, Ferranti was forced to sell £400 million worth of its assets to fill a hole in its balance sheet. Mr Guerin is now facing charges for fraud in the US amid allegations that, before Ferranti took over the US company, ISC missile technology was also supplied to South Africa in breach of sanctions.

The UAE deal has been questioned within the defence industry, on the grounds that it is an expensive way of providing Gulf states with bombs which could have been bought elsewhere off the shelf.

● The Prime Minister is to propose a registry of arms sales, administered by the United Nations to monitor weapons build-ups, when the seven leading industrial nations meet in London in July, officials said yesterday.

Cynicism and the culture of secrecy, page 23

Allies' pullout worries Kurds

Kathy Evans in Amman and Chris Stephen in Sirsenk, northern Iraq

SUGGESTIONS by US military commanders in northern Iraq that an allied pullout could begin as soon as mid-June may prompt a fresh exodus of terrified Kurds into the mountains along the Turkish and Iranian borders, according to Kurdish leaders.

The warnings come as talks between the Iraqi government and Kurdish leaders in Baghdad appear to be deadlocked, raising fears of an allied withdrawal before a full settlement to the Kurdish crisis.

Until now, the Kurdish delegation has put a brave face on the progress of the talks to ensure their continuity. Now, however, Kurdish officials in Damascus say that Masoud Barzani, who is leading the talks, is planning to return to the north for consultations with other Kurdish leaders.

The first sign that the talks were not proceeding smoothly came two weeks ago when Kurdish officials admitted the Iraqis had not accepted basic Kurdish demands on the extent of the autonomous region and the status of cities in the area, including Kirkuk.

This apparent deadlock comes as America's top officer, General Colin Powell, wound up a tour of Kurdish refugee camps on Thursday by saying that US troops may begin pulling out sooner than expected.

His remarks followed earlier comments from local US commanders that the main pullout will start on June 15.

The US Marine 24th expeditionary unit has already begun to withdraw and almost all the American special forces have now left. One of the two British Royal Marine Commando battalions, 45 Commando, is preparing to leave.

Ten of the 15 RAF Chinook helicopters deployed have already left, as has their support unit.

US commanders say that with the relief effort being scaled down because most Kurds are out of the camps, the operation can be handed over to civilians by mid-June, barring unforeseen problems.

US spokesmen stress that combat troops will remain only as long as it takes for the logistic forces to leave, and will not remain to provide security for the Kurds. Instead a UN force of 500 guards with side arms is to act as a monitoring group.

Many observers believe Kurdish civilians will panic at the prospect of any allied withdrawal, and will return to the mountains.

Hoshyar Zebari, a senior KDP spokesman in London, warned yesterday of a new exodus if Iraq thought the allied pullout was going to start soon.

"The US is sending the wrong signals, encouraging Baghdad to harden its position in the belief that the allied forces are soon to withdraw. Humanitarian assistance alone will not solve the issue, there has to be a political solution. By pulling out before a political solution, they are inviting disaster."

Hard homecoming, page 10

Fig. 38:
Less margin less space to sell.

Where margins are small, as they inevitably are in charity ads, the need is to then minimise costs. Too often creative people get carried away with 'good causes' and for the sake of their own egos want to use large spaces. They cannot work (except in the rare cases of emergency appeals) and anyone using large spaces for appeal ads is simply wasting money. Here's a small space ad for EthiopiAid, taking up the prime position of the Guardian front page solus, 20cm x 2cols. Ads like this will typically produce a small number of replies, but the replies will be generated at around break-even or a little better, meaning that names are added to the file at zero net cost.

Leaving the response rate the same adds considerably to the cost, and would turn a break-even result into a considerable failure.

But let's question the assumption that the response rate will stay the same if you spend that extra £100 per thousand.

Clearly, if you spend the extra £100 on creative elements that cannot in themselves significantly improve response, then of course the above scenario will happen. *All you will have done is increase the cost, but not the response.* Such creative elements that do not improve response can typically – but not always – be things such as *excessive* photography or illustration costs.

SPENDING MORE TO IMPROVE COST PER REPLY

But if you use that extra budget to put more 'selling power' into the package, you can actually *improve the response rate consistent with the increase in cost per response.* Thus:

■ a pack costing £600k mailed to 100,000 people at 1.2% response will produce a cost per reply of £50.

Costs have increased by 20%, but the response increase of 20%, from 1% to 1.2% to pay for it, is perfectly reasonable to expect.

You also get, importantly, the very great additional benefit of 1,200 replies from your mailing, instead of 1,000; the cost per reply remains the same so the break-evens are not sacrificed, but you actually do *more* business volume for your effort.

Does this approach really work? The answer is yes – but as I hope I have made clear above, you have to be very careful and very certain that what you are proposing will *improve* responses, not simply increase the costs. This is a very delicate judgement, and should not be attempted if you are in any real doubt.

Following this line of reasoning, it is, of course, possible to cripple a mailing by actually spending *too little* on the package. It becomes so skimpy that it lacks the necessary selling power.

THE LOW COST TRAP

There is a syndrome amongst direct marketers which, while logical, draws you inexorably into this trap. Rather than thinking about ways that creativity alone can improve pack results, the temptation is to reduce pack costs each time the mailing goes out. This works only for so long: eventually the pack reaches a point where it does not contain sufficient marketing leverage to do the job, and the result is that results get worse. This is often hidden, mostly in the early stages of this process, by the fact that large reductions in cost do indeed improve cost-per-reply. But eventually volumes begin to shrink, and after a few seasons there is no more room for savings to be made.

Believe it or not, I have actually seen cases where companies have dramatically *reduced* mailing volumes as a result of that syndrome – no power on Earth could convince them that by spending more, they would actually start to see an improvement in results. Indeed, one well-known company stopped cold direct mail completely because, after season after season of cost-reductions, the mailings ended up not working at all. To this day, that company is convinced that cold direct mail does not work, while all round it their competitors are pouring out the stuff with great success! Sometimes, the propensity of direct marketers to be logical can be as dangerous as the propensity of cats to be curious.

TURNING UP THE SELLING POWER

But now I need to add in some strong cautions and clarify what I am saying before anyone accuses me of just wanting to spend money.

As I said earlier, there are things that although they cost more do not add very much (if anything) to response rates. Here are some of the more common ways of spending money in direct marketing *without* seeing any huge return in results:

- paying for a logo in colour even though the rest of the item is black and white
- commissioning expensive illustrators because they are in fashion
- creating a lavish brochure and ignoring everything else
- adding more paper to carry product details that are of little interest to the recipient
- having to print in more colours than necessary or use shapes and types of stock that wouldn't otherwise be chosen because of the corporate ID requirements
- spending time and money on photographic backgrounds at the expense of the object being photographed
- spending money purely on artistic 'production values'

You can make your own list of favourite cardinal sins; underlying all of mine above is nothing more than a lack of understanding of what really makes a *difference* to response. So here are some of the things that really *will* make a difference, and are therefore worth spending money on:

- using unusual (i.e. not stock) envelopes
- putting more pieces of paper in the envelope, not less, so long as there's a strong message for all of them
- increasing the amount of copy, particularly the letter
- making the reply form more significant
- Yes/No envelopes in prize draw mailings
- adding flyers (for free gifts, testimonials, etc)
- using better photography if you're selling hard merchandise
- using better typography to make your message more easily comprehended

Any or all of these techniques will add a great deal more to your response than any of the techniques described in the first list – and yet too often these are the first to go when the pack cost is considered too high.

This is a great mistake. It's a bit like saying that a car is too expensive and taking out the engine to reduce the cost. If costs have to be cut, remove those things that do not make a substantial difference to performance, even if you don't have quite such a luxurious pack at the end of it.

This process – of adding rather than taking away – can be referred to as adding 'marketing leverage'. With a higher allowable, you can afford more selling effort, thus applying more leverage to the mailing. As seen above, it is the important things – such as long copy and more items – that act as the levers.

THE HIGHER THE ALLOWABLE, THE GREATER
THE CHANCE OF SUCCESS

Obviously, therefore, a direct mail pack's ability to succeed runs in direct proportion to the amount of 'selling power' you can include. The higher the allowable, the greater selling power can be included, and the more chance of success.

If the allowable turns out to be so low that all you can afford is a short letter and a reply device, your chances of success in direct mail are frankly low for this very reason.

This is why FMCG companies who try direct mail run into a massive problem: with most of their products, the allowables are so tiny as to make even the postage difficult to pay for, let alone a message at the same time.

Conversely, where the allowable turns out to be high, and the creative people take full and proper advantage of the fact, the success rate is in proportion.

ONLY SOME PRODUCTS OR SERVICES CAN EVER
BE SOLD THROUGH DIRECT MAIL

Insurance and financial products have been one of the greatest success stories of direct mail mainly because their allowables are so high.

In the old days of insurance salesmen and brokers, the seller was paid a commission by the company not only on the original premium paid, but on every *subsequent* premium paid afterwards. Slowly this system eroded, but once direct selling was adopted, this same commission payment was no longer paid to an intermediary and was left back 'in the pot', for the benefit of the company.

This made the allowables extremely high. In any event, so long as the actuaries get the odds in their favour, the cash generated by a steady income of premiums over the years is so massive that the cash alone, duly invested, makes a great deal of money. The balance sheets of most insurance companies are strong as a direct result of the economics of selling insurance – one transaction, one marketing cost, and then years of regular premiums afterwards.

With economics like this, the response rates required to make most insurance products break even are very low, and the amount spent in order to generate those responses can afford to be relatively high.

Thus the package the financial mechanics allow you to create becomes correspondingly strong. You can afford an unusual envelope, a long letter, a free gift or two, a colour brochure, a lasered reply piece and sometimes a gimmick item. Yet with all this selling power behind it, the response rates are still as a percentage low – imagine how much lower they would be with what remains for most people an inherently low-interest subject if the package itself could not generate a high degree of interest.

Fig. 39:
High margin fundraising. Not all fundraising is low margin – here's a case where the very high potential demanded a very expensive pack. A compiled list of wealthy people was put together for the NSPCC, and it was decided to mail them looking for big gifts – £1,000 was the 'prompt' level compared to the 'normal' £15. The principle of marketing leverage needed to apply – the outer envelope was personalised, the inner letter was personalised, and the expensively-bound 'brochure' not only had the recipient's name written on it, but also had bound-in copies of letters from The Prime Minister, Princess Margaret, Frederick Forsyth and other notable people. This was an expensive pack by any standards. It was not flashy, but spent money to give the impression that it was a document put together especially for the recipient. However, it was an immense financial success – the first mailing managed to get a single donation of £200,000! Clearly good targetting played the major role, but cheaper creative could have lessened the effect.

Sir Brian Batsford
Buckland House
Mill Rd
Winchelsea
E Sussex
TN36 4HJ

The Rt. Hon. The Lord Jakobovits
Chief Rabbi

Alder House
Tavistock Square
London WC1H 9HN

. . . . . . t 1989

:o you and your

have a deep and
happy to have this
enterprise to help
m, who may even

ces of the NSPCC
am also aware that
with a total

d to be involved in
essings for your

10 DOWNING STREET
LONDON SW1A 2AA

THE PRIME MINISTER

et even
n brutally
r 80

terrible
bjected to
ng for   ts - the
ying   mfort and
port we   of

ometimes   this
n how   luable one
eed to   k very
                ren. And
ull   ssional
nd   SPCC
                lready

KENSINGTON PALACE
W.8

Sir Brian Batsford

NSPCC

The National Society
for the Prevention of
Cruelty to Children

67 Saffron Hill
London EC1N 8RS
Telephone 071-242 1626

Sir Brian Batsford
Buckland House
Mill Rd
Winchelsea
E Sussex
TN36 4HJ

Dear Sir Brian,

I know you are a busy person and that the demands on
your time and resources may be many. But I am writing to
you because I believe you are in a unique position to help.

In Spring of next year, the NSPCC is planning to open
its new Child Protection Line.

Very simply, for the first time, a free, national, 24
hour telephone line will enable anyone concerned about the
protection of children - including children themselves -
to contact us at any time of the day or night.

The NSPCC Child Protection Line is a tremendously
important breakthrough for the Society. It will
provide us with a powerful new weapon in the fight to
protect innocent children from the cruelty and
violence they face every day.

A single glance at the statistics shows how pressing
the need for such a service has become. An estimated 3 to 4
children die every week in this country at the hands of
parents or guardians.

But the simple truth is that if we are to
transform our plans for the NSPCC Child Protection Line
into reality, we need urgent financial support.

Indeed, setting up the service and running it for 5
years will cost the NSPCC in excess of £6,000,000,
through training, overheads and equipment.

I am asking you to help us achieve that target, by
pledging a personal gift to the Society now, of
£1,000.

It seems a substantial sum of money, I know. But in
fact, it could cost you as little as £16.67 a month, if you
choose to covenant your gift over a period of 4 years.

To be frank, you are one of the very few people I
feel I can call on to help children in this way. But I feel
certain that, once you have read about this vitally

NSPCC | PLEDGE FORM

the details below and return this form in the envelope provided.

To: Christopher Brown, Director, NSPCC

be a donation of £1,000 to support the NSPCC Child Protection Line
(If other please indicate amount) £_____

Postcode

gift by: ☐ Covenant   ☐ Corporate Giving

eone to contact me to discuss the most tax-efficient way

number is _____
tacted in person. Please send me information about the various
donation

rown, Director, NSPCC, 67 Saffron Hill, London EC1N 8RS.

er Majesty The Queen, Her Majesty Queen Elizabeth The Queen Mother.
Her Royal Highness The Princess Margaret Countess of Snowdon.
ve Committee Michael Moore.
Christopher Brown.
84. Incorporated by Royal Charter, Charity Registration No. 216401.

THE VALUE OF CONTINUITY

Insurance falls into one of those product lines that have continuity – the income stream generated by the first sale is automatic and continuous. The allowable cost-per-reply is affected, in fact, less by the allowable on the first transaction than on the sum of the subsequent transactions – the 'life-time value'.

The great advantage of selling by a continuity method is that life-time value is *locked in*…you are not dependent on the success of further promotions to make your money. The income is automatic.

Here are some of the other areas where the income stream is continuous and automatic:

MAGAZINE SUBSCRIPTIONS

You normally get at least 12 payments, and if you get your subscriber to sign a Direct Debit (DD) your life-time value can extend considerably beyond that without too much repromotion. This is one of the highest margins possible in the business – just multiply the value of a Which? magazine subscription, over say a 24 month period, and you'll see the considerable income stream that just one subscription will produce. This is exactly why Which? mailings are so lavish – they can afford to be, and they work better as a result.

CREDIT CARDS

Once the card is issued (and here you have to take into account gross and net response – the difference being what the card issuer rejects) and usage starts you have like insurance an almost endless supply of income to pay your initial promotion costs.

One of the main problems in the past has been getting reliable statistics that show just what the life-time value really is, considering the large number of people who pay off their card in full each month and who do not therefore provide any income at all. The recent move by card issuers to charge for their cards now makes them more like magazine subscribers, dependent to some extent on renewal rates, but still locking in an income stream.

Charge cards such as Amex always had this benefit, of course. Little wonder that Amex and other credit cards are such efficient users of direct mail.

BOOK CLUBS

Probably the very first continuity sale operation ever. Here the task is to recruit a member who makes a certain commitment to buy, and then through deft re-promotion can be persuaded to buy and buy again. The success of this system is evidenced by the fact that Book Club Associates in Britain is the largest spender on media of any direct marketing company. That they can afford to 'give away' 3 books for 25p shows how much allowable is built in.

MAIL ORDER CATALOGUES

This had for some time been regarded as the 'dying' end of the mail business by those city (and direct marketing) pundits who see the glories of the Next Directory as the way forward. While Next Directory is no doubt a nice production, it is a relatively minor by-product of the massive success of agency mail order. Indeed, the Europeans

(Otto in Germany and La Redoute in France) have recognised this by buying up any available mail order catalogue concern in the UK.

The great advantage of agency mail order is, again, *continuity:* the first sale is but the start of a long relationship, wher the 'agent' continues to buy for not only herself but for others as well – the average is 1½ customers per agent. This is why, of course, the massive cost of a 900 page catalogue can be accommodated: in agency mail order, the promotional cost includes the catalogue itself (at around £5 or £6 a go), which gives an indication of the power of this method.

CONTINUITY SELLING

Continuity selling can include a variety of products. Time-Life Books, Compton and Woodhouse china collectables, Odhams Knitting Cards, are all examples of the genre. It's a bit like a Book Club – the customer buys item number one, and has either an explicit or implicit obligation to buy additional items in the series.

Because the allowable is judged against the series rather than the first sale, the promotional effort can afford to be greater than if it was limited by the first sale alone: and with more allowable giving more creative power, the responses are better. Hence the success of operations of this type.

USING FINANCIALS TO HELP CREATIVITY

It is of critical importance that creative people understand the underlying financial mechanics of these systems. It will radically affect the way you can approach the creation of a mailing.

If you know the allowable is *low*, you should create one type of mailing. If you know the allowable is *high*, you can create another type of mailing.

In fact, some of the best creative work comes from an ability to distinguish several types of financial structure which will affect the mailing you produce:

■ LEVEL 1: LOW INITIAL ALLOWABLE, LITTLE ADDITIONAL INCOME AND NOT AUTOMATIC – CAN ONLY BE PRODUCED BY FURTHER PROMOTION. This is the most difficult one because you have to produce the strongest pack you can with as little money spent as possible. Most charities fall into this camp.

■ LEVEL 2: LOW INITIAL ALLOWABLE, REASONABLE ADDITIONAL INCOME BUT INCOME HAS TO BE GENERATED. Again, difficult but if you can get statistics on repurchase rates you can begin to put a little more into the package than you could otherwise. Some charities can be in this category, but typically they will be more experienced charities where the life-time value, although not automatic, is fairly certain.

■ LEVEL 3: LOW INITIAL ALLOWABLE, GOOD ADDITIONAL INCOME EITHER SEMI-AUTOMATIC OR AUTOMATIC which includes Book Clubs, most continuity series and agency mail order. One of the easiest areas, but the initial cost of promotion needs to be watched carefully because although income is long-term, margins can be very fine and a slight shift can spell real problems.

■ LEVEL 4: HIGH INITIAL, HIGH SUBSEQUENT INCOME ON AN ALMOST ALWAYS AUTOMATIC BASIS. Insurance, credit cards, magazine subscriptions and memberships normally belong in this category, although levels of sophistication will exist within the category that will either limit or expand your creative possibilities.

If in starting your creative work you can determine in which category your client lies, you will have saved yourself a lot of later problems – either in not creating a pack which the results would never be able to justify, or in not creating a pack which uses so little of the power that could be used that results are indifferent.

The creative team needs to be able to look at the maths. No writer or art director should ever be able to say that they do not understand the term 'allowable', and no-one claiming to be truly professional in this business should start to create a pack until they know exactly what that allowable is, and what the future income stream is likely to be.

VERY HIGH ALLOWABLE PRODUCTS

There is a further category not mentioned above which should be discussed. This is the product which with the first sale alone carries a high allowable: by definition, the very high cost product.

Many people are nervous about taking the cost of products above, say £100, in direct marketing. But to the right type of file (almost always a house file, but not exclusively so) you can sell very high value products with a remarkable degree of success. The key is again within the allowable. Although you do not have the constant income stream from a continuity programme, the margin on your single sale is so high that you can afford to put *real selling power* into the piece.

This is the 'virtuous circle' working for you again. The higher the allowable, the more selling effort you can afford, the better the result you will get.

Franklin Mint have been one of the greatest exponents of this art, selling items with a price of in excess of £5,000 in a single mailing. The mailing was correspondingly lavish. You need less than a dozen responses at £5,000 a time to get your promotional costs back again, however much you spend on the package.

£1,000 GRANDFATHER CLOCK

WWAV undertook a similar exercise for Kaleidoscope, the mail order company, whose average order value was under £100. We suggested to John Wallis who was running Kaleidoscope at the time that we should do a 'one-shot' mailing selling a reproduction Grandfather Clock he had found. John looked a little worried at the idea of selling this clock, because we'd have to charge nearly £1,000 for each clock. He was less worried when we showed him the mailing: because we realised the allowable was so high, we created a correspondingly strong mailing: a 12 page brochure with superb colour photographs of every detail of this clock, and a vast amount of copy; a long letter; a large order form. It was an expensive mailing, and frankly had to be so: would anyone spend nearly £1,000 unless they were sufficiently impressed by the product?

It goes without saying that the mailing worked extremely well.

Fig. 40:
Sales worth millions.
Most business-to-business mailings are selling much greater margin products than consumer mailings, so it's surprising that there's so many cheap and nasty business-to-business mailings around. Usually a much more up-market approach is well worth taking, as with this pack for IBM, which aims to generate leads for the AS/400 computer, one of the most successful mid-range computers of all time. Prices for an AS/400 installation range from £50,000 to over £1 million, so even one successful lead from a mailing is going to be worth applying a lot of effort to get. The mailing consists not only of the personalised letter, but also a very classy silver brochure containing press cuttings, a product brochure and the 'Cost of Ownership' form – basically the reply piece made to look like a questionnaire. Clearly, for a company like IBM, image is important – but this mailing doesn't just spend money to create a nice look…it uses the budget to provide the maximum marketing effort by providing high-quality information to the reader, and by asking for a high-quality reply.

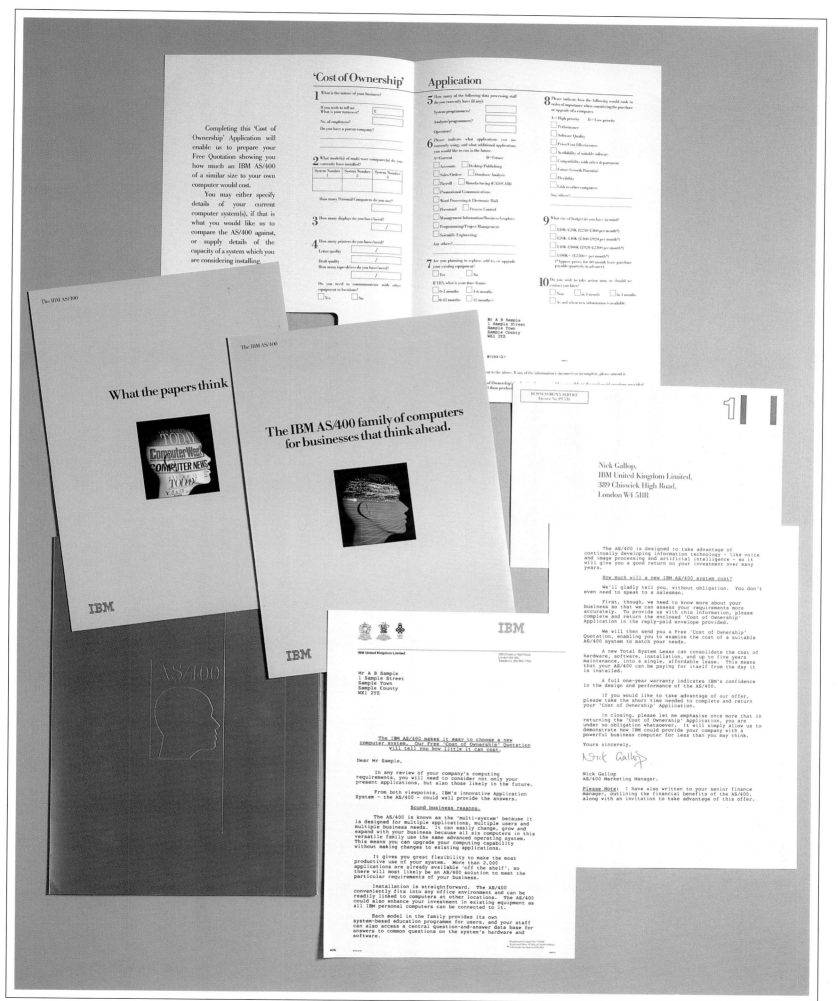

In another case, at the suggestion of Giles Pegram of the NSPCC, we created a 'big gift' mailing for the charity. Here we used a carefully researched list of wealthy people, and ended up mailing a small number of them a very expensive package. The package consisted of a number of facsimile letters from eminent people praising the work of the NSPCC, together with detailed case histories, and the need for money. It was a well argued case, heavily supported by a mass of detail. All of the information was contained in a folder, which had the recipient's name written on the front.

A CHEQUE FOR £200,000

A package costing this much for ordinary charity mailings could not hope to succeed. of course. But here we were specifically going for individual donations in excess of £1,000 or more. We would never persuade people to part with that sum of money through the post unless we were prepared to put a lot of power into the mailing.

The results exceeded anybody's expectations. Most extraordinarily of all, our list included a well-known author who had just published his latest best-seller. As a result of the mailing he sent a cheque for £200,000 ■

CHAPTER 9: SUMMARY

Prior to starting your creative work, you need to establish what the allowable is – the amount of money you can spend on each sale in order to leave a profit at the end of the promotion.

If it is low, you must ensure that you put as much selling power in as you can by reducing costs in those areas that are not truly vital; not by simply cutting out valuable selling space.

But just as importantly, if the allowable is high – either on the first sale or because you have a high degree of confidence in the subsequent income stream – then you should take every opportunity to maximise selling power.

High allowable products allow you to create the virtuous circle – high allowable, more selling power, better results.

'Life-time value' can be a critical number to know. Sometimes, profit is not generated on the first response alone, but from second and subsequent responses. Knowing how much this is likely to be would greatly affect the type of creativity you can afford to use.

Creative people should involve themselves in the financial mechanics of the products they sell: the more knowledge they have of just how much can be spent to generate a sale, the more they can judge the precise amount of selling power that can be afforded, thus greatly increasing the chances of success.

USING INCENTIVES

One of the most successful ways of increasing response is through the use of incentives. These can range from simple free gifts for an early reply up to massive prize draws. However, in order to make them work at all it is important that the creative techniques are designed to use them correctly. Even a strong incentive can fail if the creative treatment does not maximise the strength of the offer.

I N the Chapter regarding propositions, and in subsequent Chapters, I hope I made it clear that by bringing the proposition 'up front' your response rate would benefit accordingly.

Whatever proposition you chose, so long as it formed the major feature of both your headline, your format, your art direction and your copy – so long as all of those items hinged around that proposition – then it would have the greatest chance of success. Exactly the same logic applies to incentives.

If you decide to use an incentive, then in most cases the incentive should take over from the marketing proposition, such is the power of a properly used incentive.

The proposition then becomes, in fact, whatever offer you have decided on.

Clearly, therefore, the same creative rules need to apply: the creative task is to make *as much* of the proposition…in this case an offer of an incentive…as you would with a more conventional, product-related proposition.

The 'trick' is to be determined that your incentive becomes the proposition, even if this means moving away from the product or service itself in order to allow the incentive to become the 'hero' of the pack or ad. This can seem a little dangerous the first time you try it, but for the following reasons it really is the most successful method.

But before we look in detail at how to make the most of incentives, it's worth looking at incentives themselves to understand why they are so successful.

THE POWER OF INCENTIVES

The power of an incentive is quite astonishing. *By adding an incentive, you can quite easily double response rates.* And without too much effort, you can even improve responses by 500% or even more.

A properly used incentive can often take a loser and turn it into a winner.

Having said that, there exists a mass of prejudice in people's minds about incentives, even amongst some very experienced direct marketers. While I am not going to attempt to shift that prejudice, it's worth examining some of the 'problems' about incentives first.

Fig. 41:
Offer-oriented mailings.
This RSPB pack shows how single-minded you should be if you have decided to go for an incentive-led mailing. Note how the offer starts at the envelope (using a window to show colour) and then continues strongly throughout the pack. The front page of the letter is dominated by the offer (the letter is shown in more detail in figure 25) and the two colour items concentrate on other aspects of the offer – the main one talks about the magazine, the flyer sells the free gift. The reply form picks up the offers yet again, and even over the top of the application the offer is signalled one more time. People don't reply to mailings like these *just* because of the offer…in reality, the offer acts as a powerful prompt to make people do something they were thinking about doing anyway – thus the mailing doesn't take up the argument about the work of the RSPB, and concentrates on getting people to do something instead.

If you love birds and the British countryside…

DE444
Mr J B Glen
41 Kingfisher Rd
Weston Super Mare
Avon
BS22 8TZ

…there are offers inside you'll find irresistible…

URGENT
for an extra free gift
reply before close date

Join the RSPB today –
help Britain's birds and take advantage
of our special introductory offers now.

BIRDS

THE ROYAL SOCIETY FOR THE PROTECTION OF BIRDS
THE LODGE · SANDY · BEDFORDSHIRE · SG19 2DL · TEL: 0767 680551 · TELEX: 82469 RSPB · FAX: 0767 692365

DE483
Mrs S Bassett
3 Meadowbank
Worle
Weston Super Mare
Avon
BS22 9NR

BIRDS

Join the RSPB today and receive the official RSPB
96-page 'BIRDS' magazine absolutely free – 4 times per year…

1 Receive 'BIRDS' magazine 4 times per year – FREE
2 Gain free entry to over 100 beautiful RSPB nature reserves around the country, at no extra cost
3 You'll also be sent your FREE car sticker
4 And if you REPLY BEFORE THE CLOSE DATE you'll also receive 'The Complete Guide to British Wildlife' FREE (retail £7.99), a 287-page pocket guide to Britain's natural history

Dear Mrs Bassett,

Do you really care about birds and wildlife? Good! Because I'd like to invite you to become a member of The Royal Society for the Protection of Birds.

I'd also like to offer you the superb Collins 'Complete Guide to British Wildlife', a 287-page colour guide to virtually all our wildlife. Published at £7.99, it's yours absolutely free - but only if you reply before 26th February 1993.

Why am I making these offers? Quite simply, because the threats facing birds today are greater than ever, and the RSPB needs your support right now...and offers like these are a marvellous way of prompting people who really care to act now. And you get important benefits too:

* Your RSPB membership card gives you FREE admittance to over

YOURS FREE
IF YOU REPLY BY
26 FEBRUARY 1993

The complete guide to
British Wildlife

Patron Her Majesty the Queen President Ian Prestt Chairman of Council Adrian Darby Chief Executive Barbara Young
0000141

INVITATION to MEMBERSHIP

for Mr J B Glen

Joining the RSPB does more than just help protect Britain's birds and wildlife…it brings you important benefits too!

1 Free entry to over 100 RSPB nature reserves
Your membership card entitles you to entry, at no charge, to over 100 beautiful RSPB nature reserves where you'll see Britain's birds and wildlife at their best

2 'BIRDS' magazine 4 times per year
As an RSPB member, you'll automatically receive award-winning 'BIRDS' magazine, published every quarter, with nearly 100 pages in each issue, packed with colour photography

3 Free RSPB car sticker
An attractive self-adhesive car sticker to show you care about Britain's birds, sent to you with your membership pack

FREE – but only if you reply before the close date
The Collins 'Complete Guide to British Wildlife', a superb 287-page colour guide to almost every bird, flower, mammal, fish and even fungus in Britain. Published at £7.99, it's yours free if you reply before 26 February 1993

THIS IS YOUR MEMBERSHIP ACCEPTANCE FORM. DETACH AND POST IN ENVELOPE PROVIDED.

Membership Acceptance for:

Mr J B Glen
41 Kingfisher Rd
Weston Super Mare
Avon
BS22 8TZ

DE444
SEE OVERLEAF FOR MEMBERSHIP TYPE FOR YOU

00312/0000139/4

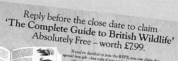

Reply before the close date to claim
'The Complete Guide to British Wildlife'
Absolutely Free – worth £7.99.

The complete guide to
British Wildlife
N Arlott · R Fitter · A Fitter

Urgent

The Royal Society for the Protection of Birds
FREEPOST
The Lodge
Sandy
Bedfordshire
SG19 2BR

A stamp will save us paying postage. Thank you.

Action for Birds

PRODUCED ON RECYCLED PAPER

DO INCENTIVES CHEAPEN THE IMAGE?

Firstly, there is no evidence to suggest that incentives cheapen the image. To understand why, you have to look deeper into the question of why incentives work at all.

Let us take a simple case of a press ad for a fashion mail order catalogue company, featuring a whole page full of incentives, one of the stronger uses of incentivisation that you will see. In fact, there is more incentive than there is catalogue – for good reasons which I shall come back to later.

In looking at the advertisement, you might expect that almost anyone replying is interested only in the premium. The image has surely suffered, and this would be clearly shown by a poor conversion rate – the great number of enquirers attracted by the gifts would not purchase from the catalogue at a reasonable rate, because they are more attracted by the gifts than the catalogue.

Interestingly, ads like these – very strongly incentivised – regularly run against 'fashion' ads. Fashion ads are those that concentrate wholly on image, showing the types of clothes available in the catalogue, but without any mention of incentives at all. We therefore have a useful and precise comparison between the performance of incentive ads and non-incentive ads.

One would suppose that if the image is damaged, by the time the catalogue arrives there will be a marked difference between the buying performance of those people who came in on one ad and those who came in on the other.

There is another very good way of judging quality between these two approaches. Responders to both ads are credit screened as a matter of course, which produces 'accepts' and 'rejects' in the terminology of the mail order business. Again, if you hold the theory that incentives damage quality and image, you would once more expect to see a higher 'reject' rate on the incentives advertisement than on the fashion advertisement.

INCENTIVE v NON-INCENTIVE: THE FACTS

So, what actually happens?

> *The incentive advertisement works about twice as well as the non-incentive advertisement in terms of actual response: the cost per response, in other words, is about twice as bad on the fashion ad as it is on the incentive ad.*

The incentive approach in this case *doubles* the response rate.

Looking at quality, the two advertisements perform about equally when it comes to 'accepts'…people who pass the credit screen. In other words, the use of incentives does not noticeably attract people who are known to be poor quality credit risk or otherwise undesirable.

Is the image damaged? This would manifest itself in poor purchasing performance. In fact, the incentive ad will produce slightly more purchasers than the non-incentive ad – let us say for the sake of the generality that they are equal.

It is clear, then, that *the use of incentives does not appear to affect 'image'* as defined by propensity to buy one way or the other. This is also borne out by the fact that the average order values are more or less equal too.

And while you can of course argue that this is a special case, the fact remains that in almost every case I have seen – up-market, down-market, consumer or business – the use of incentives ends up with exactly the same result: better response with no real effect on quality or image.

Having said all of that, it's worth bearing in mind companies like Freemans who don't use incentive advertising at all, and yet are highly successful. And there is some evidence to suggest that in some cases, non-incentive ads produce better quality of purchases over a longer term. However, these two swallows do not make a summer; for volume of agents, most mail order companies will rely on strongly incentivised ads, simply because they work.

Of course, I don't suppose these facts will convince those people who remain firmly wedded to the idea that image is still far more important – I suppose we should be thankful that they are leaving the marketplace free for the rest of us.

THE UNDERLYING MECHANISM OF INCENTIVES

Nevertheless, it defies all reason that quality and image remains unaffected through the use of incentivisation. But as with so many other things in the contradictory world of direct marketing, you need to look much deeper into the subject and understand the underlying mechanisms.

I think what happens is something like this: when someone looks at an incentivised ad, the fact that there is a page full of "FREEs" certainly gains their attention. But after that, there are few people who will go to the time and trouble of filling out the application form and posting it unless they have a high degree of interest in the subject being promoted. They know there is no such thing as a 'free lunch'. You will always hear tales of 'premium bandits' and people who read Competitor's Journal, and they certainly exist – but in relatively small numbers.

What happens, of course, is that the incentivisation works by gaining the attention of a prospect. It then continues to work by exerting a strong marketing leverage to get that person to reply.

> *But what it does not do is make someone reply who has not the faintest interest in the product or service you are advertising to start with.*

The logic is the same as the logic behind the proposition. It works by attracting those who are most likely to buy, a point discussed in detail in Chapter 1.

Even on a full page ad of incentives it really doesn't take the reader long to work out that it's an ad for a catalogue (particularly as you're surrounded by similar competitive ads) and therefore the reader is hardly likely to be fooled. The facts seem to demonstrate this point clearly.

Clearly, few things in life are as strong as free gifts. The sheer power of the word FREE remains unalloyed, however many times it is used. Used in an ad or a mailing, a free gift will attract the attention of a very much larger number of people than you

Fig. 42:
Incentive v non-incentive.
These 2 ads for Grattan show the alternatives between incentivised and non-incentivised propositions. The free gift ad clearly uses free gifts (a wide choice of them, one of the more successful free gift techniques). Note how they totally dominate the space – there's not even a picture of the catalogue in sight. In fact, after the gifts have been shown, there's just about room left for a coupon. The other approach uses fashion as the proposition – here, the photograph dominates, and works by attracting people who are interested in that garment and the image or 'look' it represents. Catalogue advertising like this is concentrated into short seasons, in much the same media, and thus competition is intense. Both of these approaches have their place, but free gift ads, while rarely popular with clients, typically outperform most other approaches.

Ask the AA for a quote on your
home contents *or* **buildings insurance**
and all this comes **free**!

FREE
gift...

Subject to availability.
Please allow 28 days for delivery.

This stylish digital mini travel alarm clock is yours – absolutely free – when you ask for a no-commitment AA Home Insurance quote on your home contents or buildings insurance.

FREE
quotes...

You pay nothing for your quote... but you could save a great deal!

Because with AA Home Insurance you may qualify for further discounts on our already competitive prices. We can arrange immediate cover, and we have a range of easy payment schemes.

FREE
phone call...

Ask for an AA Home Insurance quote today on your home contents or buildings insurance.

Phone today especially if your renewal date is within 30 days – your call is free – on:

0800 900 888
Ext. 1319
Or call into your local shop.

**LINES NOW OPEN
AT WEEKENDS!**
Mon – Fri 8.30am – 8.30pm,
Sat – Sun 9am – 4pm.

AA **Home
Insurance**

Certain occupations are not eligible for cover and all applications are subject to acceptance by the underwriters.
Automobile Association Insurance Services Limited.
Reg Office: Fanum House, Basingstoke, Hants RG21 2EA.
Registered Number: 2414212, England.

*Fig. 43:
If 'Free' is good,
three is better.*

This ad is one of the most successful creative styles for AA Home Insurance, particularly in small spaces. We had found out that giving free gifts was working – so on the simple theory that one FREE was working therefore 2 more would be a good idea, we ended up putting all 3 FREE's together in the same ad. Quality suffers very little – although enquiries are of course gift-oriented, the fact is that this type of approach produces many more enquiries than non-incentivised versions, thus the net gain ends up much higher than would otherwise be the case.

would otherwise manage to. Many will turn away once they discover that the offer is of no interest to them. But you're still left with many more than you would have started out with. The result is greatly improved response.

THE POWER OF INCENTIVISATION ON ACTION – THE TIME CLOSE

After the primary function of gaining attention, the second major area where incentives work is in prompting action. Figures are not actually available, but I suspect that something over half (and it could be as many as three-quarters) of the people who are convinced by an ad or a mailing simply never get around to replying – inertia is perhaps the biggest enemy of the direct marketer.

No matter how compulsive your copy is, it really does take a dramatic effort for your reader to respond. They have to be highly motivated – and because they are either at home or in the office when they read your message, there are very many other distractions around them that you have to compete with.

The offer of an incentive in this event actually prompts them to take action, even if they have already made up their minds. It may be just sufficient to tip them over the edge – to get them to remember to find an envelope and post it off. This is why, very often, you will see free gifts or other incentives tied into a time close: a double acting dose of pressure, as it were.

THE CREATIVE TECHNIQUES BEHIND SUCCESSFUL OFFERS

I hope by now I have convinced you that incentives are a good idea – or at least, not such a bad idea as to make you think about not using them at all. However, life is not so simple as just offering a clock radio and expecting it to work. Unless handled carefully from the creative point of view incentives can be damaging: whatever you give away costs money, and the cost of the incentive must be included in the cost-per-reply.

You must ensure that you are getting back in reply terms more than enough to pay for the cost of providing and shipping the gift. Handled badly, an incentive can sometimes simply worsen the cost-per-reply rather than improve it. Your incentive offer therefore needs to be handled carefully. The sad Hoover fiasco appears to be a clear case of this not being done very well; the promotion itself worked – but who worked out the numbers?

MAKING AN OFFER

The primary creative requirement for making offers work is to bring them 'up front'. This means, quite literally, that in order to get the best results from incentivisation, you should, as observed earlier, make the incentive the *hero* of the piece.

Rather like the 'jumping straight in' that I discussed in Chapter 6, you need to do exactly the same if you are using an incentive.

This means literally:

- featuring the incentive on the envelope
- featuring the incentive on the front page of the letter
- opening the letter with your incentive
- reprising the incentive on the order form

- carrying a separate flyer devoted to your incentive
- reminding your respondent about the incentive if it's a two-stage sell and the incentive follows on as the result of purchase.

With some clients you will have a tough battle to get such a strong package through, even though you will be proved right in the end. The problem is in creating such a package, the product or service itself gets very much second billing: this can be emotionally difficult to accept.

However, this is more or less the effect you should be striving to achieve. In a typical Digest package, for example, the incentive is by far the strongest part of the pack – but beware: you can make a £130,000 prize draw the hero, but you might not be able to make quite so much of a clock radio. Clearly, there are limits.

But even with a fairly modest incentive, while you may not be able to turn the whole piece into an incentive-led package, you should always – at the very least – commence with whatever incentive you've giving away.

STARTING THE COPY WITH THE OFFER

Clearly, if you start your main copy with the offer – by main copy I shall presume the letter or the body copy of the press ad – you need at some stage to be able to link back to the product itself. We looked at this earlier in Chapter 5 in relation to a proposition coming up front, and the technique is the same.

Here's the opening of an incentive-led letter, to show just how hard you should aim to come in at the start:

"Dear Reader,

Imagine one morning, just as you've got ready to go to work, there's a knock at the door. It's the postman.

"Morning", he'd say, and would look at you with a curious gaze. "Special recorded delivery – sign here please".

You take the package and close the door. Who on earth is sending you a recorded delivery package? You open it with curiosity. It's a cheque. It's made out in your name.

It's got the sum of – you pause and look again, just to make sure you've read it right – the sum of ONE HUNDRED THOUSAND POUNDS…payable to you.

What would your reaction be? Imagine how Mr Jones of Cardiff felt when he opened such a letter. Imagine how Mrs Palmer of Staines felt when she opened such a letter. In fact, somebody somewhere in the next few months will be opening just such a letter, and getting just such a cheque – why not you?

It all depends on whether we receive your entry into our free prize draw by 11th November – so you need to act now. And you'll also have an opportunity to receive the first of THREE FREE ISSUES of xxxxxxxxx…"

This is typical of the opening of good prize draw letters. It certainly works much better than starting with the product and going on to the incentive, for the reasons I have mentioned earlier.

FREE ALARM CLOCK RADIOS

But not every package can (or should be) a prize draw package. What do you do if all you can give away is an Alarm Clock Radio or similar?

The technique is much the same, but as it lacks the excitement of getting a cheque for £100,000 through the post, you need to be a little more restrained than the example above. Even so, it is still important to lead with the offer:

"Dear Reader,

Can I send you, absolutely free, this compact Alarm Clock Radio? It's elegant, will fit perfectly on your bedside table, and will wake you at any hour you choose with a gentle warble or the soothing tones of your favourite morning radio show.

It's yours quite free – to say thank you for joining the xzxzxzxzx Health Plan – a plan that actually guarantees to accept you NO MATTER WHAT YOUR STATE OF HEALTH NOW!"

In both cases, once you have got the link between incentive and product in, the rest of the copy would then concentrate on the product features and benefits in the ways I have described earlier.

REPRISING THE OFFER

Having opened your main copy in such a way, and then having spent however long is necessary to produce compelling body copy, you would then return to the incentive as the major part of your action close.

While this works best if you can tie it in with a real time close, even in the absence of one you should still come back hard on the incentive.

As far as ad copy is concerned, almost the whole of your last two or three paragraphs would tend to be given over to an incentive-related action close:

"REPLY TODAY TO RECEIVE YOUR FREE CLOCK RADIO

To join this plan – and to receive your free alarm clock radio – simply complete the coupon below and send it off today. No stamp is needed – we pay the postage. Or, if you prefer, call us on xzxzxzxzx now. The moment we receive your application, your alarm clock radio will be sent on its way to you – absolutely free. You'll have 30 days in which to decide the plan is for you..."

In a mailing letter, you also have the PS. Unless you have something more compelling to say, your PS should *always* reprise the incentive (and, of course, in the absence of an incentive, should reprise the offer or the proposition).

ENVELOPES AND ORDER FORMS

Two other useful places to feature incentives are on envelopes and order forms. The most powerful way of using an envelope to carry a message is to feature your incentive in full colour on it – together with some brief copy saying that it's free. Of all types of message on envelopes, this one seems to work best: in fact, there are many

Fig. 44:
Tackling quantity and quality.

The stronger the incentive, the worse the quality. This doesn't mean useless, but it does mean that if you want to generate large volumes of up-front response via strong incentives, you need to think carefully about converting them. The creative needs to take both aspects into account once you get into the realms of super-incentives, of which this offer from RAC and Sun Alliance of free £1,000 Accidental Death insurance is a prime example. The initial mailing (A) is extremely simple and cheap, because it generates immense quantities of replies, but they are of indifferent quality – so we don't want to spend too much money on them. Once they reply to take up their free insurance, they are then mailed with pack (B) which aims to convert them by upgrading them to full cover. You will notice that pack (B) is much more expensive.

RAC
Insurance Services

PRIVATE AND CONFIDENTIAL

FREE Accidental Death Cover of £1,000
valid for the next 10 years – yours without obligation

It's a sad fact that accidents – particularly those which happen on the roads or other forms of travel – are a part of everyday life and could happen to any one of us at any time. So, because we are constantly looking for new products and services which will benefit our customers, and to stress the importance of accidental death cover, we have decided to offer selected customers £1,000 free accidental death insurance specially designed to cover travel accidents, for the next 10 years.

This special insurance offer is available provided you are over 18 and under 70 years of age, remain permanently resident in England, Scotland, Wales, the Channel Islands or the Isle of Man and remain an RAC Member.

Should you suffer a fatal accident whilst travelling during this time your estate will receive £1,000 free of income tax under current Inland Revenue regulations, provided you complete and return the enclosed form before 4th September 1992. A reply-paid envelope is enclosed. You will be covered from the moment we hear from you, and we will send you your certificate of cover by return of post.

We believe it's an important form of insurance many people overlook. That's why we'll also be sending you details of how you can increase this valuable cover.

So do reply today, and remember, the £1,000 free accidental death cover already reserved in your name is yours to keep.

Yours sincerely,

Martin Bateman
Managing Director
RAC Insurance Brokers Ltd

BUSINESS REPLY SERVICE
Licence No. CY245

2

RAC Insurance Offer
PO Box 500
Tamar House
St Andrews Cross
PLYMOUTH
PL1 1AY

PLEASE TREAT WITH PRIORITY

A

RAC

IMPORTANT: Your Certificate of cover and details of up to £100,000 additional insurance are enclosed.

RAC
Insurance Services

For selected Policyholders: up to £100,000 Accidental Death Cover has been reserved for you – plus a FREE gift.

I am delighted to welcome you as a policyholder to the RAC Accidental Death Travel Plan. Your Certificate of £1,000 free cover is enclosed and will be valid for 10 years, providing you are resident in England, Scotland, Wales, the Channel Islands or the Isle of Man and you remain an RAC Member.

Having added this cover to your insurance portfolio, your estate will receive this useful sum should you die as the result of an accident whilst travelling. Furthermore, it is paid income tax-free under current Inland Revenue regulations.

Unfortunately, accidents are a fact of life and they can happen at any time to anyone. The £1,000 could help your family over a difficult time, but have you thought how they might cope afterwards? Without your regular income to rely on, will they face even greater difficulties? Naturally, we hope not. Yet to ensure even greater financial help for them, you are invited to increase your protection by up to £100,000.

And because you have been specially selected to receive this offer, you will enjoy particularly advantageous benefits. However, to qualify, you must apply before the close date shown on your Notification of Increased Cover.

Acceptance guaranteed

The first of these advantages is that your acceptance into the full Plan is guaranteed provided you apply by the close date. There is no need for you to take a medical or answer any questions about your health.

Cover underwritten by leading insurers at specially negotiated premiums

The second advantage is that your cover has been arranged with Sun Alliance, one of the country's foremost providers of personal insurance.

Furthermore, we have been able to negotiate this valuable cover at a reasonable cost. Just £3.00 a month

---

TERMS OF COVER

THE RAC ACCIDENTAL DEATH TRAVEL PLAN

As an existing Policyholder you are entitled to apply for additional cover of up to £100,000 for death as the result of a travel accident.

The terms of cover stated here can only be guaranteed to Policyholders who are eligible to apply and who return the Notification of Increased Cover by the close date shown.

Your cover will come into force the moment it is received.

Your monthly premium will be payable by direct debit to ensure your cover remains continuous.

AN IMPORTANT ADDITION TO YOUR EXISTING COVER

With this Plan your estate will receive £100,000 or £50,000 (depending on the level of cover you choose). This is in addition to your £1,000 free cover, if still in force, should you die as the result of a travel related accident. Cash benefits will be paid to your estate in addition to any other compensation you might receive.

And all cash benefits are guaranteed totally free of income tax under current Inland Revenue regulations.

Cash benefits for people aged 65 or more will be halved and cover ceases altogether when you reach the age of 75.

MONTHLY PREMIUM RATES

As an existing Policyholder, you will enjoy specially negotiated monthly premium rates as follows:

	£50,000 Cover	£100,000 Cover
RAC Member only	£3.00	£4.00
RAC Member and Spouse	£4.00	£6.25

ACCEPTANCE GUARANTEED – NO MEDICAL REQUIRED

You can increase your benefits under the Plan without the need for a medical, provided you are aged 18 or over and under 70, are permanently resident in England, Scotland, Wales, the Channel Islands or the Isle of Man and you return your completed Notification of Increased Cover before the close date.

If you are already insured under a policy which principally provides benefits for accidental death or disability issued by Sun Alliance with

---

BUSINESS REPLY SERVICE
Licence No. CY245

1

RAC Accidental Death Travel Plan
PO Box 500
Tamar House
St Andrews Cross
PLYMOUTH
PL1 1AY

PLEASE TREAT WITH PRIORITY

RAC NOTIFICATION OF INCREASED COVER
UNDER THE RAC ACCIDENTAL DEATH TRAVEL PLAN

APPROVED BY UNDERWRITERS

AVAILABLE FOR:	MEMBERSHIP NO:	
	EXISTING COVER: £1,000	PREMIUM: FREE
	ADDITIONAL COVER:	ADDITIONAL COVER:
DATE OF BIRTH:	£50,000	£100,000
	RAC MEMBER ONLY £3 per month A☐	RAC MEMBER ONLY £4 per month B☐
VALID IF RETURNED BY:	RAC MEMBER AND SPOUSE £4 per month A☐	RAC MEMBER AND SPOUSE £6.25 per month B☐

Please tick the type of Policy you require.

(declaration and direct debit instruction text)

£1,000 CERTIFICATE OF COVER
FOR THE RAC ACCIDENTAL DEATH TRAVEL PLAN

INSURED:	CERTIFICATE NUMBER:
	DATE OF BIRTH:
	EFFECTIVE DATE:
	RENEWAL DATE:

AND ANNUALLY THEREAFTER

YOU ARE INSURED FOR THE PRINCIPAL SUM OF **£1,000** UNDERWRITTEN BY SUN ALLIANCE AND LONDON INSURANCE PLC.

SIGNATURE
R.A.G. Neville
R.A.G. Neville
Group Chief Executive

SUN ALLIANCE
INSURANCE UK

SUN ALLIANCE
INSURANCE UK

RAC

Take up the
RAC Accidental Death Travel Plan
and accept a gift
with our compliments

B

RAC

GUARANTEED ACCEPTANCE FOR RAC MEMBERS

This is to confirm that as an RAC Member who already has £1,000 accidental death cover you are entitled to apply for up to £100,000 additional cover under the RAC Accidental Death Travel Plan with guaranteed acceptance.

There will be no need for a medical or have to disclose any details about your state of health. You must be resident in either England, Wales, Scotland, the Channel Islands or the Isle of Man, and be aged over 18 and under 70 years of age when you apply.

To take advantage of this special concession, you must return your completed Notification of Increased Cover before the close date shown.

Signed Martin Bateman (Martin Bateman)
Managing Director, RAC Insurance Brokers Ltd.

cases of non-offer or non-incentive-related messages on envelopes simply *decreasing* response.

In addition, the order form can be greatly assisted by the introduction of the incentive. *Order forms are perhaps the most important part of mailing packs –* certainly they are the most read items by those people who are replying. But order forms too often end up as nothing *more* than an order from – and particularly with a powerful incentive pack, a dull order form can get lost.

By adding an illustration – preferably a large one at the top – together with strong and detailed offer copy, you can make the order stand out as well as making it work harder.

THE FLYER

Rather like the order form, the free gift flyer is often put in as a last thought. This is not as it should be, given the importance of the free gift.

Free gift flyers should be as powerful as any other part of the pack. A slip of paper with a picture and twenty words of copy is simply not going to be able to compete with what should be highly compelling copy selling the product.

Format, if you can manage it, should be looked at. Free gift flyers by their very nature are additional cost items in the pack, and therefore have to work hard to pay their way. If you have followed the suggestions about bringing the offer up front throughout the rest of the package, then adding more expense to the flyer may not justify itself. But flyers of unusual sizes and folds seem to work better – we once produced a mini-brochure for a Bentley we were giving away as the flyer: the brochure was 2″ square!

Like any other part of the package, the free gift needs to be sold hard.

This will require, as usual, some lengthy, well-thought-out copy. I give an example in Chapter 5 which shows the way it can be done if the gift is approached as something to be sold, not just described.

Equally, the illustration needs to do justice to the product. Preferably photographic, the illustration should have as much attention given to it as if it were the main product itself. *There is little point in hoping an incentive will work if you do not make the incentive as attractive as you can make it.*

All of this means, of course, that items like free gift flyers have to assume a creative importance that they rarely enjoy. While the letter is critical, so is the flyer. It will repay your time over and over again in response terms if you devote much care and attention to it.

Incidentally, you can use flyers as a cheap way of introducing colour into a mailing which otherwise wouldn't stand it – such as a fundraising mailing – or into mailings where full colour can be inappropriate, such as financial mailings. A small colour flyer is of course relatively inexpensive to produce.

FORMATS AND INCENTIVES

In the Chapter on Formats we saw how it was necessary to choose the right format to accord with the proposition that was being made. Exactly the same works with incentives. Strong prize draw packages are supreme examples of how the whole incentive conditions the very make-up and design of the pack itself.

The stronger the incentive, the more the format itself should become important. Giving away a free clock radio may not lend itself to a format that gives the gift primary position within the pack. But with even slightly stronger gifts, the format can begin to play its part.

And one of the most successful formats is the 'reply form at the top of the letter' format. This is where the top third of the letter becomes the reply form, allowing it to be personalised: but the important feature is the fact that you can feature the incentive. Thus the reader is immediately greeted with both the incentive and the reply form in a format that is cheap to produce.

BEWARE...

It would be wrong to give the impression that incentives are the ultimate solution to all direct marketing problems. They are not.

Even when handled as I have described, there are times when incentives do not work. There are some cases, admittedly the minority, where incentives either do not work or actually can have the negative effects on quality that people fear.

Many ideas in this book can and should be implemented without fear of damage to response. No further testing is necessary. But this is not the case with incentives. Although it is *overwhelmingly probable* that they will improve matters for you, it is vital to test the idea in the first place.

Incentives can have a savage effect on costs. If they work, all well and good. *But if they fail, then they can easily be one of the costliest failures you may have*. It's a risk and reward equation: anything that can have such a powerful positive effect on response, by Sod's Law, can have an equally powerful negative effect. Setting up incentives can be expensive, and having made an offer you are obliged to meet the demand for it, even if your mailing has failed. The Hoover experience is a salutary lesson to us all.

And the *wrong* type of incentive can give you a real headache, as well. For instance, a prize draw mailing is *not* the same as a free gift mailing – the difference between the two is substantial. Often people test a prize draw as a cheap alternative to a free gift, but a chance to win is not always as strong as a definite gift. If one doesn't work, it doesn't mean to say that a different approach might not work exceptionally well.

Test slowly and carefully. When you develop a pack using an incentive, aim low to start with. Try a modest time close gift first and slowly build up to something grander. But all the time, bear in mind the absolute need to make the very most, creatively, of the incentive you are using, otherwise failure really is guaranteed ■

CHAPTER 10: SUMMARY

*Incentives will almost always improve response by around 100%,
and sometimes more. Quality and image are rarely affected: most evidence
suggests that incentive-generated response converts as well as
non-incentive-generated response.*

*Incentives work by gaining greater attention and by promoting response.
They do not in themselves 'sell' more products; they simply ensure that you get
the maximum response from those people who are already interested.*

*Giving incentives costs money; the cost of the premium must be added to
the cost-per-reply and therefore you must at least get the equivalent
improvement in response to pay for it.*

*Incentives usually fail to achieve this improvement because they are not handled
correctly from the creative point of view. Incentives should never be left to a free
gift flyer or a panel; much more should be made of them.*

*Incentives must be brought 'up front' in the same way that propositions or
other types of offer should be brought 'up front'. Your whole creative platform
should revolve around the incentive. The stronger the incentive,
the more the creative work should feature it.*

If possible, choose formats that allow the incentive to dominate the package.

*Because incentives cost money, they may not work even with the application
of the techniques described here. You should test carefully to avoid one of
the most expensive mistakes you can make in direct marketing.
Remember Hoover!*

PART TWO
Applications

HOW TO CREATE
BETTER MAILINGS

Mailing packs are the heavy artillery of direct marketing; getting the mailing right creatively can mean the difference between success and failure. The basic rules, often ignored, are easily learned and simple to put into practice. Going beyond the basics is a more adventurous task but can bring equally significant rewards. Here's how.

MAILINGS come in all shapes and sizes, in quantities ranging from one to millions, and selling products as diverse as computers to manure. Almost every business and organisation uses mailings of one type or another: apart from 'professional' direct mail, there's the local cricket club sending out membership renewals; estate agencies touting houses; local councils informing their tax payers of the latest development plans. Even gas and electricity bills, unattractive as they are, can be considered a type of direct mail.

The common thread to all of these communications – the definition, if you like, of 'direct mail' – is that they are all designed to *elicit a response.*

The local club wants you to rejoin; the estate agent is looking for a sale; the council wants you to think well of them at the next election; the gas board wants you to pay your bill without the need for the near-traditional 'red threat' letter.

In every case, the sender is looking to make the recipient *act*:

- in a specific way
- by a specific time
- with clear expectations of future obligations or requirements

This is the very heart of a good mailing, one that the local cricket club may well unconsciously follow but one that professional direct marketing creative people often forget: your mailing is not there to inspire admiration, it is there to get people to do something. *The whole design and conception of the mailing must be built around this simple but vital requirement: get action*

WHAT RESPONSE ARE YOU LOOKING FOR?

The response your mailing is trying to achieve isn't always simply a reply through the post ordering a product. It could be a telephone call, a donation, an expression of support, an enquiry, a visit, or just a nice warm feeling. But if you are to create a successful mailing, you must be able to clarify in your own mind exactly the action you are looking to inspire. You will, I hope, have gone through the stages in the early part of this book in order to isolate propositions, offers and incentives. These are all vital considerations.

But before you physically start creating your mailing, you have to be able to

Fig. 45:
The classic fundraising mailing.
This Salvation Army package follows closely a classic format. Most low-cost mailings, and many expensive ones, will have these basic items. The outer envelope is a from-stock DL window, which contains (A) a four page illustrated letter (B) DL donation form which acts as the address carrier (laser printed and bar-coded in this case but more typically Cheshire-labelled) (C) third-voice flyer from the UK leader and (D) reply-paid envelope. These are the basic items and represent one of the lowest-cost formats available, consistent with providing enough space to get a message across. Item (E) is an 'optional extra', in this case an Easter prayer card, aimed at the typical Salvation Army supporter. For a mailing of this type, aimed at cold (rented) lists little more is either needed or would be justifiable. Only if you're going to warm (in-house) lists would you think about adding more information.

THE SALVATION ARMY, 101 QUEEN VICTORIA STREET, LONDON EC4P 4EP.

Dear Friend,

As I sit down to write and thank you for all your wonderful support, I can see an overcast sky through the window - but I am hopeful some rays of sunshine will break through the clouds to brighten this spring morning.

Springtime is all about hope...after the bitter, dreary days of winter, we all rejoice when the first buds unfurl and the earth yields up her treasures again. But please, can I ask you to imagine what it must be like for those who fear their lives will never be touched by hope again.

For the pitiful little children who have never known the warmth of love and security. For the lonely elderly folk whose days are never brightened by a kind word or friendly face. For all those so broken down by poverty and hardship that their hearts are darkened by despair.

Just as I wish for that ray of sunlight to break through the clouds, so I hope with all my heart that you can help us to bring comfort and support into their lives today.

Your heartwarming generosity has already enabled us to achieve so much...helping to heal the pain of vulnerable children like Jenny...

It took years before Jenny could learn to trust again.

To see this bouncy little girl now, you would never guess at the dreadful ordeal Jenny had suffered as a baby. Her mother - having had an unhappy childhood, then being abandoned when pregnant - vented her rage on the baby she felt had "trapped" her. If Jenny wanted anything - from a cup of water to a toy - her mother would wait until she had crawled up to it, then snatch it away, leaving Jenny crying helplessly. _When she came into our care, you can imagine how disturbed this poor little girl had become._

At first, Jenny was deeply mistrustful of adults. Withdrawn and angry, she would snatch at food and toys, screaming furiously if they were taken away from her. It took months for the caring staff at our Children's Home to teach her to trust them, and share what she was given with others.

The breakthrough came one sunny spring weekend, when the children had enjoyed an Easter Egg hunt. Jenny raced in from the garden and proudly showed off her prizes. As the Major admired the brightly coloured eggs, her heart lifted to hear Jenny's voice pipe

An Easter message from our UK Leader, John Larsson.

MAY GOD BLESS YOU AND YOUR FAMILY THIS EASTER FOR BRIGHTENING NEEDY LIVES WITH THE PRECIOUS GIFT OF HOPE

A stamp will save us paying postage. Thank you.

The Salvation Army
FREEPOST
London EC4B 4SR

DF88/L

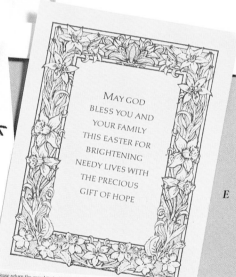

To: The Salvation Army
101 Queen Victoria Street
London EC4P 4EP

Thank you for opening your heart to help warm the lives of those in desperate need.

Mr C H Williams
81 Lincoln Road
Newark
Nottinghamshire
NG24 2BU

00125053   240

If the above details are incorrect please make the necessary alterations. Should you receive more than one copy of this appeal, please accept our apologies.
DATA PROTECTION: We will occasionally write to you about our work. However, we never give your name and address to other organisations. If you would prefer not to hear even from us, please tick.

If you've asked not to hear from us again, please accept our apologies for any extra time it takes while we update our files.

E112

Please return the complete form   13304/00014767

GIFT FORM

YES I want to make an Easter Gift to help The Salvation Army help those in need. I enclose my donation of

Other £ ___   £56 ☐   £32 ☐   £20 ☐   £15 ☐
Gifts of any size are appreciated

It is safer to send donations by cheque or postal order made payable to The Salvation Army.
OR please debit my Access/Visa/American Express/Diners with the sum of: £ _____

_____ Card Expiry Date ☐☐ ☐☐
CARD No. ☐☐☐☐ ☐☐☐☐ ☐☐☐☐ ☐☐☐☐

NAME (PLEASE PRINT) _____

SIGNATURE _____

Please accept our warmest thanks for your kind gift. As we now issue receipts only on request, please tick the box if required ☐

Q. How do you turn every £10 you give into £13.33 to help the needy?
A. A regular donation to The Salvation Army using the Covenant Form overleaf.

answer the "what response am I looking for?" question with a very simple answer. And the more complicated the answer, the less clear it is in your own mind.

Here are some typical actions that direct mailers attempt to achieve:

- Ring up to enquire
- Visit or ring to make an appointment to test
- Complete an application form for credit
- Sign an order
- Book a visit to see a site
- Ask a salesman to call to arrange an appointment
- Send a cash donation
- Renew a subscription
- Upgrade a covenant
- Complete a questionnaire
- Send for a catalogue

There are two points to note. First, each of these actions is subtly different. Second, they are not necessarily the final SALES action required – sometimes, clearly as in the case of a mailing looking to generate an enquiry, there are further stages in the sales process.

THE REAL SECRET OF SUCCESS

Why is this important?

> *Quite simply, if there is a 'secret' of successful direct mail, it lies here: have a clear image in your mind of the action you want your reader to take, and then devote your mailing to making that happen.*

That is why it is important to know the difference between the types of response you are looking for: this allows you to *concentrate* on that response to the virtual exclusion of all other considerations. And that is why if the action you are looking for is only one stage of the selling process, you should know that too: obviously, the danger in not having these things clearly in mind is that you will be confused in your own thinking and therefore unable to communicate this clearly when you come to create the mailing.

STAGE ONE: KNOW WHAT ACTION YOU ARE LOOKING FOR

To illustrate this process, let's imagine a mailing we have been asked to create. The brief is simply to get donations for charity X, which exists to protect animals. Having gone through the stages described earlier in this book, our proposition and offer is clear: "Give £18 to save a puppy or a kitten from death (otherwise we'll have to have them put down because we can't afford to keep them)".

We know from experience that a straight donation of this amount will convert at a reasonable rate in follow-ups to allow us a fundraising ratio of .9:1 on cold mailings – for every £1 we spend, we must earn 90p.

The response we are looking for is: "Send £18 now". Note that I have been very single-minded about this. I could have said: "Feel sorry for these poor animals and send us money"...but this creates mailings strong on appeal but short on response.

People who are given a problem to consider want to know what they can do about it – not just be told the problem. Starting with a single-minded statement like that concentrates the mind and disciplines everything you say towards achieving the objective you have in mind.

Is this the proposition by another name?

Sometimes, it is. But quite often there is a subtle difference between the proposition – which is what you want somebody to think or know about a product – and the action you want somebody to take. The proposition here could be expressed as: "Your £18 will save this animal's life". But it still needs the creative people to clearly translate that proposition into a definitive statement of required action – *"Send money now"*.

The difference will be more apparent if you have decided to go for covenants, for example. The proposition will be the same, but the required action is no longer 'send money' but 'complete a covenant form'. The two mailings would be noticeably different.

STAGE TWO: KNOW YOUR BUDGET LIMITATIONS

Stage one, then, is to make sure you know what action you are looking for before you start. The next stages in creating your mailing then fall easily into place. The next important feature is cost.

In Chapter 9 of the first section, you will have read about the need to make sure you are working within the appropriate cost guidelines. As I hope that Chapter makes clear, this is not always to say "it should be cheap". Quite often (and more often than you would suppose) the answer is to spend more, not less – not for reasons of creative indulgence but because if the margin on the sale allows it, the higher the amount of creative leverage you can get into your mailing, with correspondingly better results if you use your budget properly.

Let's relate that principle back to our charity mailing.

We already know that a return of .9:1 is required. We can translate this into the amount of money to spend per thousand mailings – based on a reasonable expectation of what the list will do. Like all charity mailings, we know it will have to be cheap.

(Some pure judgement at this early stage would normally be involved, given the type of charity we are discussing. With the strong emotional value of animals, colour printing should be used somewhere within the pack which would probably pay for itself in response terms.)

STAGE THREE: KNOW YOUR PROSPECT

With the required action known, and the amount of money available to achieve it, the third stage is for the creative person to identify the person they are writing to. This should be more than a dry socio-demographic description.

Your mother may well be a C2 30-55 year old, but you would hardly describe her as such. You need to consider the type of person you are writing to not just from an economic or age standpoint, but from an emotional one. In Chapter 1 you will have read about the necessity to direct your message only to those people who are most likely to respond; prior to producing your mailing, you should try to see in your mind the type of person they are. What is really motivating them to respond?

Greed?	Status?	Dreams?	Sex?	Power?
Worry?	Revenge?	Anger?	Saving money?	

It could be any of these reasons or any combinations of them that is causing the 'most likely person' to respond. I believe, with no evidence to back it up, that for most products or services only a very few motives are ever at work, and that they tend to be much the same for the people who respond to certain mailings, even if they are of different socio-economic groups.

For instance, one charity I know has great success in cold direct mail. They appeal to a certain type of person socio-economically; but more important is the fundamental motive driving those people to give: it is, quite simply, anger at the problem, followed by a strong feeling of revenge – *they wish to punish the people who caused the problem*. We actually created a mailing, very subtly, to work on this feeling.

KNOWING YOUR MARKET

To illustrate the point, let's return to our imaginary charity mailing. From the lists we are using, plus profiling work done on previous donors, we can get a good idea of the socio-economic profile. But how do we get to know the emotional side of these people?

The answer is simply to go and meet them. Talk to people you know who would give to such a charity. Study letters that previous donors have written. Talk to the client about the type of person they think it is. Talk to customer services staff, who can give you some very interesting views!

Having gone on an imaginary client visit in this case, and spoken to some imaginary donors, I think we're probably talking to older women who fall in love with these animals and who want to protect them – or who are prepared to give money to someone who will look after them on their 'behalf', as it were. It's best summed up by saying: "They would want to take these poor animals into their own homes – if they could".

Thus the three primary stages are now, hopefully, known to the creator of this mailing:

1 What action we want

2 What we can afford to spend

3 Who the person is that we're talking to

and now we can get down to business.

STARTING THE MAILING

In this imaginary charity mailing, we know what action we want:

"Give £18 now to save this animal".

We know what we can afford to spend:

Around £320 per thousand.

And we know who (emotionally) we're talking to:

Fig. 46:
A typical up-market mailing.

For mailings with higher margins than fundraising, this Compton and Woodhouse piece is a typical example. This style of mailing would be used for 'hard' products – i.e. merchandise as opposed to a service like insurance (see the next illustration) where there is a need to show the product to good advantage. To start with, we use a much larger envelope (C4 in this case) to give ourselves room. Inside, the items are the mailing letter (A), the colour reply form (B) which reiterates the offer and acts as the address carrier, (C) the reply envelope and as hero (D) the colour brochure which opens out in a 3 page gatefold (E) with masses of highly detailed copy and large colour illustrations. There are many variations on this basic theme, but while the previous fundraising example (fig. 45) wouldn't improve for having any more, this case wouldn't work that well if it was any less. Additions to this type of mailing would be mainly flyers and third-voice letters …a flyer if an incentive were to be offered, a third-voice letter perhaps from the sculptor.

GOLDEN AGE
ALEXANDRA AT THE BALL

A LIMITED EDITION FIGURE COLLECTION IN FINE BONE CHINA BY COALPORT, INSPIRED BY THE ELEGANCE OF THE EDWARDIAN ERA.

Strictly limited to 12,500 figures only

Each figure individually numbered, each with a signed Certificate of Authenticity in your name, bearing your personal figure number

Designed by Elizabeth Woodhouse

Available exclusively by direct subscription to Compton & Woodhouse, dealers in fine bone china.

Send no money with your application

'Alexandra' is made and painted entirely by hand with meticulous attention paid to every detail.

'Alexandra at the Ball'.
The figure is shown here actual size of 9¼" high.

COALPORT CRAFTSMANSHIP

METICULOUSLY SCULPTED

BEAUTIFULLY HAND PAINTED

The sweeping curve of life and movement is apparent from every angle of the figure.

THE COALPORT BACKSTAMP

STRICTLY LIMITED EDITION

E

D

An Exclusive Announcement for Compton & Woodhouse Collectors

COALPORT
BONE CHINA

An Exquisite Limited Edition Figure in the Golden Age Collection

SPECIAL CUSTOMER SAVE £13.50 OFFER

CW

Compton & Woodhouse are pleased to announce

ALEXANDRA AT THE BALL

A stunning figure in the Limited Edition Figure Collection

GOLDEN AGE

in Fine Bone China by Coalport

COALPORT
BONE CHINA
MADE IN ENGLAND
EST. 1750

COLLECTOR'S PRIORITY RESERVATION FORM
URGENT – REPLY WITHIN 7 DAYS

COALPORT
GOLDEN AGE
ALEXANDRA AT THE BALL

SEND NO MONEY NOW

Please send me 'Alexandra', a beautiful limited edition figure from the Golden Age Collection in Coalport English fine bone china, inspired by the elegance of the Edwardian era, to view in the comfort of my own home.

Sculpted by master sculptor John Bromley, who now works exclusively for Compton & Woodhouse

There are only a few remaining numbers in this strictly limited edition of 12,500 figures

Each figure individually numbered, each with a signed Certificate of Authenticity

Available exclusively by direct subscription to Compton & Woodhouse dealers in fine bone china

Special customer offer – save £13.50

Send no money with your application

Compton & Woodhouse

B

Compton & Woodhouse

Arundel House, London N15 4TR

Reserve 'Alexandra' within the next seven days and save up to £13.50 on this beautiful Coalport limited edition figure

Dear Treasured Collector,

In 1988, we issued a beautiful figurine entitled 'Alexandra at the Ball'. She was part of the 'Golden Age' Collection - our most successful fashion series ever in Coalport English fine bone china.

Since then, other customers who have seen 'Alexandra' in the homes of fellow collectors have written asking about the possibility of obtaining her for themselves. Of course, there is no possibility now for producing more of 'Alexandra' was a strictly limited edition of 12,500. And the issue has been so popular with our collectors that she has nearly completely sold out.

Why I'm able to write to you now offering you 'Alexandra at the Ball'...

I have enclosed the original brochure for you to study and I think you'll appreciate why collectors have expressed so much interest in this particular figurine.

Yours sincerely,

Rinalda Ward

Rinalda Ward
Managing Director

PS This hugely successful limited edition is about to sell out. Please send off your Reservation Form today to avoid disappointment.

A

---

send any money now, simply fill in the Reservation Form and return it to me in the envelope provided.

The Compton & Woodhouse Guarantee

Once your reservation has been confirmed and the figure sent to you, you'll have the opportunity to discover the beauty of 'Alexandra' for yourself in the comfort of your own home for 28 days.

And if for any reason whatsoever, you are not completely enchanted with 'Alexandra', you are of course assured by the Compton & Woodhouse Guarantee that your money will be refunded promptly and courteously, if you return the figure to us within those 28 days.

It would be a great pity to miss your chance to collect such a beautiful tribute to the Golden Age, simply because your Reservation Form did not get to us before the seven-day deadline. So I really do urge you to reply today.

Compton & Woodhouse Ltd
FREEPOST
Arundel House
London
N15 4BR

C

A childless lady who would like to give this animal a home.

It may help if you physically write this all down before you start the mailing. Sometimes quite a lot of the process may already be done for you through the brief. But if the brief does not contain this information *you should not attempt to start the mailing until you are confident that you have clear simple answers* to all three questions.

SELECTING THE FORMAT

The first creative process you need to address is to develop the format you will use. In Chapter 8 of the previous section we saw how the format could be 'designed' by the nature of the message to be communicated. At this stage the true creative imagination needs to be brought into play.

Going back to our example, we know that the message is a fairly simple one. We're not asking for a complicated action, nor is it a complex message. This is fortunate, because the budget will not allow a complex package anyway.

We know, then, that the pack should be simple. But should it be just another mailing pack?

THE VIRTUE OF DIFFERENCE

In Chapter 8, I referred to 'change of pace' – the idea that if all mailings look the same then results will tend to diminish through, literally, boredom. In the fundraising market it becomes increasingly important to create packages that are *different*, mainly because the target audience for fundraisers tends to be the same – and therefore they are being mailed considerable quantities of appeals.

The 'classic' fundraising package consists of a D/L envelope, letter, flyer and donation form: this basic format has been around for many years and is the cheapest way of getting a message into the post. D/L envelopes can be bought off the shelf very cheaply, and enclosing and mailing such a pack remains inexpensive.

However, this is not to say that such a classic format is correct on this occasion. In creating the fictional pack we are discussing, I would bear a single thought in mind:

> **The need to communicate a strong emotional message about animals calls for a more 'impactful' pack than the classic approach allows...**

in other words, going back to the principle that the format should be dictated by the message to be communicated, I think I need a format that will allow me to concentrate on the strong emotional message...particularly bearing in mind the type of person we are talking to. What will work for her?

From here, the creative imagination can then be turned loose, always bearing in mind the need to keep the cost at a level that won't push up the break-even to a point that becomes impossible to achieve.

The ideal format will be one that allows the strong emotional impact of animals to play its part: I would tend towards a 'portfolio of pictures' type of pack, with perhaps four colour photographs with messages on the back. This would need a folder to hold the pictures, plus the other elements, and would then need to go in a somewhat larger outer envelope that would also allow me to use the rather strong phrase: "PHOTOGRAPHS ENCLOSED". But before I get too carried away, I'll go off and talk to production first…

This is of course only an example of how this problem could be solved. The point I am making is that the decision to go for a certain format is the first real creative decision you will need to take, and it must be taken not out of blind inspiration or because someone showed you an interesting format at a trade fair, but because the message you are trying to get across can be got across more effectively *if the format itself is driven by the message*. The two should be inseparable.

THE MAJOR ELEMENTS OF THE PACK

Having chosen the basic format, we now need to return to the elements that should go into the pack.

We have seen in earlier Chapters the virtues of multiple pieces of paper in the pack. Essentially, 'the more you tell the more you sell' works just as well for sheets of paper as for copy. This supposes, logically enough, that you have a) enough story to tell and b) you use the paper sensibly to tell a real story. Every extra sheet you use *adds cost* – and you must be convinced that the cost of carrying that message is *justified* by the force of the message you are carrying.

I also referred to the recent fashion for one-piece formats. While they have their place, their use should be greatly restricted and hardly ever used for addressed direct mail, or even for door drops.

Graeme McCorkell has a splendid phrase: direct mail is 'tactile' – unlike any other medium, you can literally 'feel' direct mail. The very act of opening an envelope should be exciting – you should enjoy the drama of pieces coming out, unfolding, revealing new and interesting stories…so long as your budget permits it.

Adopting this approach then, what are the major elements?

THE OUTER ENVELOPE

This is not merely a carrier but the first thing your recipient sees. There is much debate about whether a message on the outer envelope helps or not – most of the time, it does. Certainly graphic treatments seem to work – bright yellow suggesting urgency, special Postage Paid Impression (PPI) marks, colour pictures, particularly 'show throughs' can be very successful – using oversized windows to reveal messages on the inner material, or using special windows to reveal details of free gifts. You can even use real postage stamps.

Most useful of all is to use envelopes of different or unusual sizes: large, odd shapes work very well, but so can unusually small ones too. This is part of the 'change of pace' argument. You need to be very careful about cost particularly if using an odd size as this involves a special making. But equally, don't be too frightened either: taking a control and refolding it for an unusual envelope can *dramatically* improve response.

(If you want to see a collection of superb envelope ideas, Tompla in Spain have an unusually imaginative collection.)

There remains a myth about outer envelopes that is worth killing off. The

Fig. 47:
A financial package.

Financial products need more words than pictures, to help explain the features of complex products. This means that financial mailings tend to share similar characteristics, but within the basic format there are of course huge variations. This Sun Alliance/Barclays mailing shows the essential elements. A non-standard square envelope (to make it stand out) contains (A) the personalised 4 page letter and (B) the personalised application form. App forms for financial products are inevitably more complex than other types of mailings and require a lot of space. The main product brochure (C) opens into a detailed product explanation (D) and has an all-important Questions and Answers on the back (E). There are 3 flyers in this pack – (F) is a free gift flyer, (G) is a Guarantee of Acceptance. Both of these flyers would feature in most financial packs. (H) is optional – it's a by-product of the production process used for this mailing and it's used here for 3 case histories. Note, incidentally, the very restrained use of colour and illustration in this pack, to give it a trustworthy financial feeling (see Chapter 7).

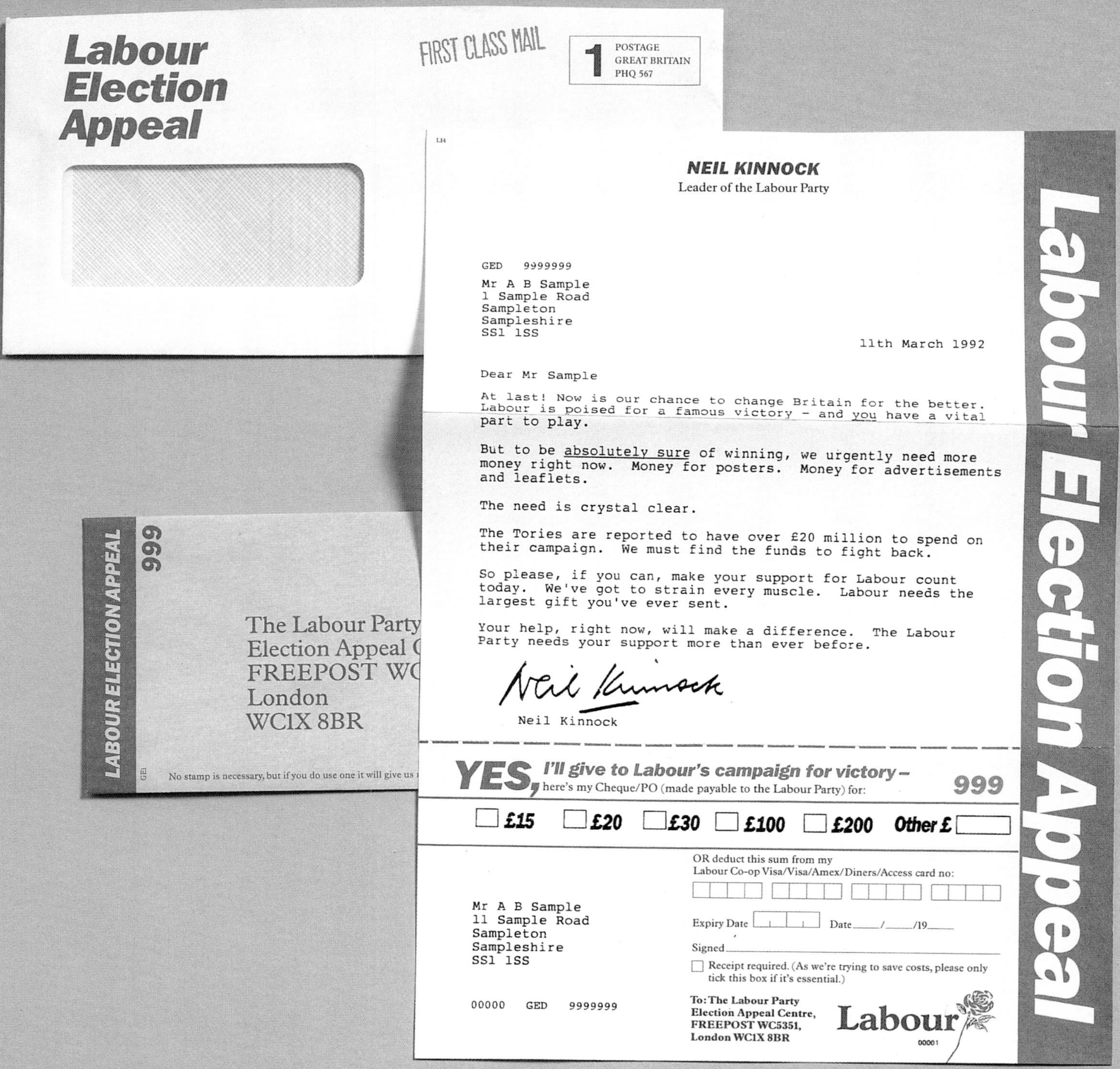

Labour Election Appeal

FIRST CLASS MAIL

1 POSTAGE
GREAT BRITAIN
PHQ 567

Labour Election Appeal

LH

NEIL KINNOCK
Leader of the Labour Party

```
GED    9999999

Mr A B Sample
1 Sample Road
Sampleton
Sampleshire
SS1 1SS

                                           11th March 1992

Dear Mr Sample

At last! Now is our chance to change Britain for the better.
Labour is poised for a famous victory - and you have a vital
part to play.

But to be absolutely sure of winning, we urgently need more
money right now.  Money for posters.  Money for advertisements
and leaflets.

The need is crystal clear.

The Tories are reported to have over £20 million to spend on
their campaign.  We must find the funds to fight back.

So please, if you can, make your support for Labour count
today.  We've got to strain every muscle.  Labour needs the
largest gift you've ever sent.

Your help, right now, will make a difference.  The Labour
Party needs your support more than ever before.
```

Neil Kinnock

Neil Kinnock

LABOUR ELECTION APPEAL
999

The Labour Party
Election Appeal C___
FREEPOST WC___
London
WC1X 8BR

GEl

No stamp is necessary, but if you do use one it will give us ___

YES, I'll give to Labour's campaign for victory –
here's my Cheque/PO (made payable to the Labour Party) for: **999**

☐ **£15**   ☐ **£20**   ☐ **£30**   ☐ **£100**   ☐ **£200**   **Other £** ☐

OR deduct this sum from my
Labour Co-op Visa/Visa/Amex/Diners/Access card no:

☐☐☐☐ ☐☐☐☐ ☐☐☐☐ ☐☐☐☐

```
Mr A B Sample
11 Sample Road
Sampleton
Sampleshire
SS1 1SS
```

Expiry Date ☐☐ / ☐☐   Date ___ / ___ /19___

Signed _____

☐ Receipt required. (As we're trying to save costs, please only
tick this box if it's essential.)

```
00000   GED   9999999
```

**To: The Labour Party
Election Appeal Centre,
FREEPOST WC5351,
London WC1X 8BR**

Labour 🌹

00001

Labour Election Appeal

Fig. 48:
Mailings with a difference (1).

Here's an alternative mailing that consists of a single sheet of paper, which contains a very short letter (6 paragraphs long) with an integral reply form. The only other piece is the reply envelope. The outer envelope is basically plain (the First Class Mail stamp is actually printed). Here, the appeal was extremely simple. We were writing only to Labour Party donors, and a General Election had been announced a few days beforehand. With the papers full of political argument there was little point in going into politics. All that was needed was a simple 'send money now'. Thus this mailing was simple not for cost reasons, but because it just didn't need any more 'weight' ... more would have taken away from the drama and excitement. In financial terms, this mailing was hugely successful.

purpose of the message/design is *not* to get the envelope opened: 80% of direct mail is opened anyway. The purpose is to get the recipient into the right frame of mind – they are well aware that they are being 'sold' to, so you need to use the outer envelope to give some idea of what you are saying. This is important: *few things are more annoying than 'junk mail' envelopes pretending to be something they aren't.* 'Private and Confidential' on the outside of a common or garden offer is, I think, one of the greatest let-downs.

THE LETTER

In studies, the majority of people look for the letter in the package first. Yet surprisingly, a large number of mailings are still sent out without a letter. There are some absolutes about direct mail, and this is one of them: *you must have a letter, and you must have a very strong reason for not making it a long one.*

This whole subject is a complex one, and I devote the next Chapter to a detailed look at the techniques of the letter because it occupies such an important role.

THE ORDER FORM

I deliberately give this third place in the list of components because it is a fundamental part of the pack – much more so than the brochure. When money is tight, a good pack can consist of simply a letter and an order form inside an envelope. Indeed, when the subject is simple, little more than this is needed.

The first thing to observe about the order form is that it is a far more important piece of paper than most creative people give it credit for. Too often it is treated as an afterthought – yet, if you follow my argument at the beginning of this Chapter, where we saw that the whole purpose of the piece was to get a reply, then the order form becomes one of the most important items in the pack – in fact, the most important. *All your efforts are concentrated on getting this piece of paper signed and returned, and therefore it must be treated as such, creatively.*

Interestingly, if you succeed in doing this, you create a much stronger sense of urgency in the pack. A strong order form demands the reader looks on this pack not simply as a communication, but as something that needs to be acted upon.

One way in which this can be done is to make it the 'hero' of the pack. Use of colour, copy, illustration and format choice should make the order form stand out. Indeed, in the choice of format the order form can be made a dominant part of the pack. One excellent way of doing this, particularly if money is tight, is to make the order form an integral part of the letter – putting it at the top or bottom of the first page. In such a position it is hardly likely to be missed, and of course has the added benefit of allowing a high degree of personalisation to be used at minimal cost – as you personalise the salutation you can personalise the reply piece at the same time. The copy on the order form needs as much care and attention as the design. A good order form will repeat the offer, will resell the proposition…it won't just be 'the small print', which too often it becomes. If your design is right, there should be a reasonable amount of room on the order form to allow your copy to do the reselling task. Bear in mind that your prospect, once they reach the order form, is very close to buying.

Where appropriate, have a picture of the product on the order form, to remind the reader of exactly what they're buying. This is important in mail order, and is particularly effective with charity packs, where an appealing picture of a dog/child/granny/whale etc can be very powerful.

Don't do the 'Supermarket Till' trick – a disinterested check-out girl who doesn't care if you buy or not. Rather than the bored 'yeah?' of some order forms, you should aim to show interest and give encouragement: "What an excellent choice" should be the emotional flavour of your order form.

One last word on an order form: once it's designed, please try filling it in and getting it inside its reply envelope. It's surprising how many otherwise good examples are impossible to fill in properly and don't fold into the reply envelope without the most arduous contortions. This is an unnecessary barrier to response.

THE REPLY ENVELOPE

The reply envelope is also part of the reply process, and like the order form is often treated as the poor relation. There is no need to have a dull, unimaginative reply envelope – as prize draw 'YES/NO' envelopes vividly demonstrate. Creative thought should be given to making the most of this item – either by putting messages on the envelopes, or changing the format of the envelope in some way: the 'NO' envelope traditionally contains an insert, tucked in under the flap, which has a brief letter printed on it, starting with:

"Frankly, I'm puzzled why you should say 'NO'..."

On fundraising return envelopes, there is usually a phrase that says:

"No stamp is needed, but if you use one it helps reduce our costs."

A little thought can turn the reply envelope into a powerful selling piece.

THE BROCHURE

If you have enough budget, then a brochure of some form is useful. It will improve response, but it is by no means a critical item. By brochure, however, I do not necessarily mean a lavish production at proportionally high cost. Indeed, a 'brochure' is not necessarily a traditional 4 colour item at all.

The brochure should be seen as an adjunct to the other items with its own specific supporting role to play, rather than as the hero.

Usually, its role is to provide authority and credibility to the statements in the rest of the mailing. What I mean by this is that most of the material in the envelope is more like a personal communication. The letter, hopefully, is typewritten; but what it gains in personal communication, it can lose in not being official enough.

A typeset brochure, complete with picture, charts and other items of information, has a higher status and gives the rest of the mailing a believability and authority that it would otherwise lack.

Seen like this, the brochure stops becoming a dominant force around which the mailing is created, and starts to become what it should rightly be. As a result of approaching the brochure this way, you find you devote more budget and creative effort to those elements, particularly letters and incentive flyers, that actually have a much stronger role to play. This has the effect of improving cost-efficiency.

In this role, *the brochure has to share the selling task* with those other items, so what you say in the letter copy you may well be saying in the brochure (given that even with the luxury of long copy there are still only so many selling points you can create) – but you would of course say it differently. The tone of the copy itself will be different. The chatty colloquial style of the personal letter should be replaced by the more formal language of the official brochure; see Chapter 5 on 'Copy Style'.

There is no need, then, to become concerned if after having written the letter you have run out of things to say in the brochure. And never fall into the trap of leaving things out of the letter because "I was going to say that in the brochure". Both items *must stand on their own feet* and contain the entire selling message, albeit phrased differently – an excellent way to practice flexibility in copy styles.

In terms of visual and format approach, the brochure is where you can display the most creativity, usually to good effect – cost permitting. The word itself... 'brochure'...produces an image of an eight-page A4 colour leaflet; indeed, many end up just like that.

However, the possibilities are far wider: broadsheets, posters, newsletters, miniature booklets – all are possible formats that you should consider. There is indeed substantial evidence to suggest that along with odd-shaped envelopes, unusual brochure formats can produce some good results.

The broadsheet approach is always well worth looking at. The broadsheet is basically a large sheet of paper (sometimes as big as A1) covered in your selling message, a bit like a poster. This is then folded down to fit the envelope: the sheer impact of the opened sheet is considerable, and cunning designers can have fun 'tracking' the reader through the various unfoldings.

But whatever format is appropriate, the brochure should always benefit from illustrations, photographs, charts, diagrams and any other graphic device that will illustrate the copy argument that you are making. Again, the style should match the format. You may have chosen a format based on:

a broadsheet	*a pop-up*
a miniature booklet	*a video*
a newsletter	*a portfolio of pictures*
an official document (semi-legal)	*a quotation*
a simple leaflet	*a reprint*
a poster	*a gatefold leaflet*

or whatever else is most likely to keep within the atmosphere of the mailing you are creating: clearly, you should then design the piece to maximise the effect of the format. If you have chosen a newsletter as your brochure style, then obviously it makes sense to make it look like a newsletter. Less obviously, but to make the point more clearly, if you choose a quotation format to do the job of your brochure (as you would for a loan

Fig. 49: Mailings with a difference (2).
In certain cases, you can always break the 'rules' wide open when the need is there. Here's a mailing to tempt people to try a brand new Porsche 928, selling for around £60,000. However good your copy and art direction is, you'll find it extremely difficult to recreate the awesome thrill of driving such a car. Solution? Simply put the thing on to video. But look how this pack still keeps to the basic principles...there's a letter, a reply card and even a brief product brochure. 'Gimmick' mailings like these need to be used very carefully – the costs are astronomical and they don't always work as well as you think (with videos, for instance, you have to find a player to watch the thing...with an ordinary mailing, all you have to do is read it). But on those rare occasions, unusual mailings can pay off.

or insurance mailing, for instance) then the style should be in keeping: little colour, restrained typography, verging on the dull.

THE FLYER

Last but not least, the final element to consider is what is loosely termed 'the flyer'. The flyer is basically any other piece of paper you care to add to the above list.

The flyer is a highly effective item. In many tests, the addition of extra information in the form of a flyer produces results that more than pay for the costs of printing and enclosing the extra piece.

You may well feel that the letter and brochure have given enough information: they probably have, but a flyer acts as a sore thumb – it sticks out and draws the reader's attention to it, and can thus act powerfully to reinforce your message.

The flyer comes in two main guises: the testimonial letter or 'third voice' letter being one of the most popular, and the free gift flyer being the second most common use.

Adding testimonials in the form of letters is a powerful but little used technique: you will be astonished at the results – but beware: they must be exact facsimiles of the original letters to carry any authority at all. The best method is to print them separately on different types of paper to make them as realistic as possible.

A variation on the testimonial letter is the 'third-voice' letter: 'third voice' because it appears to come from someone other than the writer of the main letter. This letter is very useful in fundraising: the General Secretary of the Labour Party will have credibility signing an appeals letter, but you can hardly have the Leader asking for cash.

Thus we would write a separate letter from the Leader, just talking about politics, but with a little bit at the end talking about the need for funds.

This arrangement works equally well for most other types of mailing: good 'third voices' to use are MDs, Consultants, Prize Draw Managers, Fund Managers, Designers, even The Chairman's Wife has been used on rare occasions.

Like testimonials, they should usually take the form of typewritten or handwritten letters. But other formats are sometimes used: memos are particularly good. Copies of 'internal documents' can be equally handy. Your choice of main format will to some extent dictate what kind of format you can use on your flyer: for example, the 'report from the field' format used with great success by fundraisers often has copies of telexes from the field worker.

It's important that lift letters have a very different tone-of-voice to the main letter – often the fact that they come from someone higher up in the company gives them a more formal, restrained tune.

The free gift flyer is a different task. The job it has to do is first, focus the reader's mind on the free gift, and second, 'sell' it. I have discussed some of the creative techniques that work best in Chapter 10 on Incentives. The main task is the selling of the incentive: too many free gift flyers end up as a photograph of a clock radio and one paragraph of copy under a headline that says 'FREE'. This is far from adequate.

Many other types of flyer can be devised – one of the best being newspaper cuttings. Keep in mind the basic task of the flyer – to focus attention on the strongest part of your message by using a separate item to create that focus. You can then invent flyers to do a variety of jobs.

The last word on flyers must be with Drayton Bird and a story he tells about the mailer who one season added a testimonial flyer to his control pack.

Encouraged by the result, he added a second one.

This too increased response enough to pay for itself, so he added another.

As each season went by, he added more and more, with each one earning its keep, until finally he stopped with no less than 50 testimonial flyers in the pack.

ROUGHING OUT THE PACKAGE

By now you have the basics of the mailing pack before you. What is the best order to create each piece? I assume you have been through the vital first steps:

1 The action you want

2 The amount you can spend

3 The person you're talking to

The first task is to rough out the whole package, visually. At this point, you now know the sort of format you want and the elements you need given the overall proposition, so you should not be working in the dark; indeed, the package should tend to design itself.

You also need to be taking mechanical issues into account at this stage, such as size, encloseability, price, timing and any other considerations.

Typically you will rough out the items same-size on layout paper, chop them out, fold them up and enclose them in a rough envelope to see what happens.

This process is one of the most interesting parts of creating a mailing. The writer and the art director, working up the layout in this way, will begin to see the package come together item by item, and this then helps to clarify what each item needs to say or needs to look like.

Indeed, as you go through this process, it is perfectly reasonable to change your mind as the ideas become reality. What you originally thought would be a good format may, in the light of reality, turn out not to work so well after all.

BEFORE YOU WRITE A WORD

You will have noticed that throughout this process I have not yet referred to the copy. *Until the format and the elements are satisfactory, you should not write a word.*

It is far better for the writer and art director to sort out the ground plan before undertaking the specifics. By working hard on the format, many ideas occur and thoughts change. Writing copy too early will only be a waste.

Equally, the function of each item becomes clearer as you proceed. The flyer, the order form, the envelope – as you develop them, the message each should contain becomes more and more obvious.

The remaining work is curiously straightforward. Both writer and art director will now know exactly what each piece should look like and what each piece should say.

PUTTING PEN TO PAPER

The next stage is developing the package to a final 'concept'. Here, you now put rough designs on paper to convey a reasonable impression of what the final piece will look like; and the writer needs to write to main headline and sub-headlines.

All of this needs to be done together. The art director will need to headline to make sense of the visual side; the writer will need the visual to make sense of what the headlines are supposed to say.

Again, as with the format stage, the concept stage can also produce changes – and you should allow for such changes as you progress through the work. Sometimes, what you thought was a good idea doesn't actually work when you write the headline. Don't hold to the idea at any cost. Discard it and go in another direction.

THE FINAL RUN

You have now created a format both you and the production people are happy with, and you have now produced a rough concept design that includes actual headlines and sub-headlines.

In terms of time spent on the overall package, the first stage – the format stage – should be around 25% of the total time, and the concept stage should be around 50% of the total time. Taking these two stages together you're looking at around 75% of the total creative effort, before a word of body copy or the final visual is produced.

The planning stages are where the real creative tasks are done. What the format looks like and what the concept looks like so pre-determines what the detail should do that the remaining work should be little more than "filling in the gaps".

START WITH THE LETTER

Writing the letter is the best starting place for the copywriter. The letter contains the meat of the argument. For this reason it is also the hardest item to write. Once that is written and you are reasonably happy with it, writing the brochure is straight-forward, followed by the flyer and then the order form.

FIRST DRAFT AND EDITING

Once you have completed the first draft, you should let the art director have this straight away.

The copy on the order form, once written in detail, may change the order form substantially. Always give the art director first draft copy so they can then visualise the item from the copy itself rather than working blind. A good art director will normally visualise the order form 'line by line', making sure the copy and the details fit, making sure there's enough room left for people to write their names and addresses, for example. Again, you should allow for changes at this stage if necessary.

Once the art director has a first draft to work with, the writer now needs to turn back to the first draft and get busy editing.

However pleased you are with the first draft, *editing always repays*. Personally, I tend to overwrite copy and it always needs shortening. This is a habit I have encouraged in myself, because through overwriting you get in everything you want to say – and then in editing, you still leave in what you said, but you make it shorter, punchier and more pointed. This gives a more *powerful* impression to the reader.

During the writer's editing phase, the art director will be finishing up the visual to presentation standard. This is not so calm as it sounds – changes still need to be made on the way given that copy sometimes doesn't fit.

But finally you have second draft copy plus a detailed visual. Now, all it needs is for account managers, account directors, clients and production houses to wreak their own brands of havoc on it, and finally your labours will be put before the *only* person who will make any kind of sensible judgement on your work; the prospect.

HOW LONG?

How long should it take to create a mailing?

Clearly, the more experience you have, the shorter time it takes. But a reasonably skilled team should be able to work on the following as an 'elapsed time' schedule – by elapsed, I mean actual hours spent not counting the inevitable interruptions.

For even an average mailing, *between three and five solid working days will be needed* for a decent result. For more complex mailings (such as prize draw packages or insurance products) longer will be necessary. If you try to short-circuit this time, all that happens is that there is not sufficient time to go back over concepts and ideas and develop them. You will therefore get a 'first off' package which stands much less chance of success than a package that has been carefully thought out.

Practically, three or five solid working days for most people *means a lot longer.* Given the interruptions and pressures of agency life, for example, getting three solid days of work on a package can *easily* take over a week of 'real' time. Five days becomes two weeks.

Few people outside of the creative process realise the sheer time and slog that goes into creating a mailing. Every extra hour spent on a mailing is worth it – the improved results that calm editing can produce are worth the extra few hours of time taken.

Clients who force agencies into low creative fees are making very false economies. If people have to work at a rush because of financial pressures, you simply cannot expect to get good, well-thought-out work. I've seen many cases where internal review processes at the client end take longer than the time allowed for creative work; you can imagine what the results are like! ■

CHAPTER 11: SUMMARY

The secret of success in mailings is always to have in mind that you are looking to achieve action in sending the mailing. You need to think 'action' throughout.

You need to determine exactly what action you are looking for; a reply, a phone call, a visit, or even just a warm feeling. Knowing this from the outset will pre-determine your work and send it down the most appropriate creative channel. Never create a mailing without knowing clearly what it is you want to achieve.

Once action required is established, you need to know what budget you should work within, and lastly who you are writing to. Both of these factors affect the type of mailing you create. Clearly budgetary considerations have a considerable effect – but so does the sort of person you are writing to; the type of mailing you will create for a businessman will differ greatly from one aimed at older women looking for charity donations, for example.

The next step is to select the most appropriate format, given the action required, the budget and the type of person you are writing to.

Mailings are all different, but all mailings should have at least a letter. They then typically contain a brochure, an order form, perhaps a flyer. Other elements should be added as the format and message demands – never be afraid of adding too much, but be very wary of having too little.

Shape and size of envelope is one of the most important creative decisions. Too many mailings go out in DL or C4 envelopes and the result is boredom. Different shapes and sizes make unusual and attractive mailings.

Only once all of the above is determined should the actual writing and design work commence. More creative time should be spent on the conceptual phase than on the writing and design phase. This is where more real creative decisions are taken.

Time is needed. Typically, three to five days elapsed time (ignoring interruptions) will be needed to create a good mailing. Less than this and you are not spending sufficient time to work through all of the detail.

How To Write More
Successful Letters

*In all mailings, the letter is the most important part.
No mailing should ever be sent without a letter; and if money
is tight, a mailing that consists simply of a letter will do
better than anything else. It follows that the better the letter,
the better the response, and tests show this to be true.
Here's how it's done.*

I F YOU work in an office, you probably get two sorts of mail. The first sort is the rubbish, or true 'junk' mail. Typically it consists of A4 manila envelopes, enclosed in which is a lavish colour brochure, your name and address on a sticky label attached at an angle on the front. How many of these do you read? Most of it gets thrown away.

The second type is real mail. By real, I mean those with letters. Either important letters addressed to you, or not such important letters starting 'Dear Sir/Madam…' A lot more of this type of mail will get read.

This is just one way of highlighting the importance of the mailing letter. Culturally, we are trained from our earliest days to expect a letter when we get an envelope delivered through the front door. And we always associate the letter with something important; *it contains a message that needs to be read and quite often acted upon.*

Without doubt, any mailing *has to have* a letter. But more importantly, the letter you use is a critical part of the success of that package: it is, arguably, the most important part.

As mentioned in the previous Chapter, the letter is the first job a writer should tackle; it clarifies the proposition and contains all the necessary selling arguments which you can then go on to use later in other copy such as brochures.

But good letters are notoriously difficult to write well.

Like all things, there is an underlying methodology which helps. Having said that, while the following is a good workmanlike formula that will result in good, working letters, the letter remains one of the few places where the copywriter's true skill can shine. And in the hands of an outstanding writer, a letter becomes one of the most *powerful* pieces of selling prose ever written.

LENGTH OF THE LETTER

In previous Chapters the subject of copy length has been amply aired. I will have to return to the subject once more, particularly in relation to the length of a letter.

With the letter, the saying that copy length needs to be 'as long as it needs to be' has its truest meaning. For example, in a mailing sent out to the donor file following a by-election victory for the Labour Party, the letter wasn't even a letter but a telegram.

Compton & Woodhouse

Arundel House, London N15 4TR

> "Can I send you 'The Fox' – the first plate in the magnificent
> new Royal Worcester series 'Familiar Friends'…the stunning British
> wildlife studies of Archibald Thorburn – to view at home
> **without any obligation whatsoever?"**

Dear Customer,

Let me send you a beautiful new plate. It is produced in fine English bone china by Royal Worcester, one of our most famous factories.

It is edged in 22 carat gold – gold that is applied by hand to every single plate.

It is also a unique plate: available only from Compton and Woodhouse - you'll never see it in any shop.

But the reason why I believe you will delight in this plate as much as I did is its subject: the plate I would like you to look at (without any obligation whatsoever) features a superb watercolour of that most British of wild animals, (The Fox) - drawn by one of the great masters of wildlife watercolours, Archibald Thorburn.

Will you accept my invitation?

In the next three or four weeks, we shall be advertising this new 'Familiar Friends' series in the Colour magazines. As this is an edition limited to just 15,000 complete sets, I'd like you - as one of my customers - to be one of the first to acquire this prestigious new collection.

Simply say 'yes' on the enclosed application, and I will immediately reserve a plate in your name. You send no money now. And, once your plate has arrived and you've had a while to look at it, if you're not completely satisfied, simply send it back: any money you have paid will be quickly

Compton & Woodhouse Ltd. Registered Office: Arundel House, 80 Lawrence Road, London N15 4TR. Registered No. 1868906 England.

---

and courteously refunded - you have my word.

But before you finally decide, can I spend a few minutes telling you a little more about the plate...about Archibald Thorburn himself - and about the extraordinary process that has allowed us to create such a vivid and accurate portrayal of Thorburn's masterpieces?

THE OUTSTANDING WILDLIFE ARTIST OF HIS DAY

Archibald Thorburn was generally regarded, in his day (he died in 1935), as the outstanding natural wildlife artist. From his earliest years, he was a prolific painter of British birds and mammals.

Today, Thorburn's works are eagerly collected. Recently, original Thorburn paintings have commanded prices of over £10,000 in auction.

To find the originals for this collection, we went to the archives of London's Natural History Museum.

Looking through the magnificent illustrations, it was clear to me that in order to do justice to them, a way of reproducing the delicate detail and subtle colour had to be found.

EACH PLATE IS PRODUCED FROM 12 SEPARATE LITHOGRAPHIC TRANSFERS

To produce the plates with a quality that satisfied not only me, but also The Natural History Museum, we contacted a firm called Capper Rataud.

"Capper's", as they are called in the Potteries, is an old established family firm that dates back to 1905. They specialise in the unusual art of making lithographic transfers for fine china...a more expensive and time-consuming process than the ordinary silkscreening used for cheaper china.

Yet nothing else would achieve the extraordinary sense of life, and rich infusion of colour attained in these marvellous plates. It is the most fitting tribute that Compton & Woodhouse can pay to that master of detail, Archibald Thorburn himself.

THE SKILLS OF STAN SMYTHEMAN

Stan Smytheman, Capper's master craftsman, led the challenging project of recreating all the rich detail of Thorburn's original illustrations onto lithographic transfers. To show you the skill and minute attention-to-detail which goes into this meticulous process, let me tell you how one particular plate - 'The Fox' - is created.

First, the original Thorburn illustration is carefully photographed, using special cameras. Once this is done, the original is 'separated' into no less than 12 different colour transfers - each made of wafer-thin sheets of inks -

---

Fig. 50:
Anatomy of a mailing letter (1).

This illustration shows page 1 and 2 of a 4 page letter for a Compton and Woodhouse plate product (pages 3 & 4 are shown opposite). The mailing is directed at previous customers and is asking them to take plate 1 of a 10 plate collection. All of page 1 is about the main proposition – 'take the first plate as evidence of the quality of this collection'. A Johnson Box heads the letter, and the copy refers *only* to the offer. Following the salutation, the copy continues with the main offer, with very little (yet) about the product. Note how active the copy is, and note the early close in the last paragraph. Also note the way the copy doesn't end at a full stop on page 1 – it 'hangs' in mid-air to encourage you to turn the page. At the top of page 2 we go into the detail, using a link phrase… 'But before you finally decide, can I spend a few minutes telling you a little more about the plate…' The remainder of this page is product detail – note the level of detail the letter goes into. We assume the reader is extremely interested.

to capture every hue and small detail of Thorburn's illustration.

ALL THE COLOUR AND DETAIL OF THE ORIGINAL

No effort is spared to faithfully reproduce all the colour and texture of the original brushstrokes. The golden gleam of the fox's thick coat...the pure white tip of his magnificent tail...the brown roots of the old gnarled tree. Indeed, to faithfully recapture the exact pink of the flowers, Capper's skilled craftsmen actually blend three different shades together.

The transfers are then carefully placed, by hand, on the plate by the skilled craftsmen and women at Royal Worcester...a name long prized for style and excellence, and sought after by discerning collectors since 1751.

As a special finishing touch, a delicate edge of 22 carat gold is applied - also by hand - before the plate is fired in the kiln at a temperature of 820°C. In this fierce heat, the inks melt and the 12 colours merge into the superb reproduction you see on the finished plate.

GLEAMING CLARITY AND DEPTH OF COLOUR

The result is a gleaming, flawless plate with a clarity and depth of colour that I feel will surprise you when you see it 'for real'. The colour printing in the enclosed brochure (good though it is) simply cannot show the magnificence of the finished plate...the marvellous detail of the fox's soft fur...the cunning gleam of his eyes...the power of his crouching pose...

THAT'S WHY I WOULD LIKE YOU TO TAKE UP MY
OFFER: INSPECT 'THE FOX' AT HOME WITHOUT
ANY OBLIGATION WHATSOEVER. I CAN ASSURE
YOU THAT YOU'LL BE IMPRESSED!

But, of course, it is the work of Archibald Thorburn that is the purpose of the plate.

Born in Scotland in 1860, he rapidly rose to fame in his early 20's as a wildlife painter of unusual skill. His main interests were in birds and mammals - and some of his early successes were scenes from the Scottish Highlands, particularly game birds and stags.

But his particular favourites were the familiar birds and animals that in his day were common in fields and hedgerows all over Britain.

For this 'Familiar Friends' series, I have chosen, together with The Natural History Museum, 10 of Thorburn's finest paintings, featuring British wildlife that we all know and love.

There's the wise and wily Fox, regal in his den. The perky Squirrel, so full of life and movement you can almost touch him. A pair of sleek Water Voles, busy at a river bank. A Rabbit, foregoing flight for one sweet moment in the sun.

There's an Otter, beady eye ready for the slightest

ripple of a fish. A pair of Badgers exploring the world beyond their set. A Common Hare, beautifully framed against a backdrop of winter snow. A shy Dormouse, venturing into an autumn glade. Two graceful Roe Deer browsing in the forest.

And lastly, what must have been a special favourite of the artist, with his love of the Scottish Highlands: the proud Wild Cat, portrayed in all his magnificence.

ASK TO SEE 'THE FOX' NOW. DECIDE AT HOME IF YOU WISH TO START YOUR COLLECTION. BUT YOU'RE UNDER NO OBLIGATION.

I hope you'll accept my invitation. Remember, you're under no obligation if you do.

Here's what to do now - and exactly what will happen next.

Simply sign the enclosed application form. The first plate in the 'Familiar Friends' series will be reserved in your name. Once ready for despatch (this will be around 8-10 weeks...as you can imagine, the complex process involved in making these plates is inevitably a slow one), we will write to you telling you that your reserved plate is ready, and offering you the ability to pay in two convenient instalments of just £15.75 (inclusive of £1.50 post and packing) each month; or you can pay by credit card.

Once your plate arrives, you will be entitled to return it at any time within 28 days. Any money you will have paid will promptly and courteously be returned without question.

Then, about two months later, you will be sent the second plate in the 'Familiar Friends' series, on exactly the same no-obligation basis.

So in asking to see 'The Fox' you are most certainly not committing yourself to taking any more plates in the series. It's completely up to you to decide.

BUT CAN I ASK YOU TO DECIDE QUICKLY? WE WILL
START ADVERTISING 'FAMILIAR FRIENDS' TO THE
GENERAL PUBLIC IN ABOUT FOUR WEEKS' TIME. I'D
LIKE YOU TO HAVE THE FIRST OPPORTUNITY.

So, as it's a limited edition series, the earlier you apply, the greater your chances.

Simply sign the enclosed Reservation Form and we'll look after everything else.

Best wishes,

RWard

Mrs Rinalda Ward
Managing Director

P.S. Please remember - I do not want you to send any money with your Reservation. And when the time for payment comes, you can pay on your credit card or in two convenient instalments of just £15.75 - including postage and packing.

Fig. 51:
Anatomy of a mailing letter (2).

Pages 3 and 4 of the Compton and Woodhouse mailing letter. On page 3 the detail of the product continues. Incidentally, product detail like this (and that on page 2) rarely comes in a brief - information of this kind, which is very important to the reader, usually has to be dug out by the writer. Half way down page 3 note the reprise of the main offer, in a centred paragraph printed in blue. A second reprise and call to action starts at the top of page 4 in the third paragraph, also printed in blue. The remainder of the copy is all action, and in particular features a 'what will happen' section, explaining to the reader what happens when they reply. There are further reiterations of the action sequence down to the end. The PS is used to reinforce part of the offer - in this case, the 'send no money' and credit terms. Note throughout the letter the use of typewriting rather than typesetting, other than for the Johnson Box (see following page) and the general letter layout with the use of indented and centred paragraphs to break up the text. 2 colours are used, primarily to enable the signature to appear in blue.

Total copy length was about 100 words. Here, the message was simple. Little could be added as the papers were full of the story that morning. Thus it was as long as it needed to be.

Conversely, in Bob Stone's excellent book 'Successful Direct Marketing' there is an example of a 12 page letter, conveying you on an imaginary trip around the world. Given the size and excitement of the subject, you will find that when you read the letter that 12 pages is possibly a little too short.

The skill of the writer is an important factor, too. To write a 12 page letter is easy; *but to write 12 pages that somebody will read is an entirely different proposition.* It is the ultimate test of the writer's craft and few writers possess the talents to sustain interest for so long.

The best measure of required length is simple. Sit down, write the letter, make sure you've said everything you need to say, say it in a compelling, detailed and exciting way, *then stop when you've finished.* The physical length of the resulting letter is unimportant.

(If you're reading this Chapter first, you will now need to read Chapter 1 – "Why Things Work" – for a more detailed explanation of why long copy works.)

THE FAMOUS FOUR

Having said that physical length is unimportant, we do need to enter the practical world of direct mail. A 12 page letter is expensive to produce, while a 4 page letter (normally A3 folded down to 4 A4 sides) is cheap. Thus the habit has arisen of many mailing letters ending up as 4-pagers – a comfortable length long enough to do most jobs, and short enough to be economic to print.

The advent of laser printed formats of ever-increasing complexity has started to change this, however. Writers are increasingly constrained by such formats and in order to produce a letter, space is sometimes one of the more important factors. This is not necessarily a bad thing, but beware: if you have to write letters that are too short because of format constraints, then it's time to insist that the format is changed to accommodate a longer letter.

THE PLACE OF THE LETTER WITHIN THE MAILING

On the subject of formats, some modern in-line processes cause the writer of the letter a particular problem. The letter, given its importance, should almost always be seen as the 'main' piece when the mailing is opened (the exception being prize draws or heavily incentivised mailings, where the incentive piece is often the 'hero').

If a format, no matter how economical, pushes the letter into third or fourth place, then I would suggest you do not use that format. The danger is that you can end up with a mailing that looks like just another glossy brochure, with the letter so hidden that the point of it is lost.

LETTER STRUCTURE

The key to making letters easier to write is to follow a specific structure. The AIDCA formula works well here; but we can be even more specific about structure because almost all good letters will tend to follow it.

The fundamental structure is as follows:

1 THE BEGINNING…basically, this is the offer or the proposition.
2 THE DETAIL…this section expands on the offer but also contains much more detail about the product/service.
3 THE REPRISE…here, you resell the proposition or the offer.
4 THE CALL TO ACTION…the most important part.

1: THE BEGINNING

Logically enough, we shall start at the beginning – for all writers the hardest part. Where should a good letter start?

The answer is to not start at the beginning of the letter at all, but some way before it. You need, first, a headline or the equivalent. I have discussed headlines at length in Chapter 3 and it all applies here. But headlines can differ in letters.

In the case of the NSPCC letter, shown in fig 52, the headline:

"Will you give £18 this Christmas to help save a child's life?"

is the main starting point of the letter and it benefits visually from being in childish handwriting.

There are further variations. What is called a 'Johnson Box' is an extended headline, contained in a box above the beginning of the letter. Usually, it is somewhat more than a headline – almost a mini-precis.

You may have noticed at the beginning of each Chapter of this book a short summary of what follows. This is in effect a Johnson Box. The art of a good Johnson Box is to use length, rather than writing a more conventional 'punchy' headline.

It is normally contained within a box of asterisks:

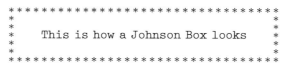

```
* * * * * * * * * * * * * * * * * * * * * * * * * * * * * * * *
*                                                             *
*                                                             *
*          This is how a Johnson Box looks                    *
*                                                             *
*                                                             *
* * * * * * * * * * * * * * * * * * * * * * * * * * * * * * * *
```

or within plain rules, or on a coloured background or visually differentiated in whatever way you choose, although the original asterisked version is strongest.

An alternative treatment is the star list or bullet points:

       ✱ Each feature is given a new line
     ✱ So that the reader can easily see them
      ✱ And it begins to sound good
       ✱ The more you add

Other 'headline' treatments can be:

■ Majoring on the free gift
■ A quotation, particularly a testimonial
■ A photograph or illustration

all of which can act as the headline.

There are not many cases where you should not have some form of headline at the start of your letter. The exceptions are where the personal tone would be damaged – the telegram I referred to earlier simply doesn't look like a telegram if you have a headline on it – and highly targeted, highly personalised letters lose their impact if headlining techniques are used.

The time and place to use headlined letters is with pre-printed mass mailings.

WHAT DO YOU SAY?

After the headline (which will, if you refer to Chapter 3, concern itself with the offer or the proposition) the opening of the letter should *continue* with the proposition or the offer. It will normally be a straightforward expansion of the headline.

There is never a case for starting the letter elsewhere, as I show below. Even though the headline has made the proposition clear, your opening sentences need to move off from that same starting point.

This is much harder than it sounds. The most common failing in letter-writing, even for experienced writers, is the

'starting-the-copy-halfway-down-page-one problem'

for which the only known cure is dexterity with the delete function on your WP. The problems of starting copy are discussed at length in Chapter 6. Certainly the problem is most noticeable in letters; I think the 'personal' tone of letters prevents many writers from diving straight into the proposition, plus the fact that copy length is less restricted. *Almost every mailing letter I see would benefit from being chopped half-way down page one*, leaving another half page for something important.

DEAR FRIEND, DEAR READER…

Oddly enough, one of the most commonly asked questions at seminars on letter-writing is about the salutation you should employ, if non-personalised. Should it be Dear Friend? Dear Reader? Dear Customer?

I am not aware of any difference in response in using different salutations. Frankly, I think the salutation is the least of your problems – use the one you feel most comfortable with. I always use Dear Reader, on the simple theory that it is the *least* offensive of them all.

HOW MUCH SPACE SHOULD BE DEVOTED TO THE BEGINNING?

Taking a typical 4 page letter, you won't hit your proposition very hard unless you have devoted most of the first page to it. In other words, before you get on to discussing the merits of the product or the service, you should have spent around 25% of your available length in developing the proposition/offer argument.

This means that you cannot get away with a quick mention of the offer and then move onto the detail. You have to sell it, and sell it hard…

```
"Dear Reader,
If you reply to this invitation within 14 days, you will be
sent, quite free and without obligation, a copy of a magnifi-
cent hardbacked volume entitled xxxxxxxxxxxxx, packed with
detail over more than 300 full colour pages written by some
of the greatest authorities on the subject..."
```

versus

Fig. 52: Letter design.

In this NSPCC letter, you can see how design elements have become an important part of the strength of the letter. Indeed, we have found that illustrating letters, particularly fundraising letters, is a highly successful technique. Points to note are the headline, in green and a childish scrawl; the use of underlining; the use of green 'marker pen' to highlight certain areas; the illustrations (all captioned); the use of hand-drawn stars for emphasis; and the use of a handwritten PS. Most of these design elements are deliberately crude to achieve the 'amateurish' effect that is so important in fund-raising – but similar techniques, not so crudely done, work just as well with letters aimed at other audiences.

NSPCC

The National Society
for the Prevention of
Cruelty to Children

67 Saffron Hill
London EC1N 8RS
Telephone 071-242 1626

<u>Will you give £15</u> this Christmas to <u>help save a child's life?</u>

Dear Friend,

October 1992

<u>That may sound dramatic but, in this country, on average three to four children a week die following abuse or neglect.</u>

And, many, many more are severely injured...seriously neglected...living in daily, hourly fear of abuse...

Children like Jane and Alice...

Their father beat his two daughters so violently that Jane had two black eyes and Alice was badly cut.

After her father brutally kicked her, Jane had to be taken to hospital with bruising on her legs and several fractured ribs.

The NSPCC took immediate and effective action to ensure the two girls were made safe.

If we had not had the funds available to help Jane and Alice - how much <u>worse</u> might the result have been?

<u>£15 could be instrumental in saving a child's life.</u>

Every day of the year abused children, like Jane and Alice, face the most appalling dangers. But somehow, at

Patrons: Her Majesty The Queen, Her Majesty Queen Elizabeth The Queen Mother.
President: Her Royal Highness The Princess Margaret Countess of Snowdon.
Chairman Central Executive Committee: Michael Moore.
Director: Christopher Brown.
Founded 1884. Incorporated by Royal Charter. Charity Registration No. 216401.

Christmas, when the rest of the country is enjoying itself, the plight of these children seems all the more pitiable.

It was Christmas Eve when the NSPCC was told about the plight of little Ellie. We found out this young girl was being left alone for days without light, heat or food in the bitter cold.

The floors and furniture were covered in filth and her only company was the cats shut in with her. There was no electricity or any form of heating. Ellie had not had a meal in the house for weeks, and couldn't remember when she last slept in a bed.

Hungry, lonely, scared...all Ellie wanted for Christmas was for her mother to come home. We made sure that in future, Christmas for Ellie would be very different indeed.

Just <u>one call</u> to the NSPCC Child Protection Helpline may mean that we can prevent at least some of this happening.

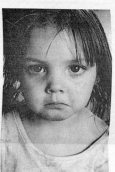

Your £15 could help pay for that first vital visit to a child whose life may be in danger - a defenceless child like Ellie.

Last year we helped many thousands of children in desperate need of protection.

That is why your help means so much. And why, as the season of goodwill approaches, I am asking you to help us carry on answering the many cries for help from children in need.

It enables us not just to protect children who have been abused...<u>but to prevent such situations arising.</u>

It is <u>essential</u> that we carry on being able to respond promptly to the calls for help.

But to do this we need <u>your</u> assistance.

The NSPCC gets very little government money. In fact, nearly <u>90% of our income comes from people like you,</u> who care very much about the wrongs being done to too many children.

And <u>we spend very little on administration.</u> The greatest

Ellie was left alone without light, heat or food in the bitter cold...

---

possible 'slice' of our income is devoted directly to helping children.

We need your help to provide -

<u>AID TO CHILDREN SUFFERING FROM PHYSICAL INJURY</u> caused by actual physical abuse by their parents or guardians...last year we responded to several thousand children in this frightening situation.

<u>HELP FOR CHILDREN WHO HAVE BEEN SEXUALLY ABUSED.</u> It is hard to express in words just how frightening and traumatic sexual assault is for the children involved.

<u>PROTECTION FOR NEGLECTED CHILDREN.</u> Too often, children are not properly cared for by their parents or guardians - and serious problems can result. Last year, we had many worrying incidents of neglect reported to us.

Without your help we cannot continue to run -

<u>THE NSPCC CHILD PROTECTION HELPLINE.</u> Anyone who suspects a child is at risk from abuse can ring one FREE national number 24 hours a day, to ask us for immediate help, which could save a child's life.

<u>CHILD PROTECTION TEAMS, CENTRES AND PROJECTS.</u> These NSPCC services are vital to the protection of children in danger. Every day the NSPCC is working - often in partnership with other professionals like the police, social services and teachers - to help and protect children who have been seriously abused or tragically neglected. It's critical that these services go on being funded.

£15 may not seem a large amount. Yet it can <u>help save a child in danger.</u>

With your help this Christmas we can perhaps make the children as happy - and safe - as they should be.

<u>Can you donate a £15 gift to help save a child's life?</u>

I know Christmas is just about the most expensive time of year. But your gift this Christmas could be critical to a child's safety.

So when you are doing your Christmas shopping, please pretend

This girl had to be taken to hospital after one of her father's beatings...

---

there's an extra child you have to buy a present for. And it's a gift they'll remember forever...a life free from the fear and misery of cruelty.

I have enclosed a simple form. Please return it as soon as possible. Your gift will be received with more gratitude than I can express.

On behalf of the many children you will be helping, may I thank you very much and wish you both a Happy Christmas and a peaceful New Year.

Yours sincerely,

Fiona Condie

Fiona Condie
NSPCC

P.S. When you remember that, on average, an estimated 3 to 4 children die every week following abuse or neglect, I am sure you will realise - just how hard our task is. We need all the help we can get for the children. Please send as much as you can today.

P.P.S. I have enclosed a car sticker which I hope you will use. We need as many people as possible to realise the need for a strong and active NSPCC, to continue protecting children from cruelty.

Thousands of children need protecting from cruelty every year.

<u>It is impractical for us to check whether you already support the NSPCC in other ways. If so, we'd like to apologise and ask you to pass this letter on to a friend who might be interested in helping the NSPCC too. Thank you.</u>

PRODUCED ON CYCLUS 100% RECYCLED PAPER

> "Dear Reader,
> You'll receive a free copy of XXXXXXX if you reply within 14
> days to this invitation – as your introduction to this brand new
> widget service..."

There is no virtue in rushing into the product benefits until you have totally convinced the reader about the offer or proposition.

Take a letter in which the opening is weak, rewrite it with more vigour by expanding upon the benefits of the offer, and you can rapidly transform a weak letter into a very strong one.

THE BENEFITS OF A TRIAL CLOSE

Trial closing has also been mentioned before, but again, in a letter, it has a particularly powerful role to play. The addition of trial closing creates in a letter a feeling of urgency and action that is impossible to replicate in any other way. Certainly, if you are using offers, then a trial close is *mandatory*.

Actually starting the letter with a trial close can work wonders. The example above actually does this. See how it sounds minus the trial close:

> "Dear Reader,
> I'd like to send you, quite free and without obligation, a copy
> of a magnificent hardbacked volume entitled xxxxxxxxxxx,
> packed with detail over more than 300 full colour pages written
> by some of the greatest authorities on the subject..."

Reasonable, but not half so strong as the original above.

In fact, trial closing comes in many different guises and writers get confused by what a trial close is. Here's a 'classic' trial close:

> "...brings you untold wealth, success and happiness for just
> £9.99. Why not send off for one right now? Just fill in the
> coupon and we'll send it to you within 21 days. But first, let me
> tell you a little more..."

This typically comes in at the end of the first paragraph or two of the copy. But trial closing can be at the very beginning, and can actually be soft:

> "Send off now for this widget, and you'll discover the secret of
> the universe..."

Here, the trial close is modified more into a call to action rather than a serious close. Yet it works as well, and it works even better allied to a time close...

> "Send off within the next 48 hours, and you'll discover the secret
> of the universe..."

Trial closing is, of course, an early *suggestion* of the need to take action. There are literally hundreds of ways of doing this, depending entirely on the task in hand and the needs of the particular job you are working on.

However, one cardinal rule is: never write more than 3 paragraphs of opening copy without some form of close coming in.

Choose the close most appropriate to the conditions, but choose one *anyway*.

2: THE DETAIL

You should now be about 25% of the way through your letter. You have written a headline/Johnson Box, you have opened with your offer, duly time closed, and expanded on it in detail.

You may now assume that your reader has become sufficiently interested in what you are saying to enter phase 2 of the letter, which is actually selling the product itself.

The *change-over phrase* has been mentioned earlier in this book:

> "But first, let me tell you more about..."

This is a convenient linking phrase for joining the two sections together.

Once achieved, you now have to sell the product/service to the reader. All of the copy techniques outlined earlier in this book apply here in full measure.

Given the additional space that most letters give you, you can exploit these techniques to their fullest. The 'brick-by-brick' technique, of adding product feature and benefit one on top of each other, is the most useful system for most subjects. You have the space to expand on the benefits. The formula is

x has y, which means z

as in

> "this plan (x) has redundancy cover (y), which means that you can continue the payments even if you can no longer work (z)"

where x is the product, y is the feature and z is the benefit deriving from that feature.

This phase of the letter can often be a 'simple' listing of all the features of the product or service. This is the most effective technique you can employ.

It sounds mechanistic, but the skill lies in writing each 'brick' so it's slightly different and interest is maintained throughout the section. Some features demand a lot of space, some features need only a little. Some will want one line, others several paragraphs. It's your judgement as a writer as to what makes the most compelling argument.

How long should this central section be? Around 50% of the total letter length is about right. The complexity or simplicity of the product will be an important consideration, but unless you can write a couple of pages of good copy about the subject, your letter will lack edge.

3: THE REPRISE

You are now 75% of the way through your letter. Following your opening, you have now carefully laid, brick by brick, the product features followed by benefits, before your reader. Your reader (if still with you) is getting convinced. Now is the time to push them over into the final stage.

Under the AIDCA formula, this would be the point at which we would think about testimonials and other convincing material. These certainly work.

In addition, the reprise technique can also add strength. Essentially, it is a re-iteration of the offer or proposition that you used at the *start* of the letter.

> "So, as you can see, your £15 really will make a huge difference to the way we can help children"

or, for a more offer-oriented letter

> "And remember, simply by applying for this card, you are automatically entitled to enter the Silver Dream Prize Draw that could win you a new Porsche".

Once again, it is not enough simply to repeat the offers. You must add colour and drama to build them up as a natural consequence of taking the action you are about to ask for.

This section should not take much space – perhaps two or three paragraphs of a 4 pager – but it is an essential linkage and creates the right framework for the last and most important section...

4: THE CALL TO ACTION

In reality, section 3 and 4 are part of the overall close, but it works better to keep them slightly apart to make sure that sufficient time is spent in reselling the offer/proposition. But having done that, you now need to work *hard* on the close itself.

The best approach is to regard the reader as totally convinced but now in that state of mind that needs a tiny push to make them get out the pen or pick up the phone.

The best place of all to study this is in a shop where even the dullest assistant can detect someone ready to buy but just need a few little 'confirmatory' pushes to get them there:

> *"I'm sure you'll be delighted with it – we sold twelve yesterday"*
>
> *"We haven't got many left"*
>
> *"If you order now, I can get it delivered this afternoon"*
>
> *"Look, if it doesn't fit, just bring it back – no problem"*
>
> *"I heard that there's a price increase coming next month"*
>
> *"That colour's perfect on you..."*

and similar phrases which we know are sales talk, but which we all readily accept because we have decided to buy – we simply need an excuse, however small.

Closes, then, fall into two sections. First is the 'excuses to buy' section as noted above. In a letter, it becomes something like:

> "Millions of people all over the world have discovered the benefits of..."
>
> "Supplies are limited..."
>
> "The earlier you start, the earlier you can benefit..."

OVERCOMING THE LAST BARRIER

. After you've given sufficient excuses to buy, this needs to be followed by the solution to the 'what happens if I reply?' problem. Here, we have to look again at what is happening in the customer's mind. We have convinced them they are ready to buy – but the last barrier is the method of purchase itself.

Fig. 53:
The PS.

The PS has a powerful fascination for the reader – they love to read the bits you 'left out'. So the PS becomes a 'hot spot' in the letter, and you should use it for important messages rather than incidental ones. Here are 6 that use the PS in a strong way, usually by reiterating the main offer or a variant on it. Remember you can also have a PPS and even a PPPS - but only do so if you have additional points of strength you want to make. Don't use a PS just because a book says so!

computer system.

    All you need to do is complete and return the Questionnaire supplied. Then, as soon as we hear from you, we'll prepare and send your personal Quotation.

    I hope you have found this information of interest. I look forward to hearing from you soon and will send your free Cost of Ownership comparison as quickly as I can.

Yours sincerely,

Andrew Selwood
AS/400 Product Manager

N.B.

You may feel that other computer systems seem less expensive at first sight. However, the true costs involved can change dramatically when you take into account the expense of running and maintaining your system. Why not find out the facts for yourself? Accept this offer and let us send you a free Quotation.

Yours sincerely,

Roger De Haan
Chairman - SAGA Group plc

P.S. If this offer is ever repeated we cannot guarantee that the terms and conditions will remain the same - so do reply now. And remember, you will receive a free travel cushion if you reply within the next 7 days.

Yours sincerely,

Caroline Stackhouse

Caroline Stackhouse
Shelter Regional Appeals Manager

P.S. Remember, we only have until the end of the year to raise the £100,000 we need for our National Appeal. So please send your donation right away - every penny counts!

Yours sincerely

Giles Pegram
Appeals Director

PS Because the National Training Appeal is such a vital, necessary part of offering better protection to abused children, we believe people playing a substantial role in its success should receive special recognition. Therefore, as a lasting testimony to your generosity, if you give the significant sum of £1,000, or more, you will have your name recorded on a role of honour in the NSPCC Child Protection Training Centre.

Yours sincerely,

Bob Scott
Head of RSPB Reserves Management.

P.S. Don't forget! By choosing to covenant your donation you can turn a £40.00 gift into £53.33 - at no extra cost to yourself. All you have to do is complete and return all of the attached forms.

Yours sincerely,

Manager

PS If you have any questions, please do not hesitate to talk to our helpful, friendly staff at the number shown overleaf. But don't delay calling: your preferential interest rate will only be held open for the next 14 days.

Borrow £500 to £10,000. With up to 5 years to repay.

Use this table to decide how much you can sensibly afford to repay each month. Loans are available in multiples of £50.

Amount of Loan £	12 MONTHLY PAYMENTS				24 MONTHLY PAYMENTS				36 MONTHLY PAYMENTS				48 MONTHLY PAYMENTS				60 MONTHLY PAYMENTS				Amount of Loan £
	With LoanCare Cover		Without LoanCare Cover		With LoanCare Cover		Without LoanCare Cover		With LoanCare Cover		Without LoanCare Cover		With LoanCare Cover		Without LoanCare Cover		With LoanCare Cover		Without LoanCare Cover		
	Monthly Payment £	Total Payable £	Monthly Payment £	Total Payable £	Monthly Payment £	Total Payable £	Monthly Payment £	Total Payable £	Monthly Payment £	Total Payable £	Monthly Payment £	Total Payable £	Monthly Payment £	Total Payable £	Monthly Payment £	Total Payable £	Monthly Payment £	Total Payable £	Monthly Payment £	Total Payable £	
500	50.29	603.36	46.92	563.04	28.44	682.56	26.07	625.68	21.41	770.76	19.19	690.84	NOT AVAILABLE				NOT AVAILABLE				500
1,000	105.56	1206.72	93.85	1126.20	56.89	1365.36	52.14	1251.36	42.82	1541.52	58.58	1383.60	37.13	1782.24	31.44	1909.12	34.50	2070.00	27.51	1658.00	1,000
2,000	201.12	2413.44	187.69	2252.20	113.77	2730.48	104.28	2502.72	85.64	3083.04	76.76	2763.36	74.25	3564.00	62.67	3017.76	69.00	4140.00	54.65	3277.80	2,000
3,000	301.69	3620.28	281.54	3378.48	170.66	4095.94	156.41	3753.84	128.46	4624.56	115.15	4144.60	111.34	5346.24	94.51	4520.88	103.50	6210.00	81.94	4916.40	3,000
4,000	402.25	4827.00	375.59	4504.60	227.54	5460.90	200.55	5005.20	171.28	6166.08	153.51	5526.36	148.51	7128.40	125.74	6033.52	138.00	8280.00	109.25	6555.00	4,000

The analogy with retail breaks down at this point, simply because the problem is that it is not retail. You cannot see anyone, you can't ask questions, you don't know what's going to happen next...all of the *disadvantages* of buying direct come into play.

It has to be said that they are not at this stage overwhelmingly strong, otherwise our reader would certainly not have got this far with any great interest. However, it is a fear that has to be recognised, and the clever writer will deflect those fears and help the buyer overcome the last barrier.

> "When you reply, we'll immediately prepare your personal policy document which will be sent to you in complete confidence. You'll then have 14 days in which to make up your mind. If you decide to accept the plan, you do nothing. We'll do all the work – we'll contact your bank..."

It sounds a bit like an idiot's guide on how to respond – even to the extent that I would suggest you talk about posting the reply form:

> "Complete the form below. Detach it, then place into the envelope provided – no stamp is needed – and post as soon as possible."

Bear in mind that your customer does have this underlying worry about writing off to complete strangers, and everything you can do to make this process *less* worrying, the better.

URGENCY

I cannot stress too much at this point the need for urgency all though the close: *urgency should permeate the whole section*, otherwise it becomes a flat list of instructions as to how to reply. Sprinkle 'now', 'vital', 'important' and a few other such adjectives around the close section. Add time limits where possible. Suggest that the benefits of purchase should not be delayed a moment longer.

Do not for one minute imagine that such urgency makes people literally rush about. What it does do, however, is make those people who were ready to respond actually go ahead and do it, rather than simply think it's a good idea but then leave the mailing on the mantelpiece.

Many otherwise excellent letters fail at this last hurdle. The prospect is completely convinced – but fails to take any action because the sense of urgency was not strong enough.

MOP-UP MAILINGS

The most vivid demonstration of this is when you see the results of follow-up or mop-up mailings.

Exactly the same mailing mailed to the same people after an interval of 2 or 3 weeks (often with an extended time close) can often achieve responses some 50 to 60% of the original response – sometimes as much as 100%. In other words, *there were more people who were convinced than who actually replied.* They must have lacked the final push at some point in the original mailing. The need for urgency is clearly paramount.

THE SIGNATURE

Like the salutation question, the signature question often arises. Who should sign it? It probably makes little difference one way or the other except in certain cases where the signatory is likely to be important to the responder.

On Compton and Woodhouse, where many of the collectors are female, I believe that a female Managing Director 'Mrs Rinalda Ward' is important.

But when it comes to getting the head of many organisations to sign a mailing letter, beware. They treat each mailing letter as a 'real' letter, and consequently want to make their own comments to the text, the most typical one being "good Lord, it's far too long, none of my friends would read a letter that long" (an actual comment, by the way).

Rather than run the risk of having your mailings rewritten, it is normally better to have somebody sign it who *understands* the direct mail process, even if that signature is not so impressive.

It is better for response to have a lowly marketing assistant sign a good mailing letter than to have the Chairman sign a bad one.

However, if the best you can come up with is 'Product Development Manager' then you're probably better off not bothering at all.

THE PS

Most mailing letters have a PS. The reason is because they work. Why?

A PS is 'something left out', and this has an extraordinary fascination for the human mind – so much so that the natural reaction of most people is to read it first.

The opportunity this creates is that it gives you a '*hot spot*' in the letter, only slightly less hot than the main headline. Thus the PS should be used for a repetition of the main offer or proposition, though it pays to do it in a slightly different way. Typically, a PS would contain a time-closed offer (which you may not necessarily have used in the main headline) or a similar action-oriented device.

Do not waste the opportunity of a PS. One example I saw was from a charity which had problems of de-duplication (I imagine the Chairman had two such mailings delivered at home) and which devoted the whole of the PS to an apology. A terrible waste.

ONE OR MORE PS?

Certainly it is feasible to have more than one PS.

The normal method is to have a typewritten PS followed by a handwritten PPS to give it a little bit more interest. I have seen a few rare examples of 3 PSs being used. The choice should depend on how hard you need to concentrate on your main offer.

If you have a mailing that hinges wholly around the offer, then I would suggest that double and even triple PSs have a place, as this gives you *additional ammunition* to fire. If your mailing is a softer one then the PS becomes rather bland and wouldn't stretch to more than one.

DESIGN AND TRACKING

The design of mailing letters is almost as important as the copy, though they are mostly thought of as a purely writer's medium.

There are two aspects to the design that need to be considered: first, the layout of the type on the page; second, the addition of other design elements to the text.

Before we consider these, it's worth just spending a bit of time on letter 'tracking', because the secret of successful letter design hinges on how the letter is read.

If you have a short letter of a couple of paragraphs, layout is hardly a problem. You start at the top and finish at the bottom in a matter of seconds. But long letters like four or more pagers are actually looked at and read in a highly specific sequence:

1 The front of the letter is looked at first

2 Almost immediately, the name of the person who sent it is looked for

– the reader goes immediately to the back page (and the PS)

3 The first few lines are read

4 The remaining body of the letter is scanned over

This whole process takes place in about four or five seconds. This is the process of the reader trying to find out if the letter is of real interest to him or her. If not, the letter is discarded within another five or ten seconds. If it is of interest, most of the letter will then be read – but not in 'start to finish' order. The reader continues to skip around the bits that are of interest, picking out paragraphs.

This tracking sequence is common to most people (except, sadly, people you show the letter to for approval who contrarily start at the beginning and carefully read their way through to the end) and explains why some of the ideas I have discussed above work.

1 The front of the letter is looked at...

this gives us the headline or Johnson Box rationale. A strong message here immediately gets through to the reader and sets up an expectation.

2 The reader goes immediately to the back page...

which explains the importance of the PS.

3 The first few lines are read...

showing how vital it is that the opening paragraphs of your copy are strong, and not hidden half way down page one.

4 The remaining body of the letter is scanned over...

which is where layout then becomes important.

LAYOUT

By layout, I mean the way in which the type is laid out on the page – more a typographical task than anything else. It is an important function because it ensures than when the reader skips or scans over the letter, there is something to catch the eye in every corner.

A number of layout techniques can be employed to assist this process.

1 Break up the text into short paragraphs. Five or six lines is the maximum.

2 Break up blocks of paragraphs with sub-headings. Every four or five paragraphs is about right.

3 Emphasise sections of your copy with indented paragraphs

   squeezed in like this

Fig. 54:
Using third-voice letters. Third-voice letters come from someone (or some organisation) different from the signatory to the main letter. They are typically used to amplify certain parts of the proposition, and by coming from a third voice can be used to re-express the proposition – reiteration being a key part of a successful mailing. Like main mailing letters, they should be typed, and by adopting different sizes of paper and different colours, the third voice can stand out well within the pack. They are particularly useful as endorsement letters. Here's a selection of just a few of the third-voice letters we use. Most of them are single-sided, and most are printed on paper half the size of the main letter. They can also be used for testimonials – a very effective treatment is to simply enclose a bunch of facsimile testimonials.

Mrs R Ward
Managing Director
Compton and Woodhouse
Arundel House
80 Lawrence Road
London N15

Dear Mrs Ward,

A brief note to say how pleased we all are with the
beautiful reproduction of the Thorburn plates. I am
particularly impressed with the clarity of detail that has
been captured.

I am sure the team at Cappers and especially Stan Smytheman
are to be congratulated on the lithography; and of course
Royal Worcester have worked to their usual high standard.

The Museum is proud of its Thorburn collection, and we are
delighted to see such a faithful rendition of the originals.
I am sure collectors will be equally pleased when they see
the actual plates.

Best wishes,

Rex Banks
The Natural History Museum

Christopher Brown
DIRECTOR
National Society for the
Prevention of Cruelty to Children

Dear Friend,

I am most grateful that you have decided
to help the work of the Society.

As the letter from Fiona Condie explained,
we depend very much on individual donations like
yours to keep the Society going. Having helped
us this Christmas, you will have made a most
significant contribution to our work.

I know very well that at this time of
year, there are many calls on your generosity,
all of which place a greater burden than usual
upon your resources. So your gift to abused
children is valued all the more.

You have helped extend a hand of hope to
the many children who will need us over the
coming weeks.

On their behalf, I thank you most sincerely
and wish you a Merry Christmas.

Christopher Brown,
Director

Dear santa,
mummy says we cannot be
at home anymore so you
cant find me becos I wont
be ther. Mummy says she
doesnt know where we
are going so I cannot tell
you where to come. Is it
OK please if you can come
later when we have
a house

your friend.
Nicky xx

to make them stand out

in the middle of the text.

4 Use <u>underlining</u>, *italics*, **bold** *and* ● *bullet points to create visual interest.*

5 Indent the start of paragraphs.

All of the above can be done on the WP. After that, you can add handwritten items – underlines, circles, slashes, all in a different colour, to create further emphasis.

Do you end up with a mess? If you were trained as a typist by IBM, yes you do. If on the other hand you *really* do want your letter read and acted upon as though your life and business depended on it, you end up with a *very* powerful letter.

THE IMPORTANCE OF TYPING

Last but not least, it is vital that your letter should look typed. The advent of desk-top publishing has tempted many people to start setting letters in Times Roman. This may suit the computer buffs but it fails to impress your direct mail letter reader. It is a cardinal rule of mailing letters that they appear to be typed – never typeset. Typeset letters simply become brochures and the whole point of them being personal communications is then wasted.

DESIGN

At risk of contradicting the point I have just made above, there is a strong case for adding brochure-like design elements to your letter. These are mainly illustrations.

So long as your letter continues to look like a letter, then *adding photographs certainly seems to improve results*, in some cases (such as fundraising letters) quite considerably.

Photographs have a news impact anyway. Printed on the rough recycled stock that most good fundraising mailing letters are printed on, they have a grainy impact which adds to this flavour.

If you use photographs, then ensure that each and every one of them are captioned. This point is made earlier in the book and counts just as much here.

Other methods of illustration can be usefully employed... 'illustrations' in the broadest sense:

1 Tables, bar charts, diagrams (especially for financial letters)

2 Case histories with lengthy captions and pictures of people

3 Facsimiles of letters – handwritten by other people (good as reports from the field in fundraising)

4 Testimonials

5 Press cuttings

All of these (and more) can be added to a letter by way of illustration and will serve not only to visually enhance the letter for the skip-reader, but will also greatly add to the net information content of the letter, turning it into a very powerful piece within the pack.

TO PERSONALISE OR NOT TO PERSONALISE

The question of whether to personalise the letter or not often arises. The general rule is that it is not mandatory – but it certainly helps.

It used to be the case that technical considerations meant you had to choose one item to personalise in the pack, and the best approach was that if you had that choice, it was probably better to personalise the reply piece rather than the letter.

Times have moved on and multiple personalisation is now relatively easy. Given that personalising the letter would add no extra cost to your pack, or involve you in a re-design of the whole format, then you should certainly personalise the letter.

If, however, cost becomes significant, there is not sufficient evidence to suggest that personalising the letter makes such a difference in response terms. In that case, it's not *worth* bothering with personalisation.

LETTER TESTING

All of the above will give you, I hope, a good working letter for your mailing pack. Your job at some point in the future will be to beat it.

It is curious that in the UK – as opposed to the United States – very little letter testing is done. In the US, rather than retest a whole new package, they will try a different letter approach to see if it works, leaving the rest of the pack much the same.

Granted that the volumes in the US are rather greater, that alone is no good reason to not introduce much more enlightened letter testing in the UK. It is cheap, fast, and I believe that if the right things are tested then significant improvements will be found.

Changing a few paragraphs is, of course, unlikely to achieve very much. Typically a rewrite of the same letter does not score significantly better or worse than the original, unless the original was very poor. More useful is to see if:

a) the offer can be improved

b) the proposition can be improved

c) the existing offer/proposition can be 'written-up' through stronger copy

Any one of these approaches is likely to do something and if I can leave you with one last thought at the end of this Chapter, it is that *beating* a good mailing letter is a far more satisfying achievement for a serious direct mail writer than writing a good letter in the first place ■

Chapter 12: Summary

*Unless you have little to say, short letters rarely work, long letters usually
do. A letter needs to be as long as it needs to be to do the job you want it to do.
Four pages is a reasonable length, but sometimes longer (much longer)
can work well.*

*Structuring your letter is vital for readability as well as to guide your reader
through the selling points you wish to make. The start is the critical point –
beware of starting the letter halfway down page one.*

*Use headlines or 'Johnson Boxes' to open your letter. Typically you will use your
main offer, or your proposition, as the subject of your headline, Johnson Box and
opening three paragraphs of copy.*

*Build up the selling argument in the body of your letter using the 'x has y, which
means z' formula – the product has a feature, which confers a specific benefit.
Build these up brick by brick to develop your sales story.*

*Reprise the offer/proposition and then ensure you have a strong call to action
which should take at least 25% of the letter. When you can, introduce that call to
action at the start of the letter as a trial close.*

*Use a PS, underlining, indented paragraphs, handwritten sections,
second colours and sub-heads to break up your letter to allow the skip-reader
to get your message easily.*

*Use photographs, diagrams, case histories and other illustrative material
in your letter to add to the net information content as well as to
break up the message for easier reading.*

*Consider testing major letter copy changes once you have established
a working control.*

How To Create
Stronger Press Ads

*Press advertising can create difficulties for creative people
more used to direct mail. Fortunately, the fundamental rules
are identical – the major difference is that you have a small
area to work in, rather than a number of sheets of paper.
This imposes its own special disciplines. It's worth
discovering them because creativity is one of the most
important factors in successful direct response advertising.*

I N DIRECT response press advertising, creativity assumes an importance that is much more obvious than with other types of direct marketing.

In direct mail, you have list variables, design variables, print cost variables and a host of other details that also affect the result, besides creative.

But in press ads, only two things really affect the result: first, the media choice, (which includes, importantly, the cost). Second, the creative work.

Thus the creative function becomes even more important in the world of press ads. Here's how to create them so that they work.

BACK TO BASICS

Creating press ads can often seem to be a more glamorous business than creating mailings. Creative people, with an eye on their portfolios, see the higher-profile world of press ads as a way of gaining a reputation.

Often the temptation can be to treat that press ad as an 'above the line' press advertisement, which while it may look good in the portfolio will almost certainly be a failure in direct response terms.

> *Direct response advertisements are very different to 'above-the-line' advertisements and it is a fundamental mistake to consider them as even vaguely similar.*

Fortunately, the same creative techniques that work for mailings work just as well, broadly speaking, when applied to press ads, so there need be no great difficulty in approaching the task of creating successful press ads, so long as the basic rules described more fully in earlier sections of this book, are kept to.

All of them, particularly the copy sections, have direct relevance to press ads. In particular:

1 The length of the copy is critical. Say too little, your ad will not work.

2 The headline is critical, even more so than in mailings.

3 The offer/proposition is critical.

4 The copy opening and close sections are critical.

The key problem comparing press ads with mailings is a simple one but one that has a profound effect: in a press ad you have a very limited space in which to satisfy most of these critical issues. In terms of copy length, the freedom that most writers have with direct mail is severely curtailed. Instead of four pages of a letter and several more of brochures and other items, suddenly you are restricted to a tabloid whole page or 25cm x 4...sometimes even less.

Similarly with the headline: no longer have you the luxury of spreading your message across limitless space. Now you have to make it work in a space often little larger than a couple of pages of a letter.

These are, however, best seen as problems of editing rather than as having to re-learn a whole new form of creativity. The important principle to remember is:

All the same creative rules and principles apply.

You just need to be more condensed.

This is not to say that you would, for example, write eight pages of copy and then attempt to edit it down to three hundred words for a press ad. Obviously you need to start out thinking in a more condensed way prior to commencing work.

But your planning and structure work would be exactly the same as if you were creating a mailing: it's in the execution that you need to train yourself to isolate the *truly* significant points and concentrate on those, leaving aside some, no doubt, good points that simply cannot be fitted in.

STARTING A PRESS AD

Given that you have already gone through the process of isolating the offer/proposition, the starting point for a press ad is much the same as for mailings. You need first to establish the 'format' – which in this case is not the physical shape of the mailing, but the layout. What will the ad look like?

This needs to be scribbled out between the writer and art director, and like a format design it will contain a number of vital points:

1 The headline

2 The general length of the copy

3 The illustrative features.

As with most direct mail, the majority of the 'creative' work is really done at this stage, with most of the balance of the work being essentially detail, important though the detail is.

THE RIGHT LOOK

In considering this stage of the work, what should you be aiming for?

There has been a habit for many years in the world of 'above the line' of designing ads almost like posters. This gives rise to, typically, a large, short headline, set in a type size considerably larger than that appearing in the neighbouring text, with correspondingly short copy length.

These ads may look pretty and doubtless they win awards. However, if a coupon or phone number is added to them, the total response they generate is rarely sufficient to cover the costs of the space. *People may look at them, but they certainly do not respond to them.*

There is, on the other hand, a general approach to the job of designing press ads which is rooted in a different approach – that of respecting, if you like, the environment in which your advertisement is appearing and allowing the rules of newspaper design and text to assist you.

In other words, if you give your advertisement an 'editorial' look, then you will almost certainly find that *your responses rise very dramatically* indeed. Drayton Bird reminds me: "I have never seen an editorial style ad fail to do better than an advertising style ad". This editorial approach fits in very neatly with the main creative principles outlined above – certainly the long copy approach is far more in tune with this method of creative.

You can choose the type of editorial approach you want to achieve. It does not have to be an exact copy – but it does need to share the general characteristics of the editorial approach.

In Chapter 7 on Art Direction I referred to the need to arrive at a 'visual proposition' where the art director would create the right visual atmosphere in order to overcome negatives and/or accentuate positives in the product. This does not conflict with the overall 'editorial' look that makes press ads work.

WHAT THE PAPERS SAY

It is worth looking carefully at newspaper design to see what techniques they employ. All newspapers and magazines employ the same basic approach, with only minor modifications. Certainly a Sun article will look jazzier than an Independent article, but the underlying approach is to present the story clearly – and it is the story that is important, not the way it is presented.

But editors know that their readers don't read everything in their papers. They know that they have to write a strong headline to catch the reader's interest. They know that the story has to be interesting. They know that adding illustrations and graphics helps make the story easier to understand. And they would find the idea of white space most curious. Nobody buys newspapers for their creative use of white space.

These are basic rules and every newspaper follows them. In putting together an edition for the next morning, they don't have time to carefully mull over each phrase and think deeply about design values.

It speaks volumes for the sheer professionalism of journalists, sub-editors and editors that even though working at such speed, the result each morning is a polished, lively and stimulating read – discarded a few hours later only to be started all over again.

So by studying the layout of newspapers, the general principles are easy enough to see.

Your advertisement will be appearing in this environment, and in order for it to get a good response it has to work within that context.

1. HEADLINING

Many newspaper headlines use the multiple approach described in Chapter 3 of this book. There is:

Cash if you die. Cash if you don't.

Should you choose to put your money into life insurance? Or should you put it into a plan that gives you a cash return? Today, with Lloyd's Life Linkplan, you don't need to split your money-because Linkplan gives you both.

With Linkplan, Lloyd's Life have cleared away much of the confusion surrounding life insurance and investment plans.

Designed for people who don't want to pick through complicated schemes, Linkplan combines the two most-needed types of insurance.

First, Linkplan gives you straightforward life insurance. Bluntly put, if you die, we pay out to your dependants. So they'll have the security of knowing they'll be looked after financially.

But what about you? Many ordinary life insurance policies simply take your money, and you'll never see any of it!

That's where Linkplan scores.

Because, although primarily designed to provide a lifetime of high-level life cover, your plan does acquire a cash value. This starts to build up after a period of time which depends on your present age and you can cash it in... totally tax free after 10 years! Naturally like any such plan, the longer you leave your money in, the greater the value. In the early years, values will not be very high – but after a reasonable period you'll find you have a growing asset. The tables below show you how it works. But for full information, return the coupon.

We'll send you a Personal Illustration showing you how much you're covered for if you die – and how much you could be worth if you want to cash in your policy.

But more than that – we'll offer you up to one month's free cover as well as your FREE Money Manager – no matter how much you choose to pay.

HOW THE PLAN WORKS

Linkplan starts off as straightforward life insurance. Your life is immediately covered for a substantial amount, which is guaranteed for a number of years, depending on your present age. In other words, should you die within weeks, we'll pay your dependants the amount shown against the premium you choose – even if you've only paid one or two premiums!

Then, after this 'guaranteed' period, something very much to your advantage could happen.

You carry on paying the same premiums. But your life insurance cover should start to rise!

How?

You see, we don't just hang on to your money. We'll be putting it to good use. After an initial period a high proportion of your monthly premiums goes into the Lloyd's Life Multiple Growth Fund, to build up your cash value.

After the guaranteed period, your life cover also becomes directly linked to the performance of this Fund.

And provided the Fund performs as well as expected, your life protection will increase as you get older – at no extra cost to you.

Result?

Your premiums bring you a guaranteed amount of life cover in the early years... and the prospect of an increasing amount later, because you benefit from our investment expertise. And your cover continues for as long as you pay premiums.

Not only that, but your plans cash value should go on growing too! Although fund values can go down as well as up, you'll see from the table that your cash in values over the medium to long term can be high. Thousands of pounds, in fact.

What would you do with your cash? Home improvements? A new car? A boat or the holiday of a lifetime? Or just added comfort for your retirement? The choice is yours.

GO FOR GROWTH

The Lloyd's Life Multiple Growth Fund is worth over £29,000,000. The fund buys stocks and shares around the world... some high performers, some gilt-edged government securities, and also invests in property.

So your money is put to work hard, always aiming to achieve a better return than you would normally expect from bank deposit accounts or building society accounts.

Over the past 10 years, in fact, a policyholder making monthly contributions would have seen his Fund value achieve an average annual growth rate of 13.2% net.

We've shown in the table, how much you'd be worth at this 13.2% growth rate. We also show what happens if the fund grows at 8% each year – which is conservative compared with past performance.

EASY TO START

To start couldn't be simpler. Just tick the amount you wish to pay and complete all the information requested.

Don't worry about a medical. If you're between 18 and 49 your weight and height are satisfactory, and you can say 'No' to the 3 questions on the coupon, we guarantee to accept you without one.

Of course you must answer the questions truthfully and tell us all relevant facts – facts which may affect our assessment or acceptance of your proposal. If you're not sure whether something is relevant, you should disclose it, otherwise your benefits may be affected. Then post your application to our Linkplan Administrator at Lloyd's Life, FREEPOST, Peterborough PE3 8BR. You don't even need a stamp.

APPLY WITHIN 10 DAYS

We'll then prepare you a FREE Personal Illustration showing how much your plan could bring you, based on the amount you wish to pay and your present age.

You'll also receive an offer of insurance. To start your plan, all you do is sign and return the certificate together with your monthly Direct Debiting Mandate. We promise there will be nothing complicated to fill in. So apply today. Send the coupon – you'll be under no obligation at all. We don't even ask for your signature on the coupon.

And, if you return the coupon within 10 days, you'll be eligible for up to one month's free cover and your FREE Money Manager. All in all, Linkplan is just right for you.

TAKE A MAN AGED 30*...

Wants protection for his wife, but also wants to see some cash from his policy. He puts £20 a month into Linkplan. He's instantly insured for £24,454 (guaranteed for 13 years). After the guarantee period, his life cover increases while his premium stays the same! In fact, at 65, his life cover is £114,708.

In the meantime, his policy is growing in value. He could cash it in at 45 and receive £5,924... and at 65 it's worth £54,469... all tax free.

THE 'MONEY MANAGER' CALCULATOR IN A SLIMLINE PERSONALISED LEATHER WALLET.

When we receive your completed application, we'll send you your free Linkplan information pack and Personal Illustration.

Then, when you make your first full payment we'll send you ABSOLUTELY FREE this superb leather wallet, personalised with up to three initials of your choice.

It will hold your cheque book, credit cards, stamps and bank notes safely. It contains a neat built in calculator which also enables you to keep a check on your bank balance. It notes your deposits and withdrawals so you always know just how much is in your account – something your Bank Manager would thoroughly approve of!

FREE

YOUR LIFE COVER

Monthly Contribution	Male Age	Guaranteed Life Cover	Life cover age 65 8% growth	13.2% growth
£10	18	£19,652	£38,450	£179,105
	30	£11,849	£18,703	£55,581
	49	£4,702	£4,973	£7,311
£15	18	£30,105	£58,902	£274,376
	30	£18,151	£28,652	£85,144
	49	£7,203	£7,618	£11,199
£20	18	£40,557	£79,353	£369,640
	30	£24,454	£38,600	£114,708
	49	£9,704	£10,263	£15,087
£25	18	£51,010	£99,806	£464,912
	30	£30,756	£48,548	£144,270
	49	£12,205	£12,908	£18,976
£30	18	£61,463	£120,257	£560,177
	30	£37,059	£58,497	£173,834
	49	£14,706	£15,553	£22,864

YOUR CASH VALUE

Monthly Contribution	Male Age	Cash Value age 65 8% growth	13.2% growth
£10	18	£19,517	£91,293
	30	£8,811	£26,389
	49	£1,466	£2,203
£15	18	£29,901	£139,869
	30	£13,499	£40,429
	49	£2,245	£3,375
£20	18	£40,281	£188,424
	30	£18,186	£54,469
	49	£3,024	£4,546
£25	18	£50,666	£237,001
	30	£22,872	£68,502
	49	£3,804	£5,718
£30	18	£61,046	£285,554
	30	£27,560	£82,542
	49	£4,583	£6,890

PERSONAL ILLUSTRATION REQUEST.
NO OBLIGATION – NO SIGNATURE – SEND NO MONEY.

Send within 10 days to qualify for up to one month's free Linkplan cover... and your FREE Personalised 'Money Manager.'

YES I'm interested in Linkplan. I've ticked my chosen contribution level and answered the questions. Please send me, without obligation, my information pack and my Personal Illustration that shows me how much I could be worth. I understand that no salesmen will call on me, and that I am under no obligation. I am returning this coupon within 10 days. If I accept your offer of insurance. I understand that I will receive free cover for up to one month and that when I pay my first full premium you will send me my FREE Personalised Money Manager.

I wish to contribute each month:
£10 ☐ £15 ☐ £20 ☐ £25 ☐ £30 ☐

Name (Mr Mrs Miss Ms) _____
BLOCK CAPITALS PLEASE

First Name(s) _____

Address _____

Town _____

County _____ Postcode _____

Date of Birth __/__/__ ☐ Male ☐ Female
DAY MONTH YEAR

Height ft ___ ins ___ Weight st ___ lbs ___

Occupation _____

Broker's name (if any) _____

Please tick 'Yes' or 'No' to these questions.

A. Has either of your parents died under the age of 60, other than by accidental death? YES ☐ NO ☐

B. Do you intend to fly other than as a fare paying passenger, OR do you engage in any hazardous sports or occupation? YES ☐ NO ☐

C. Have you had any medical or surgical attention at any time including treatment for mental or nervous disorders, other than for minor ailments? YES ☐ NO ☐

IF ALL 'NO' BOXES TICKED: Your acceptance is guaranteed without a medical, provided you are under 50, and your height and weight are satisfactory.

IF ONE OR MORE 'YES' BOXES TICKED: No need to worry. Please tell us, on a separate sheet, as much detail as you can. In many cases, that will be sufficient, although we reserve the right to decline your application.

POST TODAY, WITHOUT A STAMP, TO:
Lloyd's Life Linkplan Administrator, FREEPOST, Peterborough PE3 8BR.

Available to UK residents only. GJN

Lloyd's Life **LINK PLAN**

Fig. 55:
Anatomy of a press ad.
Here's the whole of the 'Cash if you die' ad featured earlier. The headline has already been discussed in some detail (see fig. 11); note the use of the underline (A) as an integral part of the headline, allowing a shorter, attention-grabbing headline to work without giving up all of the essential detail contained in the underline. A 'case history' box (B) allows further details to be communicated easily. The opening of the copy (C) repeats the headline but expands on it; note the 'trial close' including a mention of the premium in the last two paras of the first section (D). The premium is mentioned up front (E), as a flash on the headline (F) and in the coupon (G). The overall look of the ad is very editorial, with four columns of close-set text – the type size is about the same as the newspaper. Note the coupon (H) with a thick dotted border and scissors; the size and dominance of the coupon helps to ensure that the ad is seen as a direct response ad. Note the reiteration of the offer in the coupon (I), together with the amount of space devoted to the 'action' sequence in the copy (J).

Fig. 56:
Getting the most from the headline.

We've seen earlier (fig. 12) about multiple headline techniques – here's an AA ad showing almost every style of multiple headline. There's a panel of copy at the top, with an overline below, followed by the main headline. There are two different flashes on each side of the main headline, and then below, in the central panel, five main copy points. The sub-headlines are given high prominence, and over the coupon is the free gift headline. Not only does this approach make the whole ad more interesting to the eye, but it allows the use of short, surprising headlines like this one. The overall feel is busy and involved – just like the newspaper layout in which it will be appearing. We've tried simplified versions of this type of thing, but it simply doesn't work.

a main headline
an overline or underline
sometimes a precis introduction.

In other words, instead of attempting to get everything into the main headline, the editor breaks it up into easily-digested chunks. A point to note here is that quite often the various chunks of headline tell the same story, but in different and extended ways. It is not a good idea to make each element of the headline totally separate.

It's interesting that variations on multiple headlining are used across the board, from The Sun to The Times.

The precis beginning is an old journalistic trick. 'Tell them what you're going to tell them, tell them, and then tell them you've told them'. Much the same applies, of course, to copywriting.

2. THE GENERAL LENGTH OF THE COPY

In creating the concept for your press ad, you must allow the maximum amount of copy that you can get in.

When roughing out an ad, it always pays to not only assume long copy, but also to actually write the sub-heads as well. Rarely do concepts work as simply a headline and a scribble or two: much of the success of the ad will lie in the detail, and you need to actually create this detail to see if it succeeds as an advertisement.

When you come to write the copy, for a detailed analysis of copy structure, you'll need to read Chapters 4 and 5 earlier in this book.

The AIDCA sequence applies exceptionally well in press ads; and indeed the same kind of general structure that works in mailing letters generally works just as well for press ads, though as observed earlier you need to be much more concentrated in your use of words.

After the opening section, the 'brick by brick' (see Chapter 4) approach works well.

As an easy way to create each selling point, or 'brick', I have found it useful to use an approach where the sub-head is written first, almost as an aide-mémoire.

Take every feature and benefit you want to talk about and then turn each feature into a separate sub-headlined paragraph. Clearly, each 'brick' or selling point needs to be brief.

This works in a newspaper context because it follows the 'telegraphic' terseness of text that is common in newspapers. The same technique simply doesn't work in a mailing letter for instance. It sounds too staccato – a virtue, though, in a press ad.

The sub-heads themselves must work hard so ensure that you make them more interesting than simple one word statements. They will, of necessity, have to be long. Make them provide a benefit, if you have room.

Your action paragraphs remain as important as ever. *Don't be afraid to use mini-headlines, particularly over the coupon or telephone number, to get the action element across as strongly as possible.*

TYPE SIZE

With this copy approach, the type size is going to have to be 'small'. It has always seemed odd to me that *the great majority of advertisements are set in a larger type size* than the newspaper or magazine they appear in.

If the reader is happy reading that type size (and I imagine they would not buy the newspaper if they were unhappy) why should we give them anything different?

3. THE ILLUSTRATIVE FEATURES

Lastly, in coming up with a concept, you need to consider the illustration requirements. Fundraising is relatively simple because often a single dramatic photograph can do a lot of work in getting your proposition across.

'Hard' merchandise needs a clear and strictly illustrative shot of the product, but will probably also require more detailed pictures to show various features.

In some cases, the whole ad can and should be dominated by illustration, when that is the main point or proposition of your ad – certainly it would be the dominant element in a merchandise ad. The editorial analogy still holds true here: in those cases, see your ad as more of an illustrative spread than a story.

How far you go depends on the product. A fashion ad requires almost all picture and very few words, for instance. An ad for a clock radio would still need a strong picture, but the copy would assume much more importance. *It really depends on whether what you have to say in the copy is more interesting than what your picture can say.* For something bought wholly on appearance, such as a fashion item, there is little the copy can usefully add in a limited space other than to describe what it's made of.

Financial products will of course tend to be very copy intensive. But photography of people – usually illustrating case histories – is useful.

Pictures of people within newspapers are very strong. Our eyes tend to go immediately to pictures of faces. It can greatly help a financial ad that would otherwise be a little heavy if it has pictures of people in it.

Illustration (as opposed to photography) tends to come into its own in the financial area much more than in other types of product, with the use of charts and diagrams to help the reader understand some of the more complex details.

PRODUCING THE CONCEPT

Taking these three elements into account, you will now have a reasonable idea of what your ad will look like.

In producing concepts, I prefer to do fewer rather than many. It is a habit of creative people to churn out dozens of concepts, but this should be avoided.

It is an ill-disciplined way of working. Besides removing the need for selectivity, it also tends to take up time that should be spent working out details such as sub-heads and copy points. I would much rather work out no more than two or three versions and if those are not good enough, I would then do some more – but never attempt to cover the walls with layout paper. It is often not much more than a waste of good layout paper.

Ads work as much in the detail as in the quality of the headline. It is just as important to get both right.

SPACE SIZES

Space sizes in press ads are another major determinant of creative success – or at least an understanding of what is possible and what isn't.

If I refer you back to earlier comments about copy length being a prime factor in success, then what is interesting about space sizes is frequently a whole page advertisement will pull a better cost per reply than a half page advertisement. Equally, a double page spread will often work better than a single page – not just in volume of replies but in actual cost-efficiency.

This is all the more surprising when you consider the large increase in cost that going to the largest space sizes involves.

Why this happens is mainly because of the sheer weight of selling argument that a large space will give you.

A whole page will contain more copy than a half page. A double page spread will contain more copy than a whole page. Therefore the larger space sizes will always tend to produce a better cost per reply than small ones, simply because more information is being given.

PAGES AND DOUBLE PAGE SPREADS

In conventional advertising wisdom, larger space sizes work better because of the greater domination of such sizes. At least as far as direct response advertising is concerned, this is not the whole story by any means.

Take a whole page ad and blow it up to a DPS and the result is likely to be a worse cost per order. You have spent around twice the space cost telling exactly the same story. Consequently you have simply raised the 'cost per fact'.

The art of choosing the right space size (and I believe this is as much a creative function as the determination of a mailing format) therefore depends on the length of story you have to tell.

Like a mailing letter, a press ad is as long as it needs to be. Sometimes, for a simple enquiry-generating ad, you have little to say and a small space will be excellent. For a one-stage insurance sale, you will almost certainly need a whole page – if not larger.

And on the subject of 'copy', in the context of press ads, the word should really be read as 'information'. It is not just words. Pictures (particularly where you are selling hard products such as figurines or clock radios) are every bit as much copy as the words, in that they add to the overall information load.

Thus while a whole page may be right for an insurance sale where you have relatively little to illustrate, a double page spread may be far more appropriate for a figurine, where not only do you need a lot of illustration, but you also need a lot of copy as well.

SPACE OPPORTUNITIES AND SMALL SIZES

One of the few times when it is safe to break this rule is with special positions or

76 YEARS OLD AND LEFT TO DIE

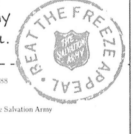

Violet was unconscious. Her lips had turned blue, and her skin was hard and cold to the touch ... her pulse was faint, but she was still alive. Just ...

Like many old folk, Violet had no ~~to visit her~~ and no friends — except ~~Timmy~~. She had ~~warm, no one~~

The Salvation Army
'Despatches' Newsletter January 1987

Violet was discovered in her home by a Salvation Army officer, slumped in a chair. She was suffering from hypothermia. Like many old folk who live alone, and who just cannot afford to keep themselves warm over the bitter winter months, Violet was tempted not to bother ... had the Captain not found her in time she would surely have died, cold and lonely in her old, worn armchair.

Last year we protected thousands of needy old folk from a horrifying, undignified and painful death from hypothermia ... with gifts of food, blankets and warm clothing ... help with heating ... and by just keeping a watchful eye.

We are determined to do the same again this winter, but we cannot do it alone. We really do need your help to Beat the Freeze — to protect those in danger, and save lives this winter. Please help. Your kindness will be very much appreciated — not just by us, but by all the needy people like Violet for whom your gift could mean the difference between life and death.

Thank you for caring and may God bless you.

★ BEAT THE FREEZE APPEAL ★

To: The Salvation Army, 101 Queen Victoria Street, London EC4P 4EP.   388
Charity Reg. No. 214779. Tel: 01-236 5222 (day), 01-764 5240 (eve).

I enclose the sum of £_____ £50 ☐ £25 ☐ £15 ☐ as my gift to help The Salvation Army
Or please debit my Access/Barclaycard/American Express/Diners with the sum of:

£_____ Account No._____

Name_____

Address_____

_____

Postcode_____ Signature_____
If you would like details of how a Tax Covenant can increase the value of your gift by one third please tick ☐
Please accept our warmest thanks.

Fig. 57:
Exploiting the editorial environment.

Small space ads have to work harder to earn their living; they're having to compete for attention and interest in the middle of a crowded and busy editorial environment. Here's a small space for Salvation Army as part of the 'Beat the Freeze' appeal, which we ran only when the weather was bad in the winter. Here we use an editorial flavour strongly, making a press cutting do the work of the headline. Detailed copy then continues the argument. The headline on this ad virtually guarantees attention, even in the middle of a broadsheet paper.

sizes. Try as hard as you might, if you are involved in fundraising, the front page solus on the Guardian (or the Telegraph, for "older appeal") is a space that will work better for you than anything else.

Equally, some short-term space opportunities can come up with the right kind of media buying that brings down the space cost dramatically. Frequently these will be sizes less that whole pages.

You can create successful direct response ads in small sizes as well as large ones. You can cram in a surprising amount of copy – small ads work best as all-copy – and if you use short, attention-grabbing headlines rather than long ones, but still use overlines to make your point clear once you have grabbed attention, then they will work well. In extreme cases, you can even drop the conventional coupon (in small sizes it doesn't pay for the space it occupies) and just ask your reader to write in or telephone.

There is an art to creating small space ads that only few people possess. The great practitioners are the 'postal bargain' advertisers, and if you want to see just how much information it is possible to pack into a small space, you should study these with care.

THE KEY TO SUCCESSFUL ADS

I have now spent quite some time on the overall look of the successful advertisement. This is because it is one of the most important things to get right, and it is consistently the one thing that most people get wrong.

The importance of the editorial concept, in its broadest sense, is that your advertisement is in an environment where you are competing against far more interesting stories than even the best you can create for your product or service.

By turning your advertisement into a 'mini' article or feature you are at least going to capture the attention, the interest and the desire of those few people who are likely to reply to your advertisement.

If you do not employ such tactics, your chances of creating successful direct response advertising become very limited.

Unless you are prepared to create advertisements within the context of the editorial environment, and eschew many of the conventional notions of art direction and advertising design, you will almost certainly fail at the task of creating press ads that work.

Art direction values are important and I am not suggesting that you simply copy a newspaper layout. It is the principle of editorial design I am encouraging: the final execution must take the form most appropriate to the 'image' you are trying to create.

ART DIRECTION

Assuming you are going to have what is essentially an editorial, long, detailed copy approach, then the task of art direction is a more important one than in mailings.

As with the layout of a long mailing letter, in order to make your long copy approach work, the writer must work closely with the art director to ensure that the ad is not simply readable but that it also presents the right visual *atmosphere* to the reader.

Much of what I have said earlier – sub-heads, secondary headlines, bullet points – needs very careful and sensitive handling to ensure that it does not end up like a postal bargain if you are selling a more expensive item, such as insurance.

Good art direction plays an even more important part when it comes to 'hard' merchandise advertisements. As pointed out earlier, it's the *total amount of information* (not just 'copy') that makes the difference. And when you are selling merchandise, the way the item itself looks is of *critical* importance.

Here it is obviously worth spending money on getting the right quality of photography – but it needs to be the kind of photography that shows the product clearly and cleanly. Too much cleverness will simply obscure the product.

It is, however, the typography that makes or breaks most press ads, from the art direction point of view. *Poor use of type can turn even the most powerful long copy ad into an unreadable mess*. Intelligent use of type, carefully crafted, creates a visual interest for the eye that is hard to ignore.

Publishers understand that typography is a vital part of creating the right flavour and feel for their papers. Often, considerable sums of money are invested in new type styles – Eric Gill's famous Times New Roman was commissioned by The Times newspaper. Art directors of press ads should take their typography with equal seriousness, and put equal effort into making full use of the flavours and images that good typography can create.

Not all typography has to be 'good' in an artistic sense. It simply needs to be the most appropriate. Sometimes fundraising ads can be particularly effective, looking as though they were set by the paper (and in the case of an emergency appeal, they are).

Postal bargains would not be postal bargains if they looked too smart.

And financial advertisements must use conservative and elegant typography to make them reek of financial rectitude if they are to convince readers to invest money in them.

MAKING IT LOOK LIKE A DIRECT RESPONSE ADVERTISEMENT

In looking through a paper or magazine full of advertisements, you will see that most of them are 'passive' advertisements. They seek your attention but rarely ask you to do anything. Rather like TV commercials, they have become part of the background, often read for their entertainment value.

This is a problem for the direct response creative person. If a direct response ad looks too much like a conventional ad, the danger is that it too will be treated as passive information, with the result that it may get high readership, but will get poor response.

Therefore when creating an advertisement, it is vital to make clear, from the earliest opportunity, that ACTION is required by the reader.

One of the easiest ways to do this (but it usually only applies to merchandise

Fig. 58:
The value of detail.

This DPS shows how much detail, both copy and visual, should be crammed into the space – easy with a DPS like this, but it can also be achieved with single pages. Apart from the length of the copy (well broken through the use of subheads and column rules), note the number of illustrations – 7 in all – each of which has its caption; the captions are lengthy and explanatory, rather than short titles or teasers. Most of the captions are used to reiterate elements of the offer – one of the captions to the main shot says 'Display your precious Coalport coffee cups and saucers on beautiful, solid wood shelves – available only to collectors'. The headline to the whole ad follows the previously-discussed pattern, but note here how the use of design elements – and engraving of the old Coalport factory at the Ironbridge and the Coalport mark – adds to the information content and flavour. The final, complete effect is busy, involving, and irresistible to the eye. A 'cleaner' approach would not work half so well.

offers) is to use the magic phrase SPECIAL OFFER, just as the papers do with their own editorial offers. This phrase sends out a clear signal to the reader, that in looking at this ad, they are doing more than just reading. It translates the ad from being simply a shop window into the shop itself.

There are many similar techniques that achieve the same end.

Sometimes, the visual look of the ad is sufficient – postal bargains rely on this approach, together with the fact that they are located in the 'marketplace' of the newspaper. The fact that there is a coupon is important as this also sends out a strong signal.

Particularly important are the opening paragraphs of the copy. A 'trial close' early on, as with a mailing letter, gives a very early indication that action is required. It says in effect that you can actually purchase this product directly from this advertisement.

Getting this feeling is not so much a problem as it was, however, now that the supplements are full of direct response ads. In the early days of colour supplement direct response advertising, the simple addition of a 'star burst' with the words 'special offer' had an encouraging effect on response. I believe that it helped differentiate the ad immediately from the non-direct-response ads surrounding it.

By using a distinct editorial style, plus early closes and where appropriate the words 'special offer', you can achieve equal differentiation. Do not let your advertisement ever sink into the background.

THE COUPON

There are some simple rules with coupons which are so basic they are not worth breaking.

1 It should always be rectangular, in the bottom outside edge corner.

This is a) where it's expected to be b) the easiest place to cut it out from.

The fact that it's where it's expected to be is probably the more important, given the need to have direct response advertisements easily recognisable as such.

There have been cases of coupons that are long and thin across the bottom, triangular, or even in the middle of the page. One time in a thousand they may work. I would rather play the odds and leave the coupon in the conventional position. If the ad fails, then at least you know it wasn't the coupon.

2 It should have a very thick black dotted line around it, preferably with a pair of scissors.

Sometimes, when the typography is particularly elegant, the art studio will attempt to make the line around the coupon thin and elegant too. From their point of view they are doing a good job; from the response point of view they are not helping. *A thick black dotted line makes the point of the ad obvious.* It shouts, "I can be bought from", and allows the reader to read the ad in a different and more active frame of mind.

The scissors? I must confess that I don't know if they work or not. But given that they probably do help, I don't see why you shouldn't get everything on your side.

3 It should be easy to fill in.

The best way of getting creative people to design coupons that are easy to fill in is to take them to a fulfilment department to see how people *actually* fill them in.

Get them to look over the shoulders of the people opening the post first thing in the morning.

You will be immediately struck by the fact that most people, when filling in the coupons, obey the instructions to the letter. They will fill in their name on the line that says name; they will write in their postcode on the line where it says postcode. They will have clipped out the coupon exactly along the dotted line – if you make the dotted line an odd shape (which I have seen) they will cut out along the oddest shape you can imagine.

This could be read as giving you carte blanche to design the coupon as small and as oddly as you want. Yes, people will still cram their names into the smallest spaces, mainly because they want the product and they want to make sure you (i.e. the supplier) have got their details right.

Not only is it plain bad manners to treat your customers like this, I am convinced it will put some people off replying. It may not be many. But when every sale counts, I see no point in both irritating customers and running the risk of putting even a few off, just for the sake of a little extra space in the coupon.

Be a considerate designer of coupons. Incidentally, those people in fulfilment will also thank you, too. Try reading and data-prepping hundreds of coupons each day if you REALLY want to know how to design coupons!

IMPROVING RESULTS

Let's say you've run your ad and the results are neither good nor bad.

If you're within 20% of the result you want, it's usually possible by some judicious reworking to get the results acceptable, leaving the base ad alone.

1 Is the offer strong enough?

This is the area that often needs strengthening. Looking not just at the headline, but at the overall effect of the headline, copy and illustration, can you see any way of making the offer or the proposition stronger? A simple change here can produce some dramatic results. Perhaps the offer or the proposition is the wrong one.

2 If you're using incentives, have you shown them strongly enough?

In other words, is the 'FREE' big enough, bold enough and visible enough, or has it become lost? Can you put some more in? Is the selling copy on the incentive strong enough or is it just an afterthought?

3 Are the product features and benefits clear?

Sometimes the product features and benefits are hidden within a mass of copy. Pull them out, turn each one of them into sub-headlines, preferably with a little illustration, and you'll find the results should improve.

4 Is the coupon and phone number strong enough?

Not only should you pay attention to the coupon, but the phone number can be important too. Is it clear? Do you sell the idea of phoning or just mention it? Does it say that the phone call is free? Who answers – live people or machines?

Quite often, just looking at those four points can give a major improvement to results, assuming that the base ad is more or less good.

CURING MAJOR PROBLEMS

For bigger changes – as when you need to beat a control or the ad you've run is a real flop – there is only one solution: *the proposition you are using is wrong and you have to find another one*. Don't, therefore, when asked to produce a control beater, simply redesign the ad around the same proposition. *The proposition has to change.* Once you have done this, your ad may look much the same, but of course the headline will be completely different ▪

CHAPTER 13: SUMMARY

In press ads, creativity is (apart from media choice) the main ingredient of success. It is therefore vital to get the creative right. All the basic rules apply – benefits, long copy, propositions in headlines – but in a more condensed fashion. You have less space to work in.

Start by getting the overall concept – the look – right first. The overwhelming majority of successful press ads have a strong 'editorial' feel to them. They are packed solid with information (no white space), the copy is long and detailed. Follow the techniques used by newspapers and you won't be far wrong.

Headlines are all-important – they must be detailed, too, in order to communicate your proposition. You'll need overlines, underlines, even precis boxes, to get the story across in stages.

Don't worry about small type sizes. So long as you're not smaller than the general text of the paper or magazine that you're in, you will have no problem. Don't allow type sizes to get much bigger – it means you're not getting enough message in to pay for the space you're using up.

Art direction, both of illustration and typography, is vital. Good typography can do an immense amount of good in helping the proposition be communicated with the right flavour. Intelligent illustration can get across complex information – but make sure every picture is captioned.

Make the ad look like it needs action. It's not just there to be looked at.

Pay a lot of attention to getting the coupon and phone number right. Is it strong enough? Is it easy to fill in? Is it in the right place?

How To Produce More
Effective Inserts

*Inserts are an increasingly useful medium. In creative terms
they occupy a position between mailings and press ads,
sharing many of the characteristics of both. This makes them
an unusual creative challenge, particularly taking into
account the fact that inserts need to be produced at low cost
to stand any real chance of success.*

INSERTS have become more popular in recent years, largely owing to two developments.

First, media space costs have risen and ads are becoming less cost-effective. But more importantly, newspaper owners have taken inserting as a source of revenue more seriously, and have invested heavily in inserting machinery. Many major national newspapers are starting up their insert facilities. Inserting facilities have been common in magazines for years, of course.

This is in spite of the fact that many advertisers are convinced inserts are a waste, based on their own experience of seeing, for example, station floors littered with inserts that have fallen out of magazines, or hearing stories from the local newsagent who "always shakes them out before I deliver to my customers". Long may they hear such stories – it means more opportunities for those of us who have found they can often work *better* than press ads.

There are also 'pack inserts'. These are broadly the same as media inserts, but go out in other people's mailings, fulfilment packs or as statement enclosures. Like the media owners, these companies have discovered that serious direct marketers are prepared to pay good money to buy inserting space in their material.

THE THIRD MAJOR MEDIUM FOR DIRECT MARKETERS

Taking both press and pack inserts together, inserts form a substantial sector of direct marketing spend, coming third after direct mail and press in the overall picture – for some advertisers they are the main marketing effort.

The number of inserts bought each year is *vast*. Hundreds of millions of inserts will go into the press, hundreds of millions more will go into packs. Clearly, at these levels, something somewhere must be working.

The beauty of inserts is that they combine some of the best features of press and direct mail. They have low distribution cost like press; they have space for a selling message like direct mail. They have large circulation, like press; they can be targeted with reasonable efficiency, like direct mail.

KEEPING THE COST DOWN

The cost argument for inserts is, however, the one that is most compelling, be they media or pack inserts. Inserts are essentially inexpensive. Compared to mailings they are considerably cheaper, but consequently produce less response. Compared to press ads they are actually more expensive per thousand circulation, but produce more response per thousand, given the greater space for the selling message. Most direct marketers view inserts as a kind of low-cost direct mail. This means that the creative techniques required to make inserts work have to take cost into account, almost above everything else. And, if we see inserts as a hybrid between direct mail and press, this also gives us some indication of the creative methods we need to apply.

FORMAT COSTS

The driving force on insert costs is of course the format. Luckily, inserting is done in vast numbers. It is not uncommon to have print runs in the several millions, particularly if a successful design is used in both media and pack. And restrictions imposed by the insert carrier usually demand a lightweight format. Taken all together, this means that formats are technically restricted, but you can nevertheless afford some powerful formats because the print runs are so big.

It is therefore usually better to go straight to the specialist printers first to see what insert formats they have. For example, a company like Promotion Impressions has invested heavily in machinery to do the most extraordinary things at remarkably low cost, if the runs are right. Reps of print companies are always happy to come in and discuss designs with you from the very earliest stage. Not only that, but of course they bring piles of samples with them of other people's inserts which act as a handy 'swipe' file.

SPECIALIST FORMATS AND SIMPLE FORMATS

Formats from specialists tend to be the more lavish ones, often giving you multiple sheets from an in-line process. However, sometimes the need is for extremely simple formats.

A single sheet printed in black and white (sometimes a straight reprint of a press ad) can be excellent, particularly if margins are tight. One of the most common forms of insert for magazines is the A4 sheet in colour folded down to an A3 four-pager, very cheap to produce in very large quantities.

Postcards can make excellent inserts and have the added benefit of being 'self mailable' – they can be posted back without any fiddling about with folding and licking and sticking. 'Bangtails' are popular too for similar reasons. The bangtail gives an integral envelope and order form…most commonly used for statement inserts.

Mailing packs themselves can also be used, although naturally enough you leave out the address elements and would probably use a close face envelope. If you are doing a very large mailing (in excess of a couple of million) this type of insert can be useful because the costs come down on such a big run, but beware the weight and size restrictions that may face you.

MARGIN IS KING

But as ever (and much more clearly so with inserts) your design will depend on the margin within the product. *What format you choose will be almost wholly*

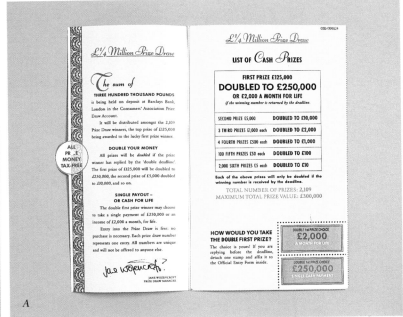

A

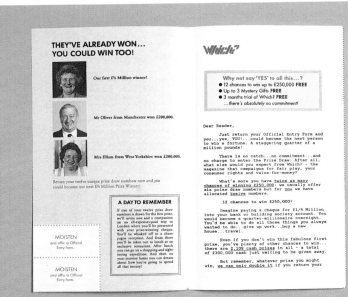

B

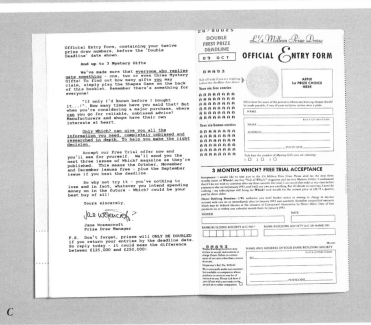

C

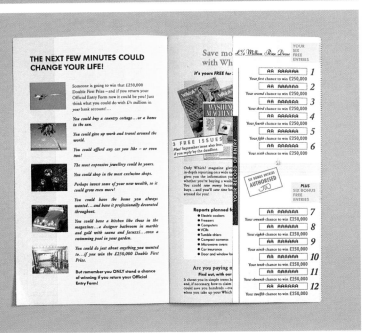

D

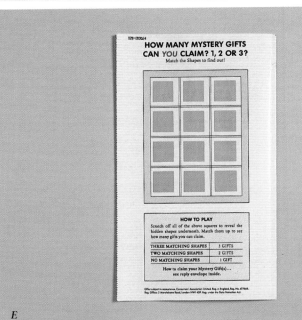

E

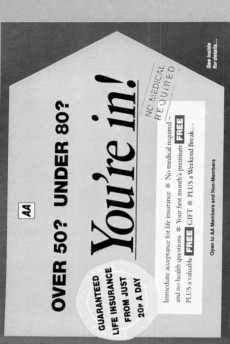

◄ Fig. 60:
Complex formats for prize draws.

This insert for Which? magazine is heavily based on existing prize draw mailing packs, and utilises a very complex (and therefore not cheap) format to present not only the basic prize draw proposition in the most dramatic way, but also to provide many of the main elements of a full-scale mailing pack. The insert is in fact lasered with prize draw numbers, which provides an opportunity to laser the name of the magazine on the front cover. Opening the 'seal' (A) displays the prize list; the next opening (B) reveals a reply envelope, winners-list and the start of the letter; (C) completes the letter and provides an entry form, complete with rub-off and (D) has product information. The back of the piece (E) has mystery gift rub-offs. These types of inserts tend to be printed on specialist in-line equipment (usually in Germany) and are clearly suitable only for certain types of product or service. Nevertheless the sheer versatility of the format creates a highly involving piece which is hard to ignore within a magazine.

Fig. 61:
Secure coupons.

This AA insert is derived directly from previously-tested propositions (see fig. 56) and contains most of the elements from that press ad. The format used folds out lengthways, and the last sheet (far right) is the entire reply-device. You complete the coupon section, detach the sheet, fold in the middle, lick the glue and stick down. A Freepost panel on the reverse side brings it safely home. 'Closed' reply devices like this are necessary when you're asking various personal questions, which most insurance products need to ask, and the respondent will be extremely upset if you don't allow it to be concealed. This is one of the easiest ways of creating a secure coupon, as all that is involved is the application of glue, which can be done during the printing phase. For a more secure version still, see fig. 63.

determined by cost. Unfortunately the same argument I used in defence of larger space sizes as far as press advertising is concerned doesn't work so well with inserts.

Inserts that are twice the size aren't, sadly, going to do twice as well. I'm not sure why this is, and I suspect it is an area where more extensive testing should be carried out, but the fact that an insert is highly visible within a magazine or newspaper, in that it intrudes upon the editorial matter, gives it an impact that is not conditional on size alone. More copy and more 'sell' will help but the first impact is so strong that the relative gain is small.

And, with pack inserts, you are usually extremely limited by weight and enclosing considerations, and therefore you will almost always end up with a small insert with little room.

SPECIFIC FORMATS FOR SPECIFIC PRODUCTS

There are some creative tasks that require specific formats. Selling a fashion catalogue is going to require colour. Selling insurance is going to need a fair amount of space. A Consumers' Association prize draw insert is heavily dependent on a laser-numbered multiple-part format that brings with it many of the attributes of a mailing – it probably wouldn't work as a single sheet, for instance.

Thus you need to balance the demands of margin with the demands of the message itself. Fortunately, this tends to become something of a self-adjusting mechanism.

A SELF-ADJUSTING MECHANISM

With an insert for a fashion catalogue, for instance, margins are tight and colour is needed. Apart from showing fashion (or a free gift) little else is needed – you can't write long copy for a product that is wholly dependent on image – all you can do is show it.

Thus an 'L' shape insert works well. It takes up a small amount of paper, there is no finishing, it has the advantage of a card reply device, and gives a reasonable colour area to get the main fashion photograph across.

A higher margin product, such as insurance, not only demands more to be said about it, but also has the necessary allowable to make a larger format affordable.

This is one reason why some products rarely work as inserts: there is a conflict between allowable and creative. Single shot merchandise usually doesn't work as inserts because the need for a large colour photograph and detailed copy demands a format that's too expensive – space is normally more cost effective.

SECRETS OF SUCCESSFUL INSERTS

Once the format has been determined, the task is to make the piece work. With inserts, there is a curious fundamental rule which is well worth knowing about:

What you put on the front and back covers of your insert
has more effect on results than anything else you can do.

Inserts are an unusual medium. They do not sit within the body of the paper or magazine, and therefore you cannot replicate the editorial effect, as you can do with press ads, to help you gain readership.

They are highly likely to fall out, in fact. Once the reader comes across the insert, the job is to make them sufficiently interested in the insert to WANT TO OPEN IT –

in other words, at the front cover stage you're like a magazine on a news stall.

Is there something on the front cover that makes the target want to open it? Once opened, the normal selling process can then take place.

So the main creative task in inserts is rather different to that of most other media – you have to get opened before you can start to sell.

This is less of a problem with single sheet inserts, such as 'L' shapes. But even here, your overall impact has to be sufficiently strong to gain attention.

GETTING OPENED

Creating strong front covers then becomes much more a design task than a copy task. Of course the copy is important. *But time and time again I have seen inserts work because the front cover design is so striking.*

In fact, for inserts alone, I would go so far as to say that it matters less about what you say on the front cover than the strength of the design you use.

And 'strength' is the right word. Considering the battle you are fighting for attention, designing insert covers is no place for the faint-hearted designer. You need an instinctive feeling for dramatic graphics. Red words out of a solid black background is the kind of thing that begins to work. But almost any design that commands attention will suffice.

It goes without saying that deliberate shock tactics to get an insert opened have to be used carefully. It's no good going over the top so that the product inside is actually just a letdown.

Intrigue is as useful as shock. For a knitting series, Chris Albert of WWAV produced an almost unbeatable front cover design that looked just like another magazine front cover, complete with fashion picture, masthead and even a summary of the contents down the side.

On more expensive insert formats, the use of rub-offs and other involvement devices, particularly with prize-draw-style inserts, works powerfully, as they gain attention quickly.

Unusual shapes are also certainly worth considering. As odd-shaped envelopes work well to overcome mailing fatigue, odd-shaped inserts work well, too. Long thin ones, round ones, even triangular ones, can all be used with success – or at least, the reasonable prospect of success, costs permitting.

BOTH SIDES

Throughout this section you will have noticed that I have referred to front 'covers', not just front cover. Inserts, of course, have two – front and back. And you have no idea which way is going to come out in front of the reader first. On a purely statistical basis, each cover has a 50% chance of being the 'front', and your design needs to take account of this.

ROYAL WORCESTER

Luxurious pink roses glisten against an exquisite gold ground on a Royal Worcester limited edition fine bone china plate

'The Queen Elizabeth Roses'

The plate measures 8" in diameter.

What could be more fitting, to commemorate the 40th Anniversary of Her Majesty the Queen's Coronation, than the issue of this unique new plate from Compton & Woodhouse featuring the pink and crimson beauty of *'The Queen Elizabeth Roses'?* Strictly limited to a hand-numbered edition of only 15,000, this beautiful plate was inspired by a similar valuable piece held in the Dyson Perrins Museum, Royal Worcester.

Hidden gold…

The glorious central bouquet of pale pinks and deep crimsons, with its exquisite border, is enhanced by the lavish use of 22 carat gold. Not just the burnished golden ground which provides such a perfect foil to the riotous display of roses, but the 'hidden' gold in the flowers themselves.

'The Queen Elizabeth Roses' is the first in the 'Royal Roses' collection. It will be sent to you on 28 days' no-obligation home approval and you may pay in two convenient monthly instalments of £15.75. Each plate bears the Royal Worcester backstamp on the base, with your individual number applied by hand, and is accompanied by a Certificate of Authenticity.

Compton & Woodhouse
Specialists in English fine bone china
Arundel House, 80 Lawrence Road, London N15 4TR.
Registered in England No. 1868906.

RESERVATION FORM

NO STAMP NEEDED · SEND NO MONEY NOW · REPLY WITHIN 7 DAYS

'The Queen Elizabeth Roses'

Please send me *'The Queen Elizabeth Roses'* to view at home without obligation. I need send no money now. I may pay in two convenient, interest-free monthly instalments of £15.75. I will be invoiced for the first instalment prior to my plate being despatched. If I do not keep it, I may return it within 28 days and I will owe nothing. I will be sent further plates in the collection on the same no-obligation basis.

Name _____

BLOCK LETTERS PLEASE

Address _____

_____

_____

Postcode _____

(Your postcode helps us to fulfil your order promptly)

The price is inclusive of VAT at 17½%. All orders are subject to acceptance by Compton & Woodhouse. Occasionally we permit other carefully-screened organisations to write to you about products we feel may interest you. If you would prefer not to hear from them, please tick this box. ☐ 01-D-QERX

Compton & Woodhouse Ltd.,
FREEPOST,
Arundel House,
London N15 4BR.

The **Compton & Woodhouse** *Guarantee*

Hand-numbered limited edition of 15,000
·
No obligation to purchase
·
Accompanied by a Certificate of Authenticity
·
Available exclusively from Compton & Woodhouse
·
Payable in convenient monthly instalments
·
Take as few or as many plates as you choose

Rinalda Ward

Rinalda Ward, Managing Director, Compton & Woodhouse

Fig. 62:
Simple but effective.

Given the high costs of inserting (compared to space) plus often marginal results, it can sometimes be necessary to make the insert as cheap as possible to produce so that a wider media choice can be used – this in turn means greater print volume therefore prices are even lower. This format, for a Compton and Woodhouse Flower Plate, is probably the simplest – consisting of a single sheet, printed both sides. The insert is essentially an adapt of a press ad – one side carries the main illustration and the headline, the other side carries the main body copy and the coupon; though, in fact, the headline is repeated on both sides. Note the self-mailable coupon – the stock is thick enough (just!) to pass Royal Mail regulations for return cards. Where no cash has to be sent, or where you're not asking for personal details, this method of reply-device is fine.

76 YEARS OLD AND LEFT TO DIE

BEAT THE FREEZE APPEAL

Violet was unconscious. Her lips had turned blue, and her skin was hard and cold to the touch … her pulse was faint, but she was still alive. Just …

… Violet had no …

Hypothermia can kill.
Will you help us Beat the Freeze?

The Salvation Army Despatches' Newsletter January 1987

Will you give £15 this Christmas to help save a child's life?

NSPCC

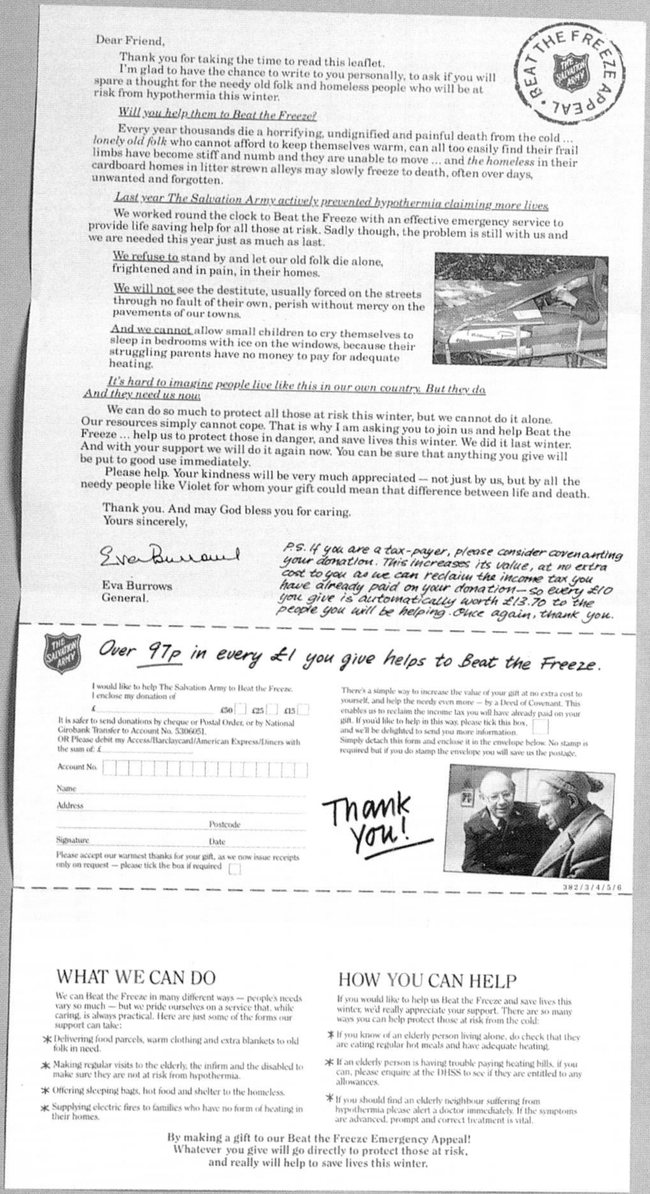

Dear Friend,

Thank you for taking the time to read this leaflet.
I'm glad to have the chance to write to you personally, to ask if you will spare a thought for the needy old folk and homeless people who will be at risk from hypothermia this winter.

Will you help them to Beat the Freeze?

Every year thousands die a horrifying, undignified and painful death from the cold … lonely old folk who cannot afford to keep themselves warm, can all too easily find their frail limbs have become stiff and numb and they are unable to move … and the homeless in their cardboard homes in litter strewn alleys may slowly freeze to death, often over days, unwanted and forgotten.

Last year The Salvation Army actively prevented hypothermia claiming more lives.

We worked round the clock to Beat the Freeze with an effective emergency service to provide life saving help for all those at risk. Sadly though, the problem is still with us and we are needed this year just as much as last.

We refuse to stand by and let our old folk die alone, frightened and in pain, in their homes.

We will not see the destitute, usually forced on the streets through no fault of their own, perish without mercy on the pavements of our towns.

And we cannot allow small children to cry themselves to sleep in bedrooms with ice on the windows, because their struggling parents have no money to pay for adequate heating.

It's hard to imagine people live like this in our own country. But they do. And they need us now.

We can do so much to protect all those at risk this winter, but we cannot do it alone. Our resources simply cannot cope. That is why I am asking you to join us and help Beat the Freeze … help us to protect those in danger, and save lives this winter. We did it last winter. And with your support we will do it again now. You can be sure that anything you give will be put to good use immediately.

Please help. Your kindness will be very much appreciated — not just by us, but by all the needy people like Violet for whom your gift could mean that difference between life and death.

Thank you. And may God bless you for caring.
Yours sincerely,

Eva Burrows

Eva Burrows
General.

P.S. If you are a tax-payer, please consider covenanting your donation. This increases its value, at no extra cost to you as we can reclaim the income tax you have already paid on your donation — so every £10 you give is automatically worth £13.70 to the people you will be helping. Once again, thank you.

Over 97p in every £1 you give helps to Beat the Freeze.

I would like to help The Salvation Army to Beat the Freeze.
I enclose my donation of
£_____ □ £50 □ £25 □ £15

It is safe to send donations by cheque or Postal Order, or by National Girobank Transfer to Account No. 5306051.
OR Please debit my Access/Barclaycard/American Express/Diners with the sum of £_____

Account No. [ ][ ][ ][ ][ ][ ][ ][ ][ ][ ][ ][ ][ ]

Name
Address
Postcode
Signature   Date

Please accept our warmest thanks for your gift, as we now issue receipts only on request — please tick the box if required □

There's a simple way to increase the value of your gift at no extra cost to yourself, and help the needy even more — by a Deed of Covenant. This enables us to reclaim the income tax you will have already paid on your gift. If you'd like to help in this way, please tick this box, and we'll be delighted to send you more information.
Simply detach this form and enclose it in the envelope below. No stamp is required but if you do stamp the envelope it will save us the postage.

Thank You!

382/3/4/5/6

WHAT WE CAN DO

We can Beat the Freeze in many different ways — people's needs vary so much — but we pride ourselves on a service that, while caring, is always practical. Here are just some of the forms our support can take:

✱ Delivering food parcels, warm clothing and extra blankets to old folk in need.

✱ Making regular visits to the elderly, the infirm and the disabled to make sure they are not at risk from hypothermia.

✱ Offering sleeping bags, hot food and shelter to the homeless.

✱ Supplying electric fires to families who have no form of heating in their homes.

HOW YOU CAN HELP

If you would like to help us Beat the Freeze and save lives this winter, we'd really appreciate your support. There are so many ways you can help protect those at risk from the cold:

✱ If you know of an elderly person living alone, do check that they are eating regular hot meals and have adequate heating.

✱ If an elderly person is having trouble paying heating bills, if you can, please enquire at the DHSS to see if they are entitled to any allowances.

✱ If you should find an elderly neighbour suffering from hypothermia please alert a doctor immediately. If the symptoms are advanced, prompt and correct treatment is vital.

By making a gift to our Beat the Freeze Emergency Appeal!
Whatever you give will go directly to protect those at risk, and really will help to save lives this winter.

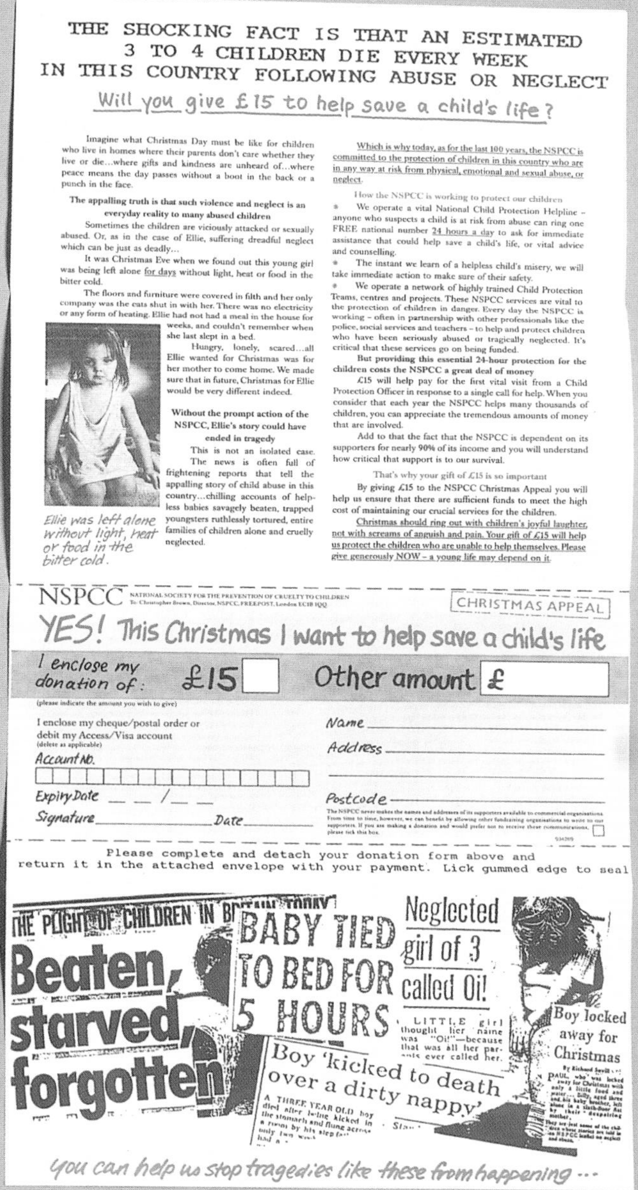

THE SHOCKING FACT IS THAT AN ESTIMATED 3 TO 4 CHILDREN DIE EVERY WEEK IN THIS COUNTRY FOLLOWING ABUSE OR NEGLECT

Will you give £15 to help save a child's life?

Imagine what Christmas Day must be like for children who live in homes where their parents don't care whether they live or die…where gifts and kindness are unheard of…where peace means the day passes without a boot in the back or a punch in the face.

The appalling truth is that such violence and neglect is an everyday reality to many abused children

Sometimes the children are viciously attacked or sexually abused. Or, as in the case of Ellie, suffering dreadful neglect which can be just as deadly…

It was Christmas Eve when we found out this young girl was being left alone for days without light, heat or food in the bitter cold.

The floors and furniture were covered in filth and her only company was the cats shut in with her. There was no electricity or any form of heating. Ellie had not had a meal in the house for weeks, and couldn't remember when she last slept in a bed.

Hungry, lonely, scared…all Ellie wanted for Christmas was for her mother to come home. We made sure that in future, Christmas for Ellie would be very different indeed.

Without the prompt action of the NSPCC, Ellie's story could have ended in tragedy

This is not an isolated case. The news is often full of frightening reports that tell the appalling story of child abuse in this country…chilling accounts of helpless babies savagely beaten, trapped youngsters ruthlessly tortured, entire families of children alone and cruelly neglected.

Ellie was left alone without light, heat or food in the bitter cold.

Which is why today, as for the last 100 years, the NSPCC is committed to the protection of children in this country who are in any way at risk from physical, emotional and sexual abuse, or neglect.

How the NSPCC is working to protect our children

● We operate a vital National Child Protection Helpline — anyone who suspects a child is at risk from abuse can ring one FREE national number 24 hours a day to ask for immediate assistance that could help save a child's life, or vital advice and counselling.

● The instant we learn of a helpless child's misery, we will take immediate action to make sure of their safety.

● We operate a network of highly trained Child Protection Teams, centres and projects. These NSPCC services are vital to the protection of children in danger. Every day the NSPCC is working — often in partnership with other professionals like the police, social services and teachers — to help and protect children who have been seriously abused or tragically neglected. It's critical that these services go on being funded.

But providing this essential 24-hour protection for the children costs the NSPCC a great deal of money

£15 will help pay for the first vital visit from a Child Protection Officer in response to a single call for help. When you consider that each year the NSPCC helps many thousands of children, you can appreciate the tremendous amounts of money that are involved.

Add to that the fact that the NSPCC is dependent on its supporters for nearly 90% of its income and you will understand how critical that support is to our survival.

That's why your gift of £15 is so important

By giving £15 to the NSPCC Christmas Appeal you will help us ensure that there are sufficient funds to meet the high cost of maintaining our crucial services for the children.

Christmas should ring out with children's joyful laughter, not with screams of anguish and pain. Your gift of £15 will help us protect the children who are unable to help themselves. Please give generously NOW — a young life may depend on it.

NSPCC NATIONAL SOCIETY FOR THE PREVENTION OF CRUELTY TO CHILDREN
To: Christopher Brown, Director, NSPCC, FREEPOST, London EC1B 1QQ

CHRISTMAS APPEAL

YES! This Christmas I want to help save a child's life

I enclose my donation of: £15 [ ]   Other amount £ _____
(please indicate the amount you wish to give)

I enclose my cheque/postal order or debit my Access/Visa account (delete as applicable)

Account No. [ ][ ][ ][ ][ ][ ][ ][ ][ ][ ][ ][ ][ ]

Expiry Date __ __ / __ __
Signature _____ Date _____

Name _____
Address _____
Postcode _____

The NSPCC never makes the names and addresses of its supporters available to commercial organisations. From time to time, however, we can benefit by allowing other fundraising organisations to write to our supporters. If you are making a donation and would prefer not to receive these communications, please tick this box. □

Please complete and detach your donation form above and return it in the attached envelope with your payment. Lick gummed edge to seal

THE PLIGHT OF CHILDREN IN BRITAIN TODAY

Beaten, starved, forgotten

BABY TIED TO BED FOR 5 HOURS

Boy 'kicked to death over a dirty nappy'

A THREE YEAR OLD boy died after being kicked in the stomach and flung across a room by his step-father only two weeks after had a …

Neglected girl of 3 called Oi!

LITTLE girl thought her name was "Oi!" because that was all her parents ever called her.

Boy locked away for Christmas

By Richard Savill

PAUL, who was locked away for Christmas with only a little food and water … fully clothed and was kept locked in a "dark, damp unheated" …

They lost both sons in the NSPCC …

you can help us stop tragedies like these from happening …

Fig. 63:
Self-made envelopes.

The insert for the Salvation Army is based on the same creative as the press ad shown in fig. 57. Once opened, the inside copy actually takes the form of a letter (which, to be honest, would probably have been better typewritten rather than typeset) and even includes a PS.

The lower section is actually an envelope, which is made (during the finishing stage of the printing) by folding back upon itself the last fold, and sticking it down. The envelope is needed in this case because, of course, we're asking for donations, and by providing the envelope we make it easier for the donor, even though this format is slightly more expensive. Note also the clarity of the reply-device in this format, located handily just above the envelope. Incidentally, this insert is printed in two colours, which not only makes it look more economical (which is good for the Army's image) but of course it is more economical. The NSPCC insert uses just the same format, but is printed using the Flexo process which makes it around 30% cheaper than the equivalent 2-colour job. The quality is poorer, but as you can see, the designer has actually exploited this by using thick handwriting and press cuttings.

This is easy on a roll-folded format where both covers are 'clean' and available for design. But on, say, a 4-pager, where you are using a self-mailing return format, the return address appears on the back cover, and it does get in the way – this means you have to work even harder to get the 'back' cover to work visually.

This may well affect your choice of format, of course. If you can avoid having the return address showing on one cover, then all the better.

ONCE OPENED...

Let us suppose that you have a design that is either sufficiently shocking or intriguing enough to get opened. What do you put inside?

Here, exactly the same techniques that apply to mailings and press ads apply. The relevant sections earlier in this book apply as much to inserts as the other media. Your copy must be long and detailed, and your headlines inside must go through the normal process of making the product or the service as desirable as possible.

However, the format you have chosen will determine whether your creative approach is more of a mailing, or more of a press ad. The less room your format allows you, the more the brevity of a press ad will be necessary; the more room your format gives you, the more you can begin to employ some of the stronger techniques of a mailing.

On a single sheet or 4-page inserts – in other words, the simpler ones – you have little room to play with and therefore you will be forced down a press ad route. Your creative approach will therefore be exactly the same as though you were preparing a press ad.

On the more complex formats, you can begin to introduce some of the mailing creative techniques, as you have a little more room to play with. This is important: a large format insert, say with four or five sheets to play with, could become very boring if it is simply a blown-up press ad. You would be missing some of the advantages of mailing creativity.

Where space allows, I would certainly recommend the use of mini-letters, testimonials and other devices imported from a mailing pack to break up the message from being just brochure-type copy. Treat your insert as being in different sections, if you like, and you will then be able to maximise the use of the space that your format is giving you.

ONE-PIECE OR MULTIPLE FORMATS

Some of the most interesting formats for inserts come from the major in-line printers. In-line in this context means a single printing process that prints, folds, collates and turns out the finished product at the end of the line. Typically these formats are all one-piece, with the selling area integral with the envelope.

Printers have made major investments to be able to provide one-piece formats. Sadly, a lot of that investment is wasted because they don't work very well.

Certainly the theory is sound. The fact that there are no additional enclosing and finishing costs means that the piece itself is cheap.

Some years ago we tried such a format for mailing purposes and even with the very large cost advantage, a conventional multiple part format worked better. We then tried them as inserts and compared with formats that came out as multiple pieces, they didn't work as well either.

The conclusion is simple. *Multiple part formats work better than one-piece formats and should be used wherever possible.* Fortunately for the in-line printers, the latest technology now not only folds and collates in-line, but also cuts up the sheet into separate pieces. The creative opportunity then becomes more akin to designing a mailing than an insert.

THE REPLY DEVICE

The reply device on inserts presents many useful creative possibilities. Whichever type of format you have chosen, almost all will offer at least some form of self-mailing reply piece. My first introduction to the mysterious world of inserts was with Guy Oliver, now at Kingfisher, but then with Odhams Mail Order. The inserts being used were simple 4-page affairs but the reply device was one of those complicated fold-up ones.

You had little arrows on the back with instructions to 'fold here', and there was even an instruction panel, complete with diagram, that informed the potential buyer to 'fold A over B, tuck into C' and generally gave an air of a highly complex operation.

I couldn't believe that such a system would work. Guy and his then assistant, Dave Rees (still at Odhams) took me round fulfilment one day. In the incoming post area were masses of neatly folded replies, all with the As and Bs tucked neatly into their Cs, which goes to show that some form of self-mailable device, even a complicated one, is better than none at all.

'Self-mailability' is one of the main characteristics of inserts, and apart from the extra impact they give you, is the main reason why they produce better responses than press ads, where you have to go and find your own envelope.

With simple A4 folded formats such as described above, the self-folding type can easily be used. Once you get into anything more ambitious, integral envelopes are now easily produced by the specialist printers, where the end of an insert is folded over, glued along three edges and the fourth printed with a remoistenable glue to create an envelope. The addition of a perforation makes it even better.

Some types of product require an envelope: life insurance, where you may have asked some sensitive questions; cash-with-order; fundraising. Other types of product will probably only need a card. Here, the creative opportunities are even more wide open. A sheet of light paper can be folded over and glued down to create a return postcard. Tip-ons can be used. Whatever the options, the main point to bear in mind is that the provision of either a reply envelope or a reply card is a major part of the success of inserts. If you simply have an insert with no reply facility, you're wasting a major opportunity ■

Fig. 64:
Leading from the front.
The front cover of this insert for the Sun Alliance Cash Escalator Plan shows how strong an insert front cover needs to be to capture attention in the first place. Not only does the insert employ the main proposition – free gifts – very strongly, it also uses visual strength to ram the point home. The use of strong, bright colours may appear to contradict the point made in Chapter 7 on Art Direction, where muted colours are recommended for financial products, but the need for attention-grabbing design on an insert is paramount; hence these colours are virtually day-glo! This illustration shows both the 'front' and the 'back' of the insert; note the use of essentially the same offer on both sides – you cannot tell if your insert will come out in front of the reader one way or the other, so you make the insert double-sided to allow for it falling out either way.

CHAPTER 14: SUMMARY

Inserts are essentially an inexpensive medium and therefore the format you choose has to reflect the need to keep costs low. There are also mechanical constraints, such as size or weight, imposed by the media owner.

The choice of the format is, like a mailing, the primary creative task. Although there are cost restraints, you're usually printing in very large quantities and therefore some quite extensive formats can be available.

The best place to start is by asking the specialist printers to come and see you to show you their formats, plus samples of how other people have used them.

Probably the most important creative job is designing the front covers (both of them, front and back, as inserts can be seen from either end). These should employ intrigue, even shock, in order to gain attention and stand out. They must act essentially as 'openers' to your main message.

Once inside, the creative job is very similar to creating either an ad or a mailing – depending on whether you have a simple format or a complex one. Simple formats should be treated as ads, complex ones more like mailings – you should consider the use of letters, for instance.

An integral reply device is an important part of an insert, and perhaps one of the reasons why you will usually get a higher response (in raw replies, not necessarily in cost per reply) than with a press advertisement. The format will determine the device you have but you should never design an insert that does not incorporate such a feature.

How To Create
Television Commercials
That Get Response

*TV stands to become a major direct response media in the UK
and is becoming so faster than most people realise. The key to
success is basically in the creative treatment and shows even
more starkly than usual the gulf between conventional
advertising techniques and direct marketing. Here's how to
create and produce TV commercials that really do work –
in other words, they generate business worth more than
the cost of the commercial.*

P ERHAPS one of the most exciting developments in direct marketing in the UK in
the last few years has been the emergence of TV as a viable direct response
medium – and by viable, I mean cost-effective from a purely direct marketing point of
view: with the right approach, it will produce replies at a cost per reply that is as good,
and sometimes better, than press or mailings.

This has been a development that is exciting for some, anyway. It has happened
so quickly that many people have still not caught on to it; and the methods of making it
work are such a direct challenge to accepted creative thinking that, fortunately, many
people's prejudices will continue to keep them off the air for some time to come.

I will be so bold as to make a prediction. *Within 5 years, TV (and probably radio)
will become in the UK one of the MAJOR direct response media*, ranking up with direct
mail, press ads, inserts and the telephone as a significant vehicle for a wide variety of
offerings – fundraising, insurance, subscriptions, and mail order.

This has already happened in the US. South Africa is ahead of us. France
has pioneered many of the insurance developments in TV. What's holding back
development in the UK?

JUNK TV?

It's not, surprisingly, media costs. The main barrier to progress has been people's
reluctance to learn from *creative* experience abroad and apply the lessons to the UK. At
WWAV, around the middle of 1991, we decided to see if we could make TV work. Quite
simply, we studied all the commercials we could find from the United States, France
and South Africa, and listed the common elements.

It was not difficult to work out which creative treatments were consistently
working. We applied the lessons to the UK and, not surprisingly, they work just as well
here as anywhere.

A word of warning, though. *This type of TV is not the glamorous end of the business.* I have even heard someone describe it as 'junk TV', because the means of making it work are rooted in direct response practice rather than in conventional TV wisdom. If you're looking for glory and big budgets, go get a job at Saatchi and Saatchi. If you're looking instead to be one of the creative pioneers of one of the biggest breakthroughs in direct marketing, be prepared to be unconventional and let *measurable* business success determine your actions.

What follows is essentially what we at WWAV have learned so far. It cannot at this early stage of development be definitive, as much more is left to learn. However, all the techniques mentioned are AT LEAST what is needed: they were devised by watching other commercials and then applied successfully in the UK.

Development should not mean going backwards – do not try to 'reduce' what I am talking about here. You must resist the siren call of above-the-line TV techniques. Development should be along the lines of enhancing what is here, and making it stronger, not weaker.

LENGTH

If you have been carefully reading this book you will have seen that one of my fundamental principles is that of length: or, more properly, *amount of selling information.* Without a minimum of 'sell', no direct response medium can ever work. It is the lack of such length that is normally the most easily-identified cause of failure, and happily one that is easy to put right.

Mailings with lots of information in them work better than mailings without. Long letters work better than short letters. Long copy in press ads and inserts outperforms short copy.

> *It will therefore come as no surprise to learn that the fundamental creative lesson of television is, simply, length. Short commercials rarely work. Long commercials usually do.*

Again, I must qualify this by saying that if your message is a simple one, a long commercial could well be just 10 seconds. But such lengths are the exception. Normally, in order to make your commercial pay for itself, you need commercials of AT LEAST ONE AND A HALF MINUTES, AND IDEALLY TWO MINUTES in length.

For people brought up on a diet of 30 second commercials, this can seem like a very long time. But, of course, it depends entirely on what you do with that length.

LENGTH, AIRTIME, TVRs

But right now, we need to consider the media impact of the statement that you need long commercials. Clearly, if you were going to be using peak airtime, a 90 second or 120 second commercial will cost so much as to render the exercise, very probably, uneconomic.

A brief diversion into the mysteries of TV airtime costings will help. Most TV is bought as 'TVRs' – Television Ratings. A '1' Rating is one per cent of all the homes able to catch that commercial. According to the research into viewership that TV companies provide, they are able to tell you what number of ratings any one commercial will get, depending on the time of day and in what programme the commercial is shown.

Fig. 65:
A working TV commercial. This commercial for a Dry Cooker from Scotcade shows the basic structure for successful TV commercials. This 90 second commercial starts with a 'flag' – an announcement that this is a direct response commercial, giving the phone number. The commercial then goes into a demonstration of the Dry Cooker, amplified by the use of captions. The call to action comes in as quickly as possible, with the use of a phone number very prominent, which is then followed by detailed instructions on how to order. This is the basic format for all broadcast commercials; you should only consider deviating from this if you have good evidence that other formats are likely to work equally well. Incidentally, this demonstration type of approach is most appropriate for 'hard' merchandise; a presenter approach is most appropriate for financial products – see fig. 68 a little later in this Chapter.

See overleaf ▶

VO: *Here's a special offer from Scotcade that you can order right now by calling this number and using your credit cards.*

It's the Dry Cooker – a healthier, easier way to cook. It bakes…

…roasts…toasts…grills…and sizzle fries…

all this without any added oil or fat. The secret is dry heat. There are no wires or special attachments.

It just sits on your stove like an ordinary pan. Super hot air circulates inside the sealed cooking chamber and the special air cushion protects your food from burning.

So without any added oil or fat, you can sizzle fry…roast a whole chicken…grill chops…sausages…bacon…bake bread, pastries, cakes or even potatoes.

The Dry Cooker comes with special heat resistant handles. The non-stick inner pan ensures easy quick cleaning. The Dry Cooker is made of steel to…

…ensure years of delicious healthy cooking – all for just £19.99 covered by our money back guarantee.

Order right now and we'll also include this 7 piece stainless steel scissors set, usually sold by us for £7.99. It's yours absolutely free.

To order your Dry Cooker and free scissors set by credit card at this special offer price of £19.99…

…ring Scotcade now on 0274 522 999.

That's 0274 522 999…and start healthier cooking.

NSPCC
CHRISTMAS
APPEAL
0800 444 222

This airtime is donated by SmithKline Beecham

VO: *This is an appeal from the NSPCC to ask you if…*

Your £15 could help
save a child's life
0800 444 222

…you can make a Christmas donation now to help save a child's life.

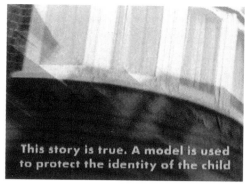

This story is true. A model is used
to protect the identity of the child

Tragically, in this country, three to four children die each week…

…victims of violence or neglect. Many more are beaten or abused, even abandoned…

…like little Ellie, left alone for days without light, heat or food in the bitter cold. Hungry, lonely, scared, all Ellie wanted for Christmas was…

Your £15 could help
fund our Child Protection Helpline

…for her mother to come home. Luckily, she was found in time. Last year, the NSPCC helped over 53,000 children. Please give what you can before another child is hurt. Your £15 could help fund our Child Protection Helpline.

Your £15 could help
us counsel a child

…where anyone can call if they fear a child is at risk. Your £15 could help us counsel a child suffering from the agony of emotional cruelty.

Your £15 could help
pay for that first vital visit

Your £15 could help pay for that first vital visit to a child whose life may be in danger…

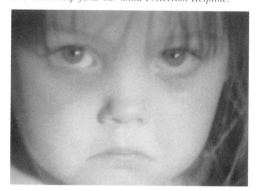

…a defenceless child like Ellie. So when you write your Christmas list, please imagine…

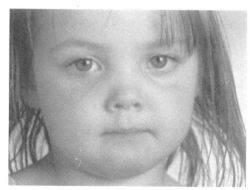

…there's an extra child to buy a present for, and send them a gift…

0800 444 222

…they'll never forget – the hope of a life free from terror or pain. Just write or ring 0800 444 222 to give £15…

NSPCC

VISA

NSPCC TV Appeal
Freepost London EC1B 1QQ
0800 444 222

…or whatever you can spare. We're waiting for your call now. Thank you.

Therefore a commercial in the middle of News at Ten will get, say, 20 TVRs; the price you pay for that commercial will then reflect the TVRs you are getting. A commercial shown at some point in the early morning will probably not even get 1 TVR, as so few people (according to research) are watching. And again, the price you pay for that commercial will relate to the low TVRs.

The greater the number watching, the more you pay. The fewer watching, the less. And below 1, it's clearly not worth buying because no-one is watching – or are they?

ZERO-RATED AIRTIME

The mystery here is that even on so-called zero-rated or low-rated airtime, a substantial number of people are actually watching TV. This is not the place to argue over the accuracy of TV viewership research. In my opinion it is hopelessly inaccurate – but in direct marketing we do not greatly care, because of course we can count the responses, rather than relying on statistically small audience surveys.

The result of all of this is that to make your commercials work, you need to buy into the low-rated time segments, not the high-rated ones at all. This means they are inexpensive. This also means that you can easily afford long commercials, which are mandatory for success.

You then have the perfect combination, from the direct marketer's point of view, of long copy and low media cost. Little wonder TV, if bought and executed in this fashion, is proving so successful.

COSTING YOUR COMMERCIAL

Another fondly-held myth about TV is production costs. Yes, you can easily spend £250,000 on a 30 second commercial; and if you are undertaking a major rebranding exercise then who is to say that you would be wrong to do so? The return on that type of investment is, presumably, large enough to warrant that kind of expenditure.

Costing a *direct response* TV commercial has to be a different proposition.

First, given that the media cost is going to be low, you cannot afford to have the production rise out of proportion to the media cost. Second, the fact that you are using relatively low-viewership time segments means that while you will be pleased with the cost-per-response, the volume is not likely to overwhelm you. You will have a small number of replies to amortise your production costs over, and therefore they need to be kept low for this reason too.

What should you pay?

It would seem that between £30,000 and £40,000 at current prices for a two minute commercial is about right. This means you cannot afford creative treatments that will be expensive.

Rather than film, you'll probably be on videotape. Rather than location, you'll probably be in a studio. Rather than stars, you'll be booking unknown actors. Rather than major sets, you'll looking at a simple background.

(Bear in mind that a 120 second commercial does not cost proportionally more

Fig. 66:
The first successful fundraising commercial.
This commercial for the NSPCC was the first in the UK to prove that fundraising by TV was an economic proposition. There were two main creative reasons for its success – first, the length...the commercial lasts one and a half minutes, three times as long as 'normal' commercials, allowing a reasonable time to get the maximum message into the commercial. Note the high information content, particularly about the work of the NSPCC, which is amplified by the use of captions to get the point home. The second reason for its success was the way it stuck closely to the original 'Give £15 to save a child's life' proposition (see fig. 52). In other words, rather than just offering problems, it offered solutions. The emotional content is powerful too, thanks to superb direction from David Bailey who gave his services free; this adds to the powerful proposition. This commercial, incidentally, won the 1992 Gold Award from the Direct Marketing Association.

◀ *See previous page*

than a 30 second commercial – the set-up costs are the same and therefore commercial length plays very little part in the overall cost.)

GET A PRODUCER

There are two keys to getting your commercial in at the right price. First is, of course, the script. It has to be inexpensive to start with – so any situations or actions have to be carefully thought about to ensure that costs will not be excessive.

The second key is getting a good producer. Never attempt to produce your own commercial. The country is full of excellent, highly professional TV producers who know where to go, who to talk to, and how to get it done. Their charges are reasonably modest, and if you involve them at the very beginning of the commercial, they can advise you as you go along on ways of keeping costs down. Listen to their ideas on scripts, as well. They may be able to suggest a different treatment which is just as effective but will cost less to shoot.

And, given that few people in direct marketing have much real knowledge of TV production, a good TV producer will be able to add their years of experience to yours, and come up with what should be a powerful combination.

STARTING YOUR COMMERCIAL

The process of creating a TV commercial is physically rather different from that of creating mailings or ads, though the underlying principles are much the same.

In physical terms, you are aiming to create a 'storyboard', which is TV's equivalent of a rough visual and copy. This consists of a series of TV-shaped frames where the main action sequences are roughed out and the script relating to that section is written in underneath.

In order to achieve this, you need to establish:

1 The general format of your commercial

2 The main selling points you want to communicate.

1: COMMERCIAL FORMATS

Given the length of the commercial, the format almost inevitably becomes *like a miniature 'programme'*, rather than a commercial.

From a response point of view, this is the best way to script your commercial. Rather than worrying about 'creative' values and clever photography, simply follow the example of how the TV station itself would treat the spot as an announcement, if you like. This then suggests a number of approaches:

The news approach: here a presenter, sitting at a desk, will go through the selling points as with a news programme.

The demonstration approach: with or without a presenter, the product is demonstrated in use. 'Tomorrow's World' is the style.

The interview approach: a person or persons talk about the product or service.

The documentary approach: the story is created with film clips – particularly suitable for fundraising.

These are just four of many possibilities. *The point to bear in mind in all of them*

Fig. 67:
Going for two minutes for complex propositions.
Length of commercial is vital. The minimum length for a successful commercial is 90 seconds; but in this commercial for the RNLI it runs to a full two minutes. The main reason is that the offer is for membership, which involves detailing various items that a member will receive. Because of the importance of explaining the offer carefully, some thirty seconds (the length of an 'ordinary' commercial) is devoted to this action sequence. Note the time that the telephone number is displayed for. Like the earlier Scotcade commercial (fig. 65), the basic format of 'announcement, explanation, action' is followed carefully.

See overleaf ▶

SFX: …gale warning – severe gale force 9 increasing storm force 10…"

VO: This is an invitation to become a supporter of the Lifeboats for just £15 a year – by ringing this number now.

Here's how your £15 will help. Day or night, lifeboat crews are ready to go to sea, whatever the weather.

They're ordinary people with ordinary jobs. Yet when the call comes, these brave men and women will head out to sea, in often terrifying conditions. They'll battle with the elements…

…risking their own lives to save the lives of others. Their bravery is astonishing. Even more extraordinary is that they are volunteers. To face conditions like this, all they ask is the look of relief on the face of a survivor…

…the support of loved ones who wait behind and the help of supporters around the country. We rely entirely on voluntary contributions. Just £15 covers the cost of keeping a lifeboat at sea for 20 minutes.

Your support right now could make the difference between life and death. Last year, we saved over 1300 lives. We need all the help we can get.

Just dial 0800 200 150 now to become a supporter of the RNLI. Joint membership is £15 per year.

As a member, you'll be sent lifeboat magazine 4 times a year…

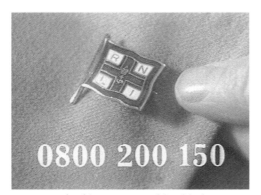

…your membership…your enamel lapel badge…

…and a sticker for your car or boat.

The number is 0800 200 150. We're waiting by the phones. Thank you.

VO: *Here's an important AA announcement about your home.*

If you're shocked by rising home insurance costs, call 0800 900 888 now to see if it's cheaper with the AA.

Presenter: *Take the AA Homequote service. As Britain's largest personal lines intermediary, we've got the power to get you a very good deal.*

Almost everything in your home…furniture…carpets…is covered for up to £30,000 without valuations. So you're covered for theft…

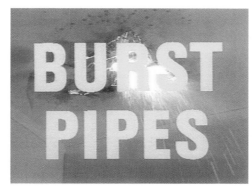

…and damage due to fire, burst pipes…even your garden furniture is covered against loss.

You're also protected against accidental damage to larger electrical goods. And if you claim, you'll be paid repair costs or today's replacement values.

There's special cover for freezer food spoilage, fraudulent use of credit cards, and loss of cash.

We'll even cover you for up to £1 million personal liability. When you call…

…0800 900 888 we'll use our computer to access our panel of leading insurers – and we'll come back to you with our very best deal. But we'd like to give you even more…

…so you'll also get up to £25,000 of legal expenses cover to help in appropriate legal disputes…for example bad workmanship or a dispute with a neighbour…there's a 24 hour legal advice line and a 24 hour disaster line…

…to help you find local help fast. We can quote for buildings insurance too. Remember, don't renew your home insurance until you've called us. Ring free of charge on 0800 900 888. Our trained staff are waiting…

…for your call. And we'll normally give you a quote then and there. So, if you're worried about rising home insurance costs call AA Homequote and we'll find you our best deal. Call 0800 900 888 today.

is that you are creating a short programme, not a long commercial.

Some approaches will suit some products, of course. An insurance product is ideally suited to the news approach or the interview technique. The demonstration approach is typically used for merchandise.

From the type of product or service you are selling, the format will usually become reasonably obvious.

Creative people need to be very wary of not getting caught up in the 'glamour' of TV. As I said earlier, making commercials like these is very different to making conventional commercials. Humour, for example, is one of the most obvious characteristics of an 'above-the-line' commercial. Yet humour in direct response TV is unnecessary and undesirable: your task is to inform, not to entertain. One of the reasons why it has taken DRTV so long to get off the ground is because creative people have viewed the commercial in the *conventional* way – with the result that the commercial is a failure. Having said that, there *is* a place for humour, as a viewing of the best DRTV from the United States will show. But if you choose to use humour, it *must* be relevant to the sale, not just added for the sake of entertainment. It should be used with extreme caution and should be done very well indeed.

At the same time as you settle on the format, you need also to determine the length – 90 seconds or 120 seconds. What does not work is writing a 90 second and then expanding it to a 120 second. This is the equivalent of taking a whole page ad and blowing it up to fit a DPS without changing the copy. You've added to costs but *not* added to the information content.

Equally, writing a 120 second and then having to cut it down to 90 seconds will prove to be a painful process.

Choose at the start. And your choice will be largely dictated by the second main issue:

2: MAIN SELLING POINTS

You need to determine early on what the main selling points are. Here, the process is not so different to writing a letter, or an ad, or an insert. The basic formula of 'x has y which means z' – the product (x) has a feature (y) which confers a benefit (z) – works just as well.

The best way to start is to simply *list all of the selling points* you want to feature in the commercial, and then turn this into a rough script first. In doing this, you need to bear in mind:

a) it has to be spoken, not read

b) it is linear – what is said last is often the most important thing, and the viewer cannot 'skip-read'.

THE SPOKEN WORD

The fact that it is spoken, not read, it vital. Direct marketing writers are wordsmiths, not scriptwriters. They do best with plenty of room. Room is the last thing you have in a commercial. You need to be very brief, very to the point, and you have to 'hear' the commercial as you write it, rather than read it. *The best test is to read it out loud and see what it sounds like.* Emphases you imagined when writing the script often disappear once spoken, necessitating some rewriting.

The 'linearity' is also important. The commercial starts at the beginning and moves inexorably onwards to its end – which may sound obvious but is clearly not the case with, say, a press ad, where the reader can (and almost certainly does) start in the middle, read the end, and then go back to the beginning. A commercial has the odd characteristic of having as much strength at the end as at the beginning. Important selling points, such as premia, can be equally strong at the end of the commercial.

TURNING THE SCRIPT TO THE STORYBOARD

By this stage, you have essentially chosen the format and you have written a rough working script containing the main selling points.

You now have to determine what actions will go with those selling points; a visual demonstration of the selling points is the most logical and usually the most effective thing to do. As the presenter of the voice-over explains the point, the video needs to emphasise or illustrate it. It is at this stage that you will develop the storyboard.

Of course, this process can be simultaneous; but the thinking has to take place in roughly this order or you will find yourself becoming hopelessly confused.

The act of roughing out the storyboard will tell you if the script is working. Usually it doesn't, and you have to change as you go along, getting the right combination on action and words to make the point most tellingly. You have to beware of jumping around too much: cutting quickly from one scene to another not only becomes tiring for the viewer but adds to production costs.

The script-to-storyboard stage is where the real work goes on. If you thought creating the right format was too easy, you will find actually making that format work in a logical and, in particular, a consistent way is a hard job. Sometimes you can get three-quarters of the way through only to find that the whole format doesn't work anymore – and, of course, it's time to change it and do another one.

THE START

I have so far mentioned only the 'meat' of the commercial. There are two additional areas that are vital: the start of the commercial, and, inevitably, the end.

The start of a long, direct response commercial has a particular role to play. If I can refer you back to Chapter 3 – Press Advertising – you will, I hope, have noted the point I made about making the advertisement look like a direct response advertisement – in other words, *this advertisement requires action.*

This principle holds true even more so for direct response commercials, given that they are still so rare and that conventional commercials almost never ask for any action. The beginning of your commercial therefore has to create a 'pause' in the programming; a signal that what is coming is not an ordinary commercial but a special announcement for the viewer.

ITVA regulations currently forbid exactly that approach, or a newslike approach. This doesn't really matter, as you have to make the initial frames relevant to the product anyway.

So, how is it done?

A simple title screen seems to be one of the best ways. For instance, in selling insurance, you could easily have a screen saying:

> **'HERE'S AN ANNOUNCEMENT OF SPECIAL INTEREST TO**
> **PEOPLE LOOKING FOR HOME INSURANCE'**

You could accompany this with a voice-over. At the same time you can follow up with the phone number straight away, to give the commercial the required action element. So perhaps the second title would be:

> **'YOU CAN ASK FOR DETAILS BY PHONE AT THE END OF THIS**
> **COMMERCIAL ON 0800 000 000'**

Both of these example frames will take no more than about 5 seconds of time, and they have then acted almost as 'opening titles', helping you get into the stride of making your mini-programme.

If it was a mail order offer, you can open with almost exactly the same opening as I was describing in the Chapter on press ads:

> **'HERE'S A SPECIAL TV MAIL ORDER OFFER FROM BLOGGINS...'**

complete with caption and shot of a large cardboard box being opened.

Your opening will of course depend on the type of commercial you are making and the type of product or service you are selling. However, an opening shot such as described above vital to differentiate yourself from the 'mere' ordinary commercials that will be showing around yours.

THE END

The ending of the commercial is also important. *You need, as with all direct marketing creativity, to call for action.* But in TV, there are specific ways of doing it – and remember, time is very short.

You need to communicate a number of separate things in your ending. First and most importantly, the telephone number you want your prospects to call.

(The overwhelming majority of respondents will respond by phone. Having said that, a small number of people will still want to write in, so it is important to have a write-in address at the same time.)

Even in a 120' commercial, there is relatively little time to take in the message of the commercial and the telephone number at the same time. Therefore the telephone number needs to come in:

> *At the beginning for at least 10 seconds*
>
> *In the middle for at least 10 seconds*
>
> *At the end for at least 10 seconds*

At the beginning, you should say "this is the number to call and to have a pen and paper ready to write the number down – we'll be showing it again."

In the middle you need to say "this is the number you should call at the end of the commercial."

And then at the end you should say something very similar to "the lines are open

WWAV

Client:	NSPCC
Product:	Christmas Appeal
Title:	'Ellie'
Length:	120 seconds

VO: This is a telephone appeal from the NSPCC to ask if you can give £15 this Christmas to help save a child's life. Please take a pen and make a note of this number: 0800 28 20 28. That's 0800 28 20 28. I'll repeat it again at the end of this appeal.

SFX: Fade in music: 'O Come All Ye Faithful'.

VO: Imagine what it's like to be just 4 years old and to spend Christmas time trapped in a dark, cold, empty house.

SFX: Frightened child breathing.

VO: Nothing to eat. Nowhere to sleep. No-one to love you, least of all give you presents.

SFX: Child sobs quietly.

VO: Imagine what it's like to listen out desperately for the sound of footsteps outside, hoping against hope that your mother's coming home.

SFX: Footsteps coming closer. Child cries 'mummy'.
Footsteps fade away.

VO: That's what happened to little Ellie, abandoned for days with little light, heat or food in the bitter cold. Hungry. Lonely. Scared. All Ellie wanted for Christmas was for someone to find her.

SFX: Footsteps coming closer. Loud knocking. Man gently calls "Ellie. Is that you Ellie?"

VO: Thankfully the NSPCC found Ellie in time. But for all the thousands of abused and abandoned children we've protected, countless more need our help this Christmas. Please call us now on 0800 28 20 28 and give us what you can.

Your £15 could help fund our NSPCC Child Protection Helpline, which anyone can call if they fear a child is at risk. Your £15 could help us counsel a child suffering from the agony of emotional cruelty. And your £15 could help pay for the first vital visit to a child whose life may be in danger.

It's the best Christmas gift you could give - the chance to free a child like Ellie, from a life of terror and pain.

SFX: Child's laughter.

MVO: To help save a child's life, please call the NSPCC on 0800 28 20 28 now with your credit card and give just £15, or whatever you can afford. That's 0800 28 20 28. We're waiting by the phones. Thank you.

Fig. 69:
Direct response radio.

This is a successful radio commercial for the NSPCC, based closely on the tested TV approach (fig. 66). Here, a full 2 minutes is needed – not only to give time to build up the emotional images, but also to provide sufficient time to get the telephone number across – insufficient opportunity to respond is probably the main reason why radio doesn't usually work for direct marketers. Note the application of the 'announcement, explanation, action' sequence, along-side the very strong use of the phone number. The use of sound effects is vital, too – although the commercial itself is basically a presenter format, the use of the sound effects adds 'colour' and emotion. The great creative joy of radio, of course, is that it's so cheap to produce – you can achieve almost any effect you like with budgets in hundreds of pounds. Although the length of this commercial is 2 minutes, it's probably too short…longer times would almost certainly work better, and would become mini-radio programmes.

now and we're waiting for your call", while the number itself is superimposed as a title. The phrase is quite important: your commercial will be running at off-peak times and it may not be obvious to the viewer that they can call at that time.

The closing shot should be nothing but a phone number, together with the write-in address. This MUST stay on screen for at least 5 seconds longer would be preferable.

It goes without saying that the phone number should be an easily memorable one, and an 0800 number is ideal. The phone element of a direct response commercial is, from the response handling point of view, one of the most important areas. *Once your commercial is running the phones start ringing – and the response comes in a huge wave within seconds of the end of the commercial.* Something like 95% of your response comes in the first 30 minutes after your commercial is shown – and of that, the majority comes in the first few minutes. Clearly, you need a pretty good phone system to handle that huge, sudden load of calls.

THE NEED FOR CAPTIONS

At this stage, your storyboard has its opening title, its 'brick-by-brick' build-up of the selling arguments complete with demonstration, its ending full of phone numbers and girls with headsets waiting for your call. What more is needed?

The last thing to add is the captions.

Once more we have to return to the basic principle of long copy. In our 90 second or 120 second commercial we have crammed in as much as we could but we're still limited to a relatively short period of time. However, by adding captions as we go, we can add quite a bit of the *net information load* in the piece.

> *Your commercial should have almost continuous captions, rolling along the bottom of the screen, rolling up the screen, or fading on and off throughout.*

In some cases, what the caption says can be the *same* as the voice-over. But it is usually better to use the captions to *add* to the script, rather than just amplify it.

For example, a presenter is saying:

> *"Under this policy, you're covered for fire…theft…natural disaster…subsidence…"*

As the presenter says "fire" a caption can come up saying "£30,000 fire cover". As the presenter says "theft", the caption might say "£20,000 theft cover", and so on.

It's remarkable that the human eye can take in a lot of information in a short time, and therefore your captions can 'flash' significant points as you go. Sometimes fast flashing or fast rolling simply conveys an impression of 'a lot'…and this *alone* can be a valid selling point. The speed with which the play-list on compilation record commercials flashes past makes it nearly impossible to pick out all the tracks shown, but you certainly get the impression that you get a lot for your money.

PRODUCTION VALUES

If I have given the impression that TV direct response commercials are cheap and nasty, then you misread my intentions. If you produce a nasty, barracking commercial, you might get away with it for certain classes of product. But nobody will give funds to a con-man; nobody will buy insurance from a shyster. The production values of your commercial are, I believe, therefore very important.

The fact that you have a limited budget is going to affect what you can do. But with the right producer you can still do a lot. The right lighting, the right typography for the captions, the right choice of voice-over or actor/actress, good editing – all of these things can and do affect the final 'feel' of the commercial.

I made the point earlier in this book about the way in which good art direction can make a powerful contribution to the flavour and feel of a mailing or a press ad. *Exactly the same applies to a commercial.*

Given the lengths that I am encouraging you to use, you should not need to go hell-for-leather at the subject anyway. A calm, reasonable exposition of the product benefits is all that is needed, and in 120 seconds (two minutes of time) you should have time to do that job calmly enough.

In the same way that a letter sprinkled with exclamation marks betrays a lack of skill on the part of the writer in creating emphasis, a commercial with a blaring, shouting style betrays a lack of skill in the script. A good writer can create the force and emphasis needed through the correct use of language, the right choice of visual and caption.

BUILD-UP: HOW LONG A CAMPAIGN SHOULD YOU NEED?

In looking at the length of a campaign, you have to once more overturn conventional wisdom. Where a normal TV campaign will need to run for a period of time in order to achieve its objectives, a direct response commercial should only run once. If it does not break-even first time, carrying on running it will *not* help.

In fact, the response to the first and last commercial in a series is not too different. *There is little evidence of any 'build-up' effect at all.* Each commercial is seen on its own merits and judged on the day – it is not seen as one of a series. Repeating direct response commercials too closely together seems to have a negative effect. You need to wait a while for your audience to 'take a breather' before you start at them again.

Thus a TV promotion should be looked at as a series, not a campaign. You keep on running the commercial until, in effect, it no longer works.

Given the small amount of TV experience in the UK, I do not know at what point this occurs. As we are using off-peak airtime, I suspect the life of a commercial may be a long one. But if it is particularly successful, then the commercial will of course tire. The answer, like a mailing, will be change of pace, and a new creative treatment will probably give it an additional lease of life.

RADIO

Very little work has been done on radio direct response in the UK, but in my so far limited experience it can be made to work.

The reasons for this are that a) production costs are very low indeed – a good commercial can be produced for about £300! And b) with the eruption of local commercial stations, airtime rates are very low, even compared to off-peak TV. Some spots can be bought for as little as £25.

With this kind of cost equation working for you, you will need a small enough response to make the exercise worthwhile. And with the new stations, there should be enough volume to make the use of radio a cost-effective proposition.

The creative treatment is almost exactly the same as TV. Long spots are needed. Initial announcements will be used to differentiate the commercial from the normal.

You cannot use captions, of course. And the main problem is the phone number. On a TV commercial, you can easily write it down. Listening to the radio in the car, you will have some difficulty. It will therefore need a very memorable number, but these can be obtained from a major telemarketing bureau with ease, so this should not be a big problem.

Given what should be low costs for radio, then it is possible that even longer spots can be used – in excess of 2 minutes – which will largely overcome this problem.

I believe that for some classes of product, radio offers a low-cost medium that if given the right creative treatment will work well. We've already had some good successes with radio, using exactly these techniques.

SHORTER COMMERCIALS?

I've gone on at length about the need for long commercials – but there are cases where very short ones can work too. If you have a very simple message, requiring a very simple response, then a 10 second commercial can give you excellent results. For some years the AA has run a series of highly effective commercials that simply get you to call a number to get a quote; cheap, short, and to the point. Like long copy, long commercials only work if you've got a long story; if you've got a short story, a short commercial is fine ■

CHAPTER 15: SUMMARY

Direct response TV and radio commercials, like letters and ads, require a high information content, which means they usually need to be at least 90 seconds long and probably 2 minutes.

Straightforward presenter-type commercials are most successful; there is little place for humour in DRTV. Your commercial should be like a news announcement or a mini-programme from the TV station, within the ITVA rules.

Low production costs are vital – if you spend too much on your commercial you can never get your money back. Around £30-40,000 is appropriate, and your creative treatment must reflect the fact that you are making a low-budget commercial.

Your commercial should start with an announcement to differentiate it from a normal, non-response commercial: 'Here's a special TV offer from…'. This should then be immediately followed by the fact that the respondent can telephone a number to buy straight away.

The body of your commercial should be a simple presentation of the main selling points.

Each selling point made by the presenter or demonstrator should have if possible a caption, ideally amplifying on the point made. The eye can absorb information faster than the ear can – thus a sequence of rolling captions along the bottom of the screen will add greatly to the information content.

The time given to the phone number is critical. It should occur, on both sound and vision, as many times as it is possible to fit in – at least once at the start, once in the middle, and again at the end. A key closing phrase is to invite viewers to call now – "our lines are open now and we're waiting for your call".